URDU:
AN ESSENTIAL GRAMMAR

Urdu: An Essential Grammar is a reference guide to the grammatical structures of modern Urdu.

The complexities of Urdu are set out in short, readable sections, which are conveniently grouped under major topical headings. Explanations contain minimal jargon and emphasis has been placed on the aspects of Urdu that pose a particular challenge for English-speaking students.

Features include:

- language examples throughout in both Urdu script and romanization
- user-friendly layout
- network of cross-references between sections
- detailed contents list
- comprehensive index.

Urdu: An Essential Grammar presents a fresh and accessible description of the language. It will prove invaluable to students at all levels in schools, colleges, universities and adult classes. Its clear explanations make it ideal for independent learners too.

Ruth Laila Schmidt lectures in the Department of East European and Oriental Studies at the University of Oslo, Norway.

URDU: AN ESSENTIAL GRAMMAR

Ruth Laila Schmidt

London and New York

First published 1999 by Routledge
2 Park Square, Milton Park, Abingdon, Oxon, OX14 4RN

Simultaneously published in the USA and Canada
by Routledge
270 Madison Ave, New York NY 10016

Routledge is an imprint of the Taylor & Francis Group

Transferred to Digital Printing 2006

Typeset in Norman, Jawhar and South Asia Times by R.L. Schmidt

British Library Cataloguing in Publication Data
A catalogue record for this book is available from the British Library

Library of Congress Cataloging in Publication Data
A catalogue record for this book has been requested

ISBN 0-415-16380-3 (hbk)
ISBN 0-415-16381-1 (pbk)

This book is dedicated to
Bruce R. Pray
in recognition of his four decades of service
to the Urdu language, and his contribution
to the study of Urdu
through the establishment of the
Berkeley Urdu Language Program

TABLE OF CONTENTS

kyā kyā; kaun kaun; kōī kōī, kōī na kōī; kuch kuch, kuch na kuch

The difference between transitive and intransitive verbs; agreement of verbs; the increment -ā; transitives derived with the increment -ā; double transitives derived with the increment -ā; transitivity with compound verbs; transitivity with denominative verbs; verbs which function both intransitively and transitively; exceptions: transitives without **nē**, intransitives with **nē**

Direct causatives derived with the increment -ā; indirect causatives formed with the increment -vā; causative denominative verbs; causative verbs in requests

Adjectival use of imperfective participles; adverbial use of imperfective participles; imperfective participle + **vaqt**, 'while (VERB)-ing'; imperfective participle + **hī**, 'as soon as (VERB)'; repeated imperfective participles; imperfective participles used as nouns

Adjectival use of perfective participles; adverbial use of perfective participles; adverbial perfective participles in expressions of time; repeated perfective participles; perfective participles used as nouns; perfective participles in compound verbs

Conjunctive participles used adverbially; repeated roots in conjunctive participles

Word order in sentences; objects; noun phrases; adverbs; negative sentences; interrogative sentences

Subject-verb agreement; verb phrases; agreement with mixed subjects; agreement with transitive verbs; agreement with impersonal verbs; mixed transitivity; adjective-noun agreement

LIST OF TABLES

PREFACE

by Gopi Chand Narang

Urdu is a major language of South Asia which has been gaining in popularity since the advent of independence of India and Pakistan. It is one of the eighteen national languages listed in the Constitution of India, as well as the national language of Pakistan. Unlike Arabic and Persian, Urdu is an Indo-Aryan language akin to Hindi. Both Urdu and Hindi share the same Indic base, and at the phonological and grammatical level they are so close that they appear to be one language, but at the lexical level they have borrowed so extensively from different sources (Urdu from Arabic and Persian, and Hindi from Sanskrit) that in actual practice and usage each has developed into an independent language. This distinction is further marked at the orthographic level, where Hindi uses Devanagari and Urdu uses the Arabo-Persian script indigenously modified to suit the requirements of an Indo-Aryan speech. With this context in view, although the grammars of these languages cover much common ground, nevertheless in order to do justice to the differing sociolinguistic paradigms, separate materials have to be developed for each of these languages, which taken together form the fourth largest speech community in the modern world.

The grammatical tradition of Urdu and Hindi is now almost three centuries old, beginning with Ketelaar in the seventeenth century and continuing through Schultze, Forbes, Fallon, Platts, Shakespear, Gilchrist and others down to the nineteenth century. While Platts' work has become a classic and is reprinted time and again, the others have fallen into disuse. Lately, with inputs from modern linguistics, and the fresh impetus given by Urdu's new status as a national language as well as a cultural vehicle of the Indo-Pakistani diaspora, the need for new teaching materials is ever on the increase. The work of scholars such as Barker, McGregor, Russell, Shackle, Glassman, Pray, Naim and others has met some of the present need, however most of them have developed language-teaching books in which a discussion of the grammar is included as part of the pedagogical requirement. As far as I know, no reference grammar of Urdu (or Hindi) has so far been written, and it is precisely this gap which the present volume attempts to fill.

I have known Ruth Laila Schmidt for more than twenty years, since her study of Dakhini Urdu appeared. She is widely travelled in India and Pakistan, spending years in research and teaching. Her research in the Dardic language Shina, and her *Practical Dictionary of Modern Nepali*, have in particular been well received. She belongs to that brand of South Asian linguistic scholars who deserve attention for their sense of dedication and thoroughness. It has been my pleasure to interact with her on this grammar, and I found the work fulfilling. Though the volume is called a reference grammar, I am sure it can profitably be read from cover to cover in a systematic way. As such it breaks fresh ground, and I do hope it will serve as a model for future intrepid scholars in the difficult terrain of South Asian grammatical studies.

New Delhi
14 June 1999

INTRODUCTION

What is Urdu?

Urdu is widely spoken not only in South Asia but also in the West. Worldwide, there are nearly 55 million Urdu speakers.[1]

In Pakistan it is the national language and is used in instruction in most government schools, at the lower levels of administration, and in the mass media.[2] The number of Urdu speakers in Pakistan has been estimated at almost 11 million with the largest number in the province of Sindh, followed by Panjab.

Urdu is also one of the one of the 18 national languages of the Union of India. There are almost 44 million Urdu speakers in India, with the largest numbers found in the state of Uttar Pradesh, followed by Bihar, Maharashtra, Andhra Pradesh and Karnataka. Delhi is also a significant centre not only of Urdu speakers but of Urdu literature and publishing.

Urdu is also spoken in Bangladesh, Afghanistan and Nepal, and has become the culture language and lingua franca of the South Asian Muslim diaspora outside the subcontinent, particularly in the Middle East, Europe, the United States and Canada.

Historically, Urdu developed from the sub-regional language of the Delhi area, which became a literary language in the eighteenth century. Two quite similar standard forms of the language developed in Delhi, and in Lucknow in modern Uttar Pradesh. Since 1947, a third form, Karachi standard Urdu, has evolved.

What does this work cover?

Urdu: An Essential Grammar is intended to present as complete a description of the grammar of Delhi Standard Urdu as is possible in the space available. It does not cover Urdu phonology or the writing system. The inventory of grammatical structures has been compiled from existing textbooks as well as from texts typically read in second- and third-year Urdu classes.

This work is a reference grammar rather than a pedagogical grammar. Grammatical constructions are grouped by topical headings: nouns, pronouns, adjectives, adverbs, verbs, etc., with a network of cross references to other sections. It is intended to serve a resource to which to refer as one reads texts; to

1 Sources: The Summer Institute of Linguistics *Ethnologue*, Census of India 1991, Census of Pakistan 1981, *Encyclopedia Britannica* (*Britannica Online*).

2 Tariq Rahman, *Language and Politics in Pakistan*, Karachi: Oxford University Press, 1996.

look up complex grammatical constructions, or review more elementary constructions; and with the help of the table of contents, index and cross-references, to look up individual sentences and analyse them without reading the whole book. Ideally one should be able to start anywhere in *Urdu: An Essential Grammar* and find the information one needs.

Although one can certainly read this book from cover to cover, and the author has kept that kind of reader in mind, that is not its primary purpose. This means that some constructions must be looked up in several different places. If a person wishes to make a comprehensive review of the use of **nē** with perfective tense transitive verbs, he or she must consult all the following sections: §211, §510, §629 and §809, because the **nē** construction involves a postposition, verb constructions, special forms of pronouns, and the notion of transitivity; and each of these is dealt with under its own heading. Cross references are provided to make the search easier.

Transcription system

The primary purpose of the transcription system, which is adapted from that presented by R.S. McGregor,[3] is to provide a guide for pronunciation. The two main departures are: (a) the Arabic letters ء ع ظ ط ض ص ژ ح ث are not distinguished, and (b) long and short **e** and **o** are distinguished as: **e ē/o ō** (even though short **e, o** are allophones of / **i a u** /). The purpose for transcribing them in this way is that the environments of short **e, o** are many, complex and often require a knowledge of the spelling of the word, or its origin; thus this convention is expected to be helpful to the reader.

How should this book be used?

This work is most useful to students who already have a basic knowledge of Urdu. The reader may begin by skimming the table of contents to get an overview of what is covered and how it is organized. A reader who knows what he or she is looking for may find it here. Alternatively, one may look up key words in the index. For example, the uses of the adverb **bhī** 'also' are listed in the index under '**bhī**', 'emphatic particles', 'modal adverbs', 'both ... and', 'neither ... nor' and 'relative words followed by **bhī**'. Finally, look up any reference and follow the network of cross-references.

In the example sentences, the grammatical topic under discussion is highlighted by italicization of words in the Urdu transcription and the corresponding English translation. Occasionally, a literal translation holds the italicized equivalent. The following examples illustrate italicization.

3 R.S. McGregor, *Urdu Study Materials*, Delhi: Oxford University Press, 1992.

دفتری کام
daftarī kām
official work

اُس کا نام مجھے معلوم ہے ۔
us kā nām mujhē mālūm hai
I know his name (his name is *known* to me).

If there is no italicization in an example, it is because the structure of the Urdu original and the translation are too disparate to permit the technique, because the entire sentence would need to be italicized, or because the relevant Urdu word is not expressed in the translation. For example, **kyā** in the sentence below merely introduces a question, and is not translated.

کیا یہ گھڑا ہے ؟
kyā ye ghaṛā hai?
Is this is a water pot?

Acknowledgements

The author thanks Professor Gopi Chand Narang of the Sahitya Akademi, New Delhi (formerly of Delhi University and Jamia Millia Islamia) for checking the example sentences and for providing guidance during the writing process. Without his sharp judgement and insight into Urdu, this would have been a much poorer work. The grammatical analysis based on the example sentences is my own, and only I am responsible for any errors.

Dr. Elena Bashir and Professor Christopher Shackle read the entire manuscript and offered criticisms and suggestions. I am grateful to them both, and solely responsible for any errors or omissions which may remain.

Numerous colleagues responded to my queries for information during the three years it has taken to produce this grammar; there is not room to mention them all by name, but they are remembered with gratitude. I also wish to thank the tutors and programme evaluators of the University of California's Berkeley Urdu Language Program in Pakistan for patiently answering my many questions.

The Department of East European and Oriental Studies of the University of Oslo provided sabbatical leave as well as resources for the production of the manuscript and funds for the visit of Professor Narang to the University of Oslo.

The roman text in this book is set in the Norman font, except for the examples in Chapter 15, which are set in Jerome Bauer's South Asia Times Bold. Urdu is set in the Jawhar font produced by Kamal Mansour of Monotype, U.S.A., which was provided by Monotype as a courtesy.

SYMBOLS AND ABBREVIATIONS

x → **y**	**x** becomes **y**
x < **y**	**x** is derived from **y**
x + **y**	**y** is added to **x**
x ~ **y**	**y** is a variant or inflected form of **x**
f.	feminine
int.	intransitive
lit.	literally
m.	masculine
pl.	plural
sg.	singular
tr.	transitive
AP	active participle
PP	passive participle
VN	verbal noun

1 NOUNS

Urdu has two grammatical genders: masculine (m.) and feminine (f.). Nouns may have special gender suffixes (marking), or be unmarked for gender. Nouns are inflected to show number (singular or plural) and case (nominative, oblique or vocative).

GENDER AND MARKING

101 Gender

All Urdu nouns belong to one of two noun genders, masculine and feminine.

MASCULINE		FEMININE	
لڑکا	**laṛkā**, boy	لڑکی	**laṛkī**, girl
بچّہ	**bacca**, (male) child	چڑیا	**ciṛiyā**, bird
گھر	**ghar**, house	میز	**mēz**, table

102 Marking

All Urdu nouns may be additionally divided into two groups: those which are marked for gender (marked nouns), and those which have no special gender suffix (unmarked nouns).

Plural nouns, excepting masculine unmarked nouns, have distinctive gender suffixes. See §107.

103 Marked nouns

Nouns ending in the masculine gender suffixes **-ā** ا, **-a** ہ and **-aya** یہ are masculine:

لڑکا	**laṛkā**, boy	بچّہ	**bacca**, (male) child
مرغا	**murγā**, rooster	روپیہ	**rūpaya**, rupee, money

Extremely rarely, the suffix **-ā** is nasalized.

کنواں **kūāṁ**, well

Nouns ending in the feminine gender suffixes **-ī** ی or **-iyā** یا are feminine.

لڑکی	**laṛkī**, girl	بچّی	**baccī**, (female) child
مرغی	**murγī**, hen	چڑیا	**ciṛiyā**, bird

104 Unmarked nouns

Nouns which do not end in the above gender suffixes are unmarked, and their gender must be learned.

گھر	**ghar**, house (m.)
کام	**kām**, work (m.)
کتاب	**kitāb**, book (f.)

Special attention should be paid to nouns that look like marked nouns, but are not. A number of common masculine nouns end in **-ī**. They are either suffixless nouns that happen to end in **-ī**, or nouns formed with the occupation suffix **-ī**.

پانی	**pānī**, water (suffixless)
جہازی	**jahāzī**, sailor (جہاز **jahāz**, ship + occupation suffix)

Some feminine nouns end in **-ā**, **-a** or **-āṁ**. They are either suffixless words that happen to end in **-ā**, **-a**, **-āṁ**, or Arabic nouns in which the final **-a** ہ results from an Arabic suffix **-t** ۃ which derives a feminine noun from a masculine one:

ہوا	**havā**, wind, air (a suffixless Arabic noun)
جگہ	**jaga**, place (colloquial pronunciation of جگہ **jagah**)
والدہ	**vālida**, mother (term of reference) (< Arabic والد **vālid**, father)
امّاں	**ammāṁ**, mother (term of address)

Feminine nouns formed with the suffix **-iyā** should not be confused with masculine nouns.

چڑیا	**ciṛiyā**, bird (چڑا **ciṛā**, male sparrow + diminutive suffix)

105 Natural gender

The biological gender of people or animals denoted by a noun usually determines the gender of the noun.

ماں	**māṁ**, mother (term of address) (f.)
باپ	**bāp**, father (term of address) (m.)

ڈاکٹر	**ḍākṭar**, doctor (masculine if a man, feminine if a woman)
دستکار	**dastkār**, artisan (masculine if a man, feminine if a woman)

106 Some other clues to gender of nouns

Some other suffixes or noun patterns help to identify the gender of nouns.

Arabic loanwords

Arabic nouns ending in **-at** اَت **-iyat** یت and **-ā** ا are usually feminine.

قیمت	**qīmat**, price
حیثیت	**haisiyat**, status, capacity
حیا	**hayā**, modesty
دوا	**davā**, medicine

Verbal nouns of the pattern **tafʿīl** تفعیل are feminine.

تکلیف	**taklīf**, trouble
تصویر	**tasvīr**, picture

Arabic nouns ending in **-a** ہ are usually masculine.

حملہ	**hamla**, attack
قصّہ	**qissa**, story

However, **vālida** والدہ, 'mother'; **tāliba** طالبہ, 'female student'; **dafa** دفعہ, 'time', are feminine. Note also that not all masculine nouns ending in **-a** are borrowed from Arabic, as there is an increasing tendency to write **chōṭī hē** ہ in place of final **alif** ا : **ghanṭa** گھنٹہ for **ghanṭā** گھنٹا, 'hour' (indigenous Urdu); **pata** پتہ for **patā** پتا, 'address' (Persian); **kamra** کمرہ for **kamrā** کمرا, 'room' (Portuguese).

Persian loanwords

Nouns ending in the place suffixes **-gāh** گاہ and **-āē** ائے are feminine.

عبادت گاہ	**ibādatgāh**, place of worship
خاکنائے	**xāknāē**, isthmus

Nouns ending in the noun-forming suffixes **-ī** ی and **-gī** گی are feminine.

دوستی **dōstī**, friendship
زندگی **zindagī**, life

Nouns ending in the place suffix **-istān** or **-stān** ستان are masculine:

پاکستان **pākistān**, Pakistan
ریگستان **rēgistān**, desert

Indigenous Urdu words

Most indigenous nouns ending in **-ū** or **-ō** و are masculine.

بھاؤ **bhāō**, market price
آلو **ālū**, potato
ڈاکو **ḍākū**, robber

However, personal names in rural areas are often formed by adding **-ū** for men and **-ō** for women:

تاجو **tājō** (a woman's name)
رمضانو **ramzānū** (a man's name)

Nouns ending in the noun-forming suffixes **-pan** پن and **-pā** پا are masculine.

بچپن **bacpan**, childhood
لڑکپن **laṛakpan**, boyhood; childishness
بڑھاپا **buṛhāpā**, old age

Nouns ending in the diminutive suffix **-ī** ی ~ **-iyā** یا and the noun-forming suffix **-i** ی are feminine.

پہاڑی **pahāṛī**, small hill (from **pahāṛ** پہاڑ , mountain)
چڑیا **ciṛiyā**, bird (from **ciṛā** چڑا , male sparrow)
سلائی **silāī**, seam, sewing (from **silnā** سلنا , to be sewn)
لمبائی **lambāī**, length (from **lambā** لمبا , long)

Nouns ending in the abstract noun-forming suffixes **-āhaṭ** آہٹ , **-āvaṭ** آوٹ and **-yat** یت are feminine.

گھبراہٹ	**ghabrāhaṭ**, confusion
رکاوٹ	**rukāvaṭ**, obstacle

NOUN PLURALS

107 Forms (nominative case)

There are different plural suffixes for masculine marked, feminine marked and feminine unmarked nouns. Masculine unmarked nouns have no plural suffixes.

(a) The suffixes **-ā** and **-a** (masculine marked) change to **-ē**:

لڑکا ← لڑکے	**laṛkā** → **laṛkē**, boys
بچہ ← بچے	**bacca** → **baccē**, children

If the suffix **-ā** is nasalized (**-āṁ**), the plural suffix is nasalized as well.

کنواں ← کنوئیں	**kūāṁ** → **kūēṁ**, well

(b) The suffix **-aya** (masculine marked) changes to **-aē** ~ **-ē**:

روپیہ ← روپئے ، روپے	**rūpaya** → **rūpaē**, **rūpē**, rupees

(c) Masculine unmarked nouns have no plural suffix:

گھر ← گھر	**ghar** → **ghar**, houses

(d) The suffix **ī** (feminine marked) changes to **-iyāṁ**:

لڑکی ← لڑکیاں	**laṛkī** → **laṛkiyāṁ**, girls

(e) Indigenous feminine nouns ending in **-iyā** take the plural in **-iyāṁ**.

چڑیا ← چڑیاں	**ciṛiyā** → **ciṛiyāṁ**, birds

(f) Feminine unmarked nouns add the plural suffix **-ēṁ**:

کتاب ← کتابیں	**kitāb** → **kitābēṁ**, books
دوا ← دوائیں	**davā** → **davāēṁ**, medicines

Reduction of penultimate short vowel

When suffixes consisting of long vowels, including the nominative and oblique plural and the vocative, are added to roots containing two or more short vowels, the penultimate short vowel of the root is reduced or lost.

عورت	**aurat**, woman + **-ēṁ** → **aurtēṁ**, women
بہن	**bahen**, sister + **-ēṁ** → **bahnēṁ**, sisters

Table 1: Plural of nouns

	Singular		Plural	
Masc. marked	لڑکا	**laṛkā**	لڑکے	**laṛkē**
	کمرہ	**kamra**	کمرے	**kamrē**
	روپیہ	**rūpaya**	روپئے ، روپے	**rūpaē, rūpē**
	کنواں	**kūāṁ**	کنوئیں	**kūēṁ**
Masc. unmarked	گھر	**ghar**	گھر	**ghar**
Fem. marked	لڑکی	**laṛkī**	لڑکیاں	**laṛkiyāṁ**
	چڑیا	**ciṛiyā**	چڑیاں	**ciṛiyāṁ**
Fem. unmarked	کتاب	**kitāb**	کتابیں	**kitābēṁ**

108 Non-count (mass) nouns

Non-count (mass) nouns do not have plural forms.

بہت پانی
bahut *pānī*
a lot of *water*

ہمارے پاس کافی چینی ہے -
hamārē pās kāfī *cīnī* hai
We have plenty of *sugar*.

If one has occasion to speak of more than one variety of non-count nouns, they may be pluralized. However plural amounts of non-count nouns are usually qualified by the measure or container used to hold them. See §116.

ہمارے پاس دو طرح کی دالیں ہیں ۔
hamārē pās dō tarah kī *dālēṁ* haiṁ
We have two kinds of *lentils.*

INFLECTION OF NOUNS

Nouns may occur in the nominative, oblique or vocative case.[1]

109 Nominative case

Nominative nouns most commonly occur as the subjects of verbs. (In perfective tenses, however, the subjects of transitive verbs take the postposition **nē**, and are in the oblique case. See §629.)

لڑکا یہاں رہتا ہے ۔
***laṛkā* yahāṁ rahtā hai**
The boy lives here.

روپیہ کل ملے گا ۔
***rūpaya* kal milē gā**
The money will be available tomorrow.

A nominative noun may occur as the direct object of a sentence.

میں کام کرتا ہوں اور روپیہ کماتا ہوں ۔
maiṁ kām kartā hūṁ aur *rūpaya* kamātā hūṁ
I work and I earn *money.*

110 Oblique case

Whenever a noun is followed by a postposition (for example, **kō** کو , 'to'; **kā** کا, 'of'; **mēṁ** میں , 'in'; **sē** سے, 'from', etc.), it occurs in the oblique case. The ergative postposition **nē** نے also takes the oblique case of nouns. (See Chapter 5 for information about postpositions; see §211 for pronouns before **nē**.)

1 The term 'case' is used in this work to refer only to bound nominal suffixes (nominative, oblique and vocative) described below and in Chapter 2. Other grammarians treat grammatical postpositions (Chapter 5) as case markers. According to this school of thought, a noun followed by the ergative postposition **nē** is in the ergative case; a noun followed by **kō** is in the dative case, and a noun with no postposition is in the nominative-accusative case.

Oblique singular

Only masculine marked nouns have a special oblique singular suffix.

(a) The suffixes **-ā** and **-a** (masculine marked) change to **-ē**:

لڑکا ← لڑکے کا	**laṛkā →**	**laṛkē kā**
کمرہ ← کمرے کا	**kamra →**	**kamrē kā**

If the suffix **-ā** is nasalized (**-āṁ**), the oblique suffix is nasalized as well.

کنواں ← کنوئیں کا	**kūāṁ →**	**kūēṁ kā**

(b) The suffix **-aya** (masculine marked) changes to **-aē** ~ **-ē**:

روپیہ ← روپئے کا ، روپے کا	**rūpaya →**	**rūpaē kā, rūpē kā**

(c) Feminine nouns and unmarked masculine nouns do not change.

گھر ← گھر کا	**ghar →**	**ghar kā**
لڑکی ← لڑکی کا	**laṛkī →**	**laṛkī kā**
کتاب ← کتاب کا	**kitāb →**	**kitāb kā**

Examples

لڑکے کا بھائی کراچی میں ہے -
***laṛkē* kā bhāī karācī mēṁ hai**
The boy's brother is in Karachi (lit. the brother of the *boy* is in Karachi).

اِس کنوئیں کا پانی ٹھنڈا ہے -
is *kūēṁ* kā pānī ṭhanḍā hai
The water of this *well* is cold.

گھر کا کرایہ تین ہزار روپئے ہے -
***ghar* kā kirāya tīn hazār rūpaē hai**
The rent of *the house* is three thousand rupees.

کتاب کی قیمت دو سو روپئے ہے -
***kitāb* kī qīmat dō sau rūpaē hai**
The price of *the book* is two hundred rupees.

Oblique plural

All plural nouns have oblique suffixes (except Perso-Arabic nouns with borrowed Persian or Arabic plural, or dual, suffixes; §1405; §1503-§1504). The oblique plural forms are derived from the nominative plural forms as shown below.

(a) The plural suffixes **-ē** and **-ēṁ** change to **-ōṁ**:

لڑکے ← لڑکوں کا		**laṛkē →**	**laṛkōṁ kā**
کمرے ← کمروں کا		**kamrē →**	**kamrōṁ kā**
کنوئیں ← کنوؤں کا		**kūēṁ →**	**kūōṁ kā**
روپے ← روپوں کا		**rūpē →**	**rūpōṁ kā**
کتابیں ← کتابوں کا		**kitābēṁ →**	**kitābōṁ kā**

(b) The plural suffix **-īyāṁ** changes to **-īyōṁ**:

لڑکیاں ← لڑکیوں کا	**laṛkiyāṁ →**	**laṛkiyōṁ kā**

(c) The suffix **-ōṁ** is added to the suffixless masculine unmarked forms:

گھر ← گھروں کا	**ghar →**	**gharōṁ kā**

Examples

اِن کنوؤں کا پانی ٹھنڈا ہے -
in *kūōṁ* kā pānī ṭhanḍā hai
The water of these *wells* is cold.

گھروں کے کرائے مختلف ہیں -
***gharōṁ* kē kirāē muxtalif haiṁ**
The houses have various rents (lit. rents of *the houses* are various).

لڑکیوں کا بھائی کراچی میں ہے -
***laṛkiyōṁ* kā bhāī karācī mēṁ hai**
The girls' brother is in Karachi (lit. the brother of the *girls* is in Karachi).

کتابوں کی قیمتیں مختلف ہیں -
***kitābōṁ* kī qīmatēṁ muxtalif haiṁ**
The books have various prices (lit. prices of *the books* are various).

Table 2: Oblique case of nouns

SINGULAR	NOMINATIVE		OBLIQUE	
MASC. MARKED	لڑکا	**laṛkā**	لڑکے	**laṛkē**
	کمرہ	**kamra**	کمرے	**kamrē**
	روپیہ	**rūpaya**	روپئے ، روپے	**rūpaē, rūpē**
	کنواں	**kūāṁ**	کنوئیں	**kūēṁ**
MASC. UNMARKED	گھر	**ghar**	گھر	**ghar**
FEM. MARKED	لڑکی	**laṛkī**	لڑکی	**laṛkī**
	چڑیا	**ciṛiyā**	چڑیا	**ciṛiyā**
FEM. UNMARKED	کتاب	**kitāb**	کتاب	**kitāb**
PLURAL	**NOMINATIVE**		**OBLIQUE**	
MASC. MARKED	لڑکے	**laṛkē**	لڑکوں	**laṛkōṁ**
	کمرے	**kamrē**	کمروں	**kamrōṁ**
	روپئے ، روپے	**rūpaē, rūpē**	روپوں	**rūpōṁ**
	کنوئیں	**kūēṁ**	کنوؤں	**kūōṁ**
MASC. UNMARKED	گھر	**ghar**	گھروں	**gharōṁ**
FEM. MARKED	لڑکیاں	**laṛkiyāṁ**	لڑکیوں	**laṛkiyōṁ**
	چڑیاں	**ciṛiyāṁ**	چڑیوں	**ciṛiyōṁ**
FEM. UNMARKED	کتابیں	**kitābēṁ**	کتابوں	**kitābōṁ**

111 Oblique nouns resulting from dropping of kō

The postposition **kō**, 'to', 'at' is often dropped in expressions describing movement to a destination. The noun remains in the oblique case. See §507.

Nouns in time expressions also appear in the oblique case. See §1309, §1311.

112 Expressing totality

Numbers, time words and the pronoun **sab** may occur in the oblique plural to express totality or an indefinitely large amount. In numbers 20 or lower, it tends to express totality; in higher numbers it expresses an indefinitely large amount.

The following words have special stems before **-ōṁ**.

BASIC FORM		STEM BEFORE **-ōṁ**		STEM PLUS **-ōṁ**	
دو	**dō**, two	دون	**dōn-**	دونوں	**dōnōṁ**
سو	**sau**, hundred	سینکڑ	**saiṁkaṛ-**	سینکڑوں	**saiṁkaṛōṁ**
سب	**sab**, all	سبھ	**sabh-**[2]	سبھوں	**sabhōṁ**

Totality

پانچوں مہمان آ گئے -
***pāṁcōṁ* mehmān ā gaē**
All five guests came.

اُنہوں نے سبھوں کو بلایا -
unhōṁ nē *sabhōṁ* kō bulāyā
He called *every single one of* them.

Indefinitely large amounts

سینکڑوں درخت
***saiṁkaṛōṁ* daraxt**
hundreds of trees

وہ گھنٹوں روتی رہی -
vo *ghanṭōṁ* rōtī rahī.
She went on crying *for hours*.

Totality may also be expressed by a phrase in the pattern: **X kā X**, where **X** is a repeated noun, noun phrase or the pronoun **sab**. In this expression, the oblique plural is not used.

چھ کے چھ مہمان آ گئے -
***chē kē chē* mehmān ā gaē**
All six guests came.

آگ میں جنگل کا جنگل جل گیا -
āg mēṁ *jangal kā jangal* jal gayā.
The entire forest burned in the fire.

سارے کے سارے درخت جل گئے -
***sārē kē sārē* daraxt jal gaē**
Every last tree burned.

سب کا سب لُٹ گیا -
***sab kā sab* luṭ gayā**
Every last thing was looted.

113 Vocative case of nouns

The vocative singular suffix is identical with the oblique suffix. The vocative plural suffix is **-ō** و .

The vocative is used only towards persons or objects identified with persons, and does not occur very often. Vocatives may be introduced by the vocative interjections, **ō** او , **ai** اَے , 'o' or **arē** ارے , 'hey' (§1217).

2 This stem is actually derived from **sab hī** (**sab**, 'all' + **hī**, emphatic particle).

The nominative form of **bēṭā**, 'son' is sometimes used in place of the vocative, addressing both boys and girls.

Table 3: Vocative case of nouns

SINGULAR	NOMINATIVE		VOCATIVE	
MASC. MARKED	لڑکا	**laṛkā**	لڑکے	**laṛkē**
MASC. UNMARKED	بھائی	**bhāī**	بھائی	**bhāī**
FEM. MARKED	لڑکی	**laṛkī**	لڑکی	**laṛkī**
FEM. UNMARKED	بہن	**bahen**	بہن	**bahen**

PLURAL	NOMINATIVE		VOCATIVE	
MASC. MARKED	لڑکے	**laṛkē**	لڑکو	**laṛkō**
MASC. UNMARKED	بھائی	**bhāī**	بھائیو	**bhāiyō**
FEM. MARKED	لڑکی	**laṛkī**	لڑکیو	**laṛkiyō**
FEM. UNMARKED	بہن	**bahen**	بہنو	**bahnō**

Examples

بیٹے ، اِدھر آؤ -
***bēṭē*, idhar āō**
Son, come here.

او رکشے والے !
ō *rikśē vālē*!
O *rickshaw driver*!

بچّو ، سنو -
***baccō*, sunō**
Listen, *children*.

بھائیو اور بہنو !
***bhāiyō* aur *bahnō*!** [3]
Brothers and *sisters*!

3 See 'Reduction of penultimate short vowels' under §107 for loss of penultimate **-e-** in **bah(e)no**.

REPETITION OF NOUNS

114 Simple repetition

The doubling of nouns expresses variety or multiplicity.

اِس دکان میں طرح طرح کے مسالے ملتے ہیں -
is dukān mēṁ *tarah tarah* kē masālē miltē haiṁ
Various kinds of spices are available in this shop.

ہم نے فقیر کو گلی گلی ڈھونڈا -
ham nē faqīr kō *galī galī* ḍhūṁḍā
We searched for the faqir in *lane after lane*.

115 Repetition with an echo word

Nouns (and other parts of speech) are sometimes repeated with a rhyming echo word, often one beginning with **v-** و. Echo words beginning with **v-** have no meaning of their own; their function is to generalize the meaning of the first word. Sometimes an echo word has a meaning of its own, but its independent occurrence is much less frequent than its occurrence in the compound.

چابی وابی
cābī vābī
something like a key (< **cābī**, key)

دھوم دھام
dhūm dhām
pomp and show (< **dhūm**, pomp; **dhām**, splendour)

NOUNS AS UNITS OF MEASURE (116)

Nouns describing measure, quantity and price may behave like adjectives and precede the nouns they qualify. Used in this way, they are not followed by the possessive **kā**. Marked masculine measure nouns (**camca**, **rūpaya**) take plural suffixes when they denote a plural number. Feminine measure nouns (**piyālī**, **bālṭī**) do not.

پچاس روپئے میٹر
pacās *rūpaē* mīṭar
fifty *rupees* (a) metre

دو چمچے چینی
dō *camcē* cīnī
two *spoons* (of) sugar

چار پیالی چائے
cār *piyālī* cāē
four *cups* (of) tea

دو بالٹی پانی
dō *bālṭī* pānī
two *buckets* (of) water

However, if the noun is not used like an adjective, it inflects in the usual way:

مجھے پانی کی دو بالٹیاں چاہئیں ۔
mujhē pānī kī dō *bālṭiyāṁ* cāhiēṁ
I need two *buckets* of water (two different buckets, both containing water).

When nouns showing units of measure, time or money are preceded by numbers, they do not take the oblique plural suffix.

سو دفعہ سے زیادہ
sau *dafa* sē zyāda
more than one hundred *times*

میں دو گھنٹے میں آؤں گی ۔
maiṁ dō *ghanṭē* mēṁ āūṁ gī
I will come in two *hours.*

دو دن کے بعد آنا ۔
dō *din* kē bād ānā
Come after two *days.*

But:

کچھ دنوں کے بعد آنا ۔
kuch *dinōṁ* kē bād ānā
Come after a few *days.*

OTHER PARTS OF SPEECH USED AS NOUNS (**117**)

Many adjectives can also be used as nouns. See §319.

A few Perso-Arabic loanwords, including **naujavān** نوجوان , 'young man'; **ɣairmulkī** غیرملکی , 'foreigner'; **numāinda** نمائندہ , 'representative', and nouns denoting nationality, are classified as both nouns and adjectives. See §319.

Participles are essentially verbal adjectives. Both imperfect and perfect participles may be used as nouns (though it is infrequent). See §906, §911.

The infinitive is a verbal noun and is used as a noun in sentences. See §639.

2 PRONOUNS

There is no distinction between the masculine and feminine genders in Urdu pronouns. The same pronoun is used for both 'he' and 'she' (the verb phrase often provides the information, however). There is on the other hand a distinction between proximate and distant in the third person: Urdu distinguishes between a 'he/she/it' which is close at hand, and a 'he/she/it' which is at a distance.

Urdu pronouns may refer to singular or plural people or things. Plural pronouns referring to people may refer to two or more people (grammatical plural), or to a single person respectfully (polite plural).

Like nouns, pronouns may occur in the nominative case (for example as subjects of sentences) or in the oblique case (followed by postpositions; §208).[1]

DEMONSTRATIVE PRONOUNS

201 ye, 'this' and vo, 'that'

The demonstrative pronoun **ye**, 'this' refers to something or someone close at hand. The demonstrative pronoun **vo**, 'that' refers to something or someone further away. The demonstrative pronouns **ye** and **vo** are identical in form to the personal pronouns **ye** and **vo** (meaning 'he', 'she', 'it').

In the nominative case, the plural forms of **ye** and **vo** are identical to their singular forms. Only the verb shows whether the pronoun refers to a singular or plural noun.

Examples

یہ کیا ہے ؟	**ye kyā hai?**	What is this?
یہ گھڑا ہے	**ye ghaṛā hai**	This is a water pot.
یہ کیا ہیں ؟	**ye kyā haiṁ?**	What are these?
یہ گھڑے ہیں	**ye ghaṛē haiṁ**	These are water pots.

In the oblique case, however, **ye** and **vo** have distinct singular and plural forms.

1 See Chapter 1, footnote 3 for a definition of the term 'case' as used in this work.

Nominative and oblique demonstratives

	NOMINATIVE		OBLIQUE	
SINGULAR	یہ	**ye**	اِس	**is**
	وہ	**vo**	اُس	**us**
PLURAL	یہ	**ye**	اِن	**in**
	وہ	**vo**	اُن	**un**

Examples

اِس کا نام کیا ہے ؟
***is* kā nām kyā hai?**
What is the name of *this*?

اُس کا نام کیا ہے ؟
***us* kā nām kyā hai?**
What is the name of *that*?

اُن کو کیا کہتے ہیں ؟
***un* kō kyā kahtē haiṁ?**
What do you call *those*?

ہم اِن کو گھڑے کہتے ہیں -
ham *in* kō gharẹ̄ kahtē haiṁ
We call *these* water pots.

The demonstrative pronouns also function as adjectives.

یہ گھڑا بڑا ہے -
***ye* gharạ̄ barạ̄ hai**
This water pot is big.

وہ کنواں بہت گہرا ہے -
***vo* kuāṁ bahut gahrā hai**
That well is very deep.

اِس کنوئیں کا پانی ٹھنڈا ہے -
***is* kuēṁ kā pānī ṭhanḍā hai**
The water of *this* well is cold.

PERSONAL PRONOUNS

202 Forms

Table 4: Persons and cases of personal pronouns

		Nominative		Oblique	
Singular					
1st person	میں	**maiṁ**, I	مجھ	**mujh**
2nd person	تو	**tū**, you	تجھ	**tujh**
3rd person	وہ	**vo**, he, she, it	اُس	**us**
	یہ	**ye**, he, she, it	اِس	**is**
Plural					
1st person	ہم	**ham**, we	ہم	**ham**
2nd person	تم	**tum**, you	تم	**tum**
	آپ	**āp**, you	آپ	**āp**
3rd person	وہ	**vo**, they	اُن	**un**
	یہ	**ye**, they	اِن	**in**

203 Honorific levels in second person pronouns

There are three second person pronouns: **tū**, **tum** and **āp**. The use of **tū** is very intimate, **tum** is non-honorific, and **āp** is honorific.

tū تو — is used only when addressing a small child in one's own family, one's beloved, God, as an insult, or as a reproof to a servant or subordinate. It occurs commonly in poetry (where according to convention, the poet addresses his beloved).

tum تم — is used when addressing one or more persons of lower status, children, or close family members younger than oneself. Persons of equal status may address each other as **tum** in informal social situations. When addressing small children in another person's family, one should use **tum**, not **tū**.

āp آپ — is used when addressing one or more persons of higher status, persons to whom respect is due, or family members elder than onself. It is also used by young persons to elderly persons (even if the elder is a servant), to skilled persons (of all socio-economic ranks), and by parents to children, to teach them good manners. Finally, persons of equal status generally address each other as **āp** in formal social situations, such as an office or a formal event.

āp آپ is also used as a third person polite plural pronoun meaning 'he', 'she'. This is even more honorific than **vo** + plural verb, so is used to refer to persons to whom a high degree of respect is due (including revered religious personages, especially the Prophet Mohammad (PBUH)).

Examples

تو کیا کھا رہا ہے؟ منہ کھول۔
tū **kyā khā rahā hai? mumh khōl**
What are *you* eating? Open (your) mouth (to a very small child).

(تم) بیٹھو۔
(*tum*) baiṭhō
(*You*) please sit down.

تم اِتنی رات گئے کہاں جا رہی ہو؟
tum **itnī rāt gaē kahāṁ jā rahī hō?**
Where are *you* going so late at night (to a younger family member)?

آپ بیٹھئے
āp **baiṭhiē**
You please sit down (to an elder).

آپ سے درخواست ہے کہ ہمیں اپنے فن سے نوازیں۔
āp **sē darxāst hai ke hamēṁ apnē fann sē navāzēṁ**
He (an honoured poet) is requested to favour us with his art.

204 ham used as a first person singular pronoun

The first personal plural **ham** is sometimes colloquially used in place of the singular, **maiṁ**. By referring to himself as a member of a group, the speaker makes himself slightly more anonymous. The use of **ham** may also reflect a person's assumption of social superiority or superior status. **ham** is also used in place of **maiṁ** in poetry.

ہم کو اُن سے وفا کی ہے اُمید
جو نہیں جانتے وفا کیا ہے
ham **kō un sē vafā kī hai ummīd**
jō nahīṁ jāntē vafā kyā hai
I hope for loyalty from the one
Who does not know what loyalty is (Ghālib)

205 Omission of personal pronouns

Personal pronouns, especially **tū** and **tum**, are often omitted in sentences, since the verb provides information about person, number, gender and level of respect.

کیا کرو گے ؟
kyā karō gē?
What will you (**tum**) do?

کیا کریں گے ؟
kyā karēṁ gē?
What will you (**āp**) do?

کیا کر رہا ہے ؟
kyā kar rahā hai?
What are you (**tū**) doing? (reproof)

کل جاؤں گا ۔
kal jāūṁ gā
I (**maiṁ**) will go tomorrow.

206 lōg as a plural specifier

The noun **lōg**, 'people' may be added to plural personal pronouns to specify or emphasize plurality. The resulting phrase is masculine plural.

ہم لوگ (ہیں)	**ham lōg (haiṁ)**	We (are)
تم لوگ (ہو)	**tum lōg (hō)**	You (are)
آپ لوگ (ہیں)	**āp lōg (haiṁ)**	You (are)
وہ لوگ (ہیں)	**vo lōg (haiṁ)**	They (are)

207 Nominative pronouns

Nominative pronouns most commonly occur as the subjects of verbs (except for transitive verbs in perfect tenses, where the subject takes **nē** (§510, §629).

میں یہاں رہتا ہوں ۔
***maiṁ* yahāṁ rahtā hūṁ**
I live here.

تم کہاں رہتے ہو ؟
***tum* kahāṁ rahtē hō?**
Where do *you* live?

وہ پاس میں رہتا ہے ۔
***vo* pās mēṁ rahtā hai**
He lives nearby.

وہ پاس میں رہتے ہیں ۔
***vo* pās mēṁ rahtē haiṁ**
They live nearby.

A nominative third person pronoun very occasionally occurs as the direct object of a sentence, referring to a thing.

میں نے یہ پڑھا ہے ، وہ نہیں پڑھا ۔
maiṁ nē *ye* paṛhā hai, *vo* nahīṁ paṛhā
I have read *this*, not *that*.

208 Oblique (inflected) pronouns

Whenever a pronoun is followed by a postposition (for example, **kō** کو, 'to' **kā** کا, 'of', **mēṁ** میں, 'in', **sē** سے, 'from', etc.), it occurs in the oblique case, as shown in the following examples.

The functions of location and direction, as well as many grammatical functions, are shown in Urdu by postpositions, described in Chapter 5.

The oblique case of the pronouns **ham, tum** and **āp** is identical to the nominative case.

ملک صاحب آپ کو چائے پلائیں گے -
malik sāhib *āp* kō cāē pilāēṁ gē
Mr. Malik will give *you* tea to drink.

ہم پر ذمہ داری ہے -
***ham* par zimmēdārī hai**
The responsibility is ours (lit. on *us*).

The pronouns **maiṁ**, **tū**, **ye** and **vo**, however, have distinct oblique case forms. See Table 5, p. 21.

ملک صاحب مجھ کو چائے پلائیں گے -
malik sāhib *mujh* kō[2] cāē pilāēṁ gē
Mr. Malik will give *me* tea to drink.

تجھ کو نیند آئی ہے ، منّی ؟
***tujh* kō nīṁd āī hai, munnī?**
Are you sleepy, child (lit. is sleep coming to *you*)?

اُن پر ذمہ داری ہے -
***un* par zimmēdārī hai**
The responsibility is his/theirs (lit. on him/them).

اِس میں کوئی شک نہیں -
***is* mēṁ kōī śak nahīṁ**
There is no doubt about (lit. in) *this*.

---

2 An alternate form, **mujhē** مجھے, is however more common than **mujh kō** مجھ کو. The pronouns **tū**, **tum**, **ham**, **vo** and **ye** also have alternate forms. See §210.

209 Exception to §208

First and second person pronouns occur in the nominative case before the postposition **nē** نے . See §211, Table 6.

210 The suffix ē ~ (h)ēṁ replacing kō

The postposition **kō** کو, 'to', 'at' shows (a) animate or specified direct objects and (b) indirect objects (§505). Following pronouns (including personal, demonstrative, interrogative and relative pronouns, except **āp**) it may be replaced by the suffix **ē** ~ **(h)ēṁ**. This usage is more common than the usage with **kō**, especially in the spoken language. Both usages are shown below in Table 5.

NOTE: the spelling with ہ (**chōṭī hē**) shown below is more common than spelling with ھ (**dō caśmī hē**), except in **mujh**, **tujh**. But all the alternate forms can also be spelled with ھ .

Table 5: Oblique pronouns + alternate forms of **kō**

	PRONOUN + kō		PRONOUN + ē ~ (h)ēṁ	
SINGULAR				
1st person	مجھ کو	**mujh kō**	مجھے	**mujhē**
2nd person	تجھ کو	**tujh kō**	تجھے	**tujhē**
3rd person	اُس کو	**us kō**	اُسے	**usē**
	اِس کو	**is kō**	اِسے	**isē**
PLURAL				
1st person	ہم کو	**ham kō**	ہمیں	**hamēṁ**
2nd person	تم کو	**tum kō**	تمہیں ~ تمھیں	**tumhēṁ**
	آپ کو	**āp kō**	—	—
3rd person	اُن کو	**un kō**	اُنہیں ~ اُنھیں	**unhēṁ**
	اِن کو	**in kō**	اِنہیں ~ اِنھیں	**inhēṁ**

Examples

خورشید صاحب مجھے چائے پلاتے ہیں -
xurśīd sāhib *mujhē* cāē pilātē haiṁ
Mr. Khurshid gives me tea to drink (lit. gives tea *to me*).

دلِ ناداں، تجھے ہوا کیا ہے
dil-e-nādāṁ, *tujhē* hūā kyā hai
Foolish heart, what has happened *to you* (Ghālib)

کیا تمہیں کچھ چاہئے ؟
kyā *tumhēṁ* kuch cāhiē?
Do you need anything (is anything needed *to you*)?

آپ نے اُنہیں کیا بتایا ؟
***āp nē* unhēṁ kyā batāyā?**
What did *you* tell them?

211 Pronouns before the postposition nē

When pronouns occur as the subjects of sentences, the sentence verbs agree with them in gender, number and person. There is an exception to this rule: the subjects of transitive verbs in perfect tenses agree with the direct object, and the subject is followed by the postposition **nē** (see §510, §629). When followed by **nē**, first and second person pronouns occur in the nominative case. Third person singular pronouns occur in the oblique case. Third person plural pronouns have special forms which occur only before **nē**.

Table 6: Forms of pronouns before nē

		Nominative		Pronoun + nē
Singular				
1st person	میں	**maiṁ**, I	میں نے	**maiṁ nē**
2nd person	تو	**tū**, you	تو نے	**tū nē**
3rd person	وہ	**vo**, he, she, it	اُس نے	**us nē**
	یہ	**ye**, he, she, it	اِس نے	**is nē**
Plural				
1st person	ہم	**ham**, we	ہم نے	**ham nē**
2nd person	تم	**tum**, you	تم نے	**tum nē**
	آپ	**āp**, you	آپ نے	**āp nē**
3rd person	وہ	**vo**, they	اُنھوں نے	**unhōṁ nē** [3]
	یہ	**ye**, they	اِنھوں نے	**inhōṁ nē**

3 اُنہوں نے **unhōṁ nē**, etc. is also correct, and reflects the phonology more accurately. But the spellings given here are the ones in common use.

Examples

میں نے ملک صاحب کو چائے پلائی ۔
***maiṁ nē* malik sāhib kō cāē pilāī**
I gave Mr. Malik tea to drink.

تم نے بازار سے کیا خریدا ؟
***tum nē* bāzār sē kyā xarīdā?**
What did *you* buy in (from) the market?

آپ نے سڑک پر کیا دیکھا ؟
***āp nē* saṛak par kyā dēkhā?**
What did *you* see on the road?

ہم نے اونٹوں کا کارواں دیکھا ۔
***ham nē* ūṁṭōṁ kā kārvāṁ dēkhā**
We saw a caravan of camels.

اُس نے اونٹ پر سواری کی ۔
***us nē* ūṁṭ par savārī kī**
He rode on a camel.

اُنہوں نے اونٹ پر سواری کی ۔
***unhōṁ nē* ūṁṭ par savārī kī**
They rode on a camel.

212 Possessive forms of personal pronouns

The possessive forms of pronouns are grammatically adjectives, and agree with the nouns they qualify. The possessives are shown in Table 7 on p. 24.

The possessives are marked (§301): they have suffixes that inflect to show gender and number.

میرا بھائی	**mērā bhāī**, my brother
میری بہن	**mērī bahen**, my sister
میرے والدین	**mērē vālidain**, my parents
اُس کا بھائی	**us kā bhāī**, his/her brother
اُس کی بہن	**us kī bahen**, his/her sister
اُس کے والدین	**us kē vālidain**, his/her parents

تمہارا بھائی	**tumhārā bhāī**, your brother
تمہاری بہن	**tumhārī bahen**, your sister
تمہارے والدین	**tumhārē vālidain**, your parents

Table 7: Possessive forms of personal pronouns

	Nominative		Possessive	
Singular				
1st person	میں	**maiṁ**, I	میرا	**mērā**
2nd person	تو	**tū**, you	تیرا	**tērā**
3rd person	وہ	**vo**, he, she, it	اُس کا	**us kā**
	یہ	**ye**, he, she, it	اِس کا	**is kā**
Plural				
1st person	ہم	**ham**, we	ہمارا	**hamārā**
2nd person	تم	**tum**, you	تمہارا	**tumhārā**
	آپ	**āp**, you	آپ کا	**āp kā**
3rd person	وہ	**vo**, they	اُن کا	**un kā**
	یہ	**ye**, they	اِن کا	**in kā**

REFLEXIVE PRONOUNS

213 The reflexive possessive adjective apnā

The possessive adjective **apnā**, 'one's own' is substituted for the possessive forms of personal pronouns when the subject of the sentence possesses the object. **apnā** agrees with the noun it qualifies.

احمد اپنی گھڑی دیکھ رہا ہے -
ahmad *apnī* ghaṛī dēkh rahā hai
Ahmad is looking at *his* (own) watch.

احمد اُس کی گھڑی دیکھ رہا ہے -
ahmad *us kī* ghaṛī dēkh rahā hai
Ahmad is looking at *his* (someone else's) watch.

ہم اپنے گھر میں رہتے ہیں -
ham *apnē* ghar mēṁ rahtē haiṁ
We live in *our* (own) house.

میں اپنی کتاب پڑھ رہا ہوں -
maiṁ *apnī* kitāb paṛh rahā hūṁ
I am reading *my* (own) book.

WRONG میں میری کتاب پڑھ رہا ہوں - **maiṁ mērī kitāb paṛh rahā hūṁ**
WRONG ہم ہمارے گھر میں رہتے ہیں - **ham hamārē ghar mēṁ rahtē haiṁ**

apnā can also be used after possessives for emphasis:

یہ میری اپنی گاڑی ہے -
ye *mērī apnī* gāṛī hai
This is *my own* car.

214 **xud** and **āp**, 'self'

Both **xud** and **āp** mean *X-self* (myself, yourself, himself, ourselves, themselves, etc.). **xud** is the commoner of the two.

میں خود ڈاکٹر سے بات کرنا چاہتا ہوں -
maiṁ *xud* ḍākṭar sē bāt karnā cāhtā hūṁ
I want to speak to the doctor *myself.*

میں آپ وہاں گیا -
maiṁ *āp* vahāṁ gayā
I went there *myself.*

215 **apnē āp, xud, xud baxud**

To express something that someone does by himself, without help from others, or something that happens spontaneously, **apnē āp** or **xud** may be used.

ہم نے اپنے آپ یہ پل مرمّت کیا -
ham nē *apnē āp* ye pul marammat kiyā
We repaired this bridge *by ourselves.*

ہم نے خود یہ پل مرمّت کیا -
ham nē *xud* ye pul marammat kiyā
We repaired this bridge *by ourselves.*

بجلی اپنے آپ جل اُٹھی -
bijlī *apnē āp* jal uṭhī
The electric bulb suddenly lit up *by itself.*

xud baxud, 'of one's own accord' may be used with intransitive verbs to express 'by himself', 'by itself', etc.

بجلی خود بخود جل اُٹھی -
bijlī *xud baxud* jal uṭhī
The electric bulb suddenly lit up *by itself.*

216 āpas mēṁ, 'among'

Something people do 'among' themselves (reciprocally) is expressed by **āpas mēṁ**:

لوگ آپس میں بات کر رہے تھے -
lōg *āpas mēṁ* bāt kar rahē thē
The people were talking *among themselves.*

INTERROGATIVE PRONOUNS

217 kyā, 'what?'

kyā means 'what' (referring to things). It is also used as an adjective qualifying a noun, especially before oblique case nouns, where it means 'which' (§220).

kyā shares its oblique case with **kaun**. See §220, Table 8.

Interrogative words usually come right before the verb. See §1006.

یہ کیا ہے ؟
ye *kyā* hai?
What is this?

یہ کیا ہیں ؟
ye *kyā* haiṁ?
What are these?

آپ کے دوست کا کیا نام ہے ؟
āp kē dōst kā *kyā* nām hai?
What is your friend's name?

218 kyā marking questions and exclamations

kyā may also be used as a question marker, turning a statement into a yes-or-no question. It is not translated.

کیا یہ گھڑا ہے ؟
kyā ye ghaṛā hai?
Is this is a water pot?

kyā may introduce an exclamatory sentence.

> کیا مزیدار کھانا ہے !
> ***kyā* mazēdār khānā hai!**
> *What* delicious food (it is)!

219 kaun, 'who?'

kaun means 'who?'. It is occasionally also used as an adjective, qualifying a noun. The singular and plural froms of **kaun** are distinguished only in the oblique case. In the nominative case, **lōg**, 'people' may be added to specify the plural, or **kaun** may be doubled (§225).

> دروازے پر کون ہے ؟
> **darvāzē par *kaun* hai?**
> *Who* is at the door?

> یہ کون ہے ؟
> **ye *kaun* hai?**
> *Who* is he/she?

> یہ لوگ کون ہیں ؟
> **ye lōg *kaun* haiṁ?**
> *Who* are they (these people)?

> کون صاحب بول رہے ہیں ؟
> ***kaun* sāhib bōl rahē haiṁ?**
> *Who* is speaking (sir)?

220 Oblique forms of kyā and kaun

The oblique and plural forms of the interrogative pronouns are shown in Table 8. Like **vo** and **ye, kyā** and **kaun** have special oblique plural forms which occur only before **nē**. **kyā** and **kaun** may take the alternate suffixal forms of **kō** (§210): کسے **kisē** (= **kis kō**), کنہیں **kinhēṁ** (= **kin kō**).

Table 8: Oblique and plural forms of **kyā** and **kaun**

		Nominative		Oblique		+ nē
Singular						
	کیا	**kyā**, what?	کس	**kis**	کس نے	**kis nē**
	کون	**kaun**, who?	کس	**kis**	کس نے	**kis nē**
Plural						
	کیا	**kyā**, what?	کن	**kin**	—	—
	کون	**kaun**, who?	کن	**kin**	کنہوں نے	**kinhōṁ nē**

Examples

یہ سامان کس کا ہے ؟
ye sāmān *kis* kā hai?
Whose baggage is this (lit. of *whom* is this baggage)?

یہ ٹکٹ کن کے ہیں ؟
ye ṭikaṭ *kin* kē haiṁ?
Whose tickets are these (lit. of *whom* are these tickets)?

سامان یہاں کس نے چھوڑا ؟
sāmān yahāṁ *kis nē* chōṛā?
Who left the luggage here?

The oblique forms of **kyā** occur mainly as adjectives, meaning 'which'.

آپ کس دفتر میں کام کرتے ہیں ؟
āp *kis* daftar mēṁ kām kartē haiṁ?
Which office do you work in?

یہ کن کمروں کی چابیاں ہیں ؟
ye *kin* kamrōṁ kī cābiyāṁ haiṁ?
(For) *which* rooms are these the keys?

However 'which' (of a finite number of possibilities) is usually expressed by adding the adjectival particle **sā** (~ **sī** ~ **sē**) to **kaun** (§310).

کون سا کمرہ خالی ہے ؟
***kaun sā* kamra xālī hai?**
Which room is vacant?

INDEFINITE PRONOUNS

221 kōī, 'some(one)', 'any(one)'

kōī is used both as a pronoun and an adjective. As a pronoun, it means 'someone', 'anyone'. If the sentence is negative, it means 'no one'.

دروازے پر کوئی ہے -
darvāzē par *kōī* hai
There is *someone* at the door.

گھر پر کوئی نہیں -
ghar par *kōī nahīṁ*
No one is at home.

As an adjective, **kōī** means 'some', 'any' and qualifies only count nouns. If the sentence is negative, it means 'no', 'not any'.

کیا یہاں کوئی ٹیکسی ملے گی ؟
kyā yahāṁ *kōī* ṭaiksī milē gī?
Is *any* taxi available here?

میرے پاس کوئی تصویر (تصویریں) نہیں -
mērē pās *kōī* tasvīr (tasvīrēṁ) *nahīṁ*
I have *no* picture(s).

The oblique form of **kōī** is **kisī**. **kisī** is also the form used before **nē**.

کسی کے پاس دولت ہے ، کسی کے پاس کچھ بھی نہیں ہے -
***kisī* kē pās daulat hai, *kisī* kē pās kuch bhī nahīṁ hai**
Some have wealth, (and) *some* have nothing at all.

پیسہ کسی نے چُرا لیا -
paisa *kisī nē* curā liyā.
Someone stole the money.

222 kuch, 'some(thing)', 'any(thing)'

kuch, 'some(thing)', 'any(thing)' is used both as a pronoun and an adjective. As a pronoun, it means 'something'. If there is a negative word in the sentence, it means 'nothing', 'not anything'. **kuch** does not have an oblique form.

کچھ کرو ، یار !
***kuch* karō, yār!**
Do *something*, pal!

As an adjective it means 'some', 'any' and qualifies both non-count nouns and plural count nouns. With count nouns, **kuch** + NEGATIVE means 'not some of (something)'.

وہ کچھ نہیں کرے گا -
vo *kuch* nahīṁ karē gā
He won't do *anything*.

کچھ پانی لاؤ -
***kuch* pānī lāō**
Bring *some* water.

کچھ دیر بعد آئیے ۔
***kuch* dēr bād āiyē**[4]
Please come after *some* time (a little later).

کچھ تصویریں میز پر ہیں ۔
***kuch* tasvīrēṁ mēz par haiṁ**
There are *some* pictures on the table/*some* of the pictures are on the table.

اُس کے پاس کچھ پانی بچا ہوا تھا ۔
us kē pās *kuch* pānī bacā hūā thā
He had saved *some* of the water (he had *some* water which had been saved).

kuch does not qualify uncount nouns in negative sentences.

WRONG	کچھ پانی نہیں ۔	**kuch pānī nahīṁ**
CORRECT	پانی نہیں ۔	**pānī nahīṁ** There's no water

RELATIVE PRONOUN

223 jō

The relative pronoun corresponding to **vo** and **ye** is **jō** جو , 'who', 'which'. See §1106-§1107.

REPEATED PRONOUNS

224 kyā kyā

When **kyā** is doubled, it means 'what (various) things?', and takes a singular verb.

آپ نے وہاں کیا کیا دیکھا ؟
āp nē vahāṁ *kyā kyā* dēkhā?
What things did you see there?

225 kaun kaun

When **kaun** is doubled, it means 'which (various) people?', and takes a singular verb.

---

4 One would normally expect **kuch dēr kē bād**, but after **dēr**, omission of **kē** is idiomatic.

دعوت میں کون کون آیا ؟
dāvat mēṁ *kaun kaun* āyā?
Which various people came to the party?

226 kōī kōī, kōī na kōī

kōī kōī means 'a few'.

جلسے میں صرف کوئی کوئی آیا ۔
jalsē mēṁ sirf *kōī kōī* āyā
Only *a few* came to the meeting.

kōī na kōī means 'someone (or the other)'.

کوئی نہ کوئی گھر پر ہو گا ۔
***kōī na kōī* ghar par hō gā**
Someone must be at home.

کسی نہ کسی کو معلوم ہو گا ۔
***kisī na kisī* kō mālūm hō gā**
Someone must know it.

227 kuch kuch, kuch na kuch

kuch kuch means 'somewhat'.

وہ کچھ کچھ ٹھیک ہے ۔
vo *kuch kuch* ṭhīk hai
He is *somewhat* better.

kuch na kuch means 'something (or the other)'.

اِس واقعہ کے پیچھے کچھ نہ کچھ ضرور ہو گا ۔
is vāqea kē pīchē *kuch na kuch* zarūr hō gā
Something is certainly at the bottom of (behind) this event.

3 ADJECTIVES

MARKING

Adjectives qualify nouns, as modifiers, or as predicate complements. Like nouns, adjectives are divided into two groups: those which have suffixes that change to show gender and number (marked adjectives), and those which do not (unmarked adjectives).

301 Marked adjectives

Adjectives which may take the masculine singular suffixes **-ā** ا or **-āṁ** اں are marked.

اچّھا کام	دایاں ہاتھ
***acchā* kām** (m.)	***dāyāṁ* hāth** (m.)
a *good* job	the *right* hand

These suffixes change to agree with the noun which the adjective qualifies (§303-§304).

اچّھی بات	دائیں آنکھ
***acchī* bāt** (f.)	***dāīṁ* āṁkh** (f.)
a *good* thing	the *right* eye

302 Unmarked adjectives

Unmarked adjectives have no special suffixes and do not change to show agreement.

دلچسپ کام	دلچسپ بات
***dilcasp* kām**	***dilcasp* bāt**
interesting work	an *interesting* thing

Some adjectives look like marked adjectives, but are not. In the examples which follow, **tāza** تازہ and **zinda** زندہ are Persian adjectives which end in **-a** ہ (**chōṭī hē**). Whereas nouns ending in **-a** ہ are treated as marked nouns, and change to show number and case (§103), adjectives ending in **-a** ہ do not change.

تازہ کیلا
tāza kēlā (m.)
a *fresh* banana

تازہ خوبانی
tāza khūbānī (f.)
a *fresh* apricot

Persian past participles ending in **-a** ہ are unmarked adjectives in Urdu.

تعلیم یافتہ خاتون
tālīm yāfta xātūn (f.)
an *educated* lady

Many adjectives are formed from nouns, or from other adjectives, by adding the adjectival suffix **-ī** ی , which may be of Persian origin, or an indigenous Urdu suffix. In either case, the suffix does not change.

دیسی گھی
dēsī ghī (m.)
indigenous clarified butter, 'desi ghee' (< **dēs** دیس , country)

دیسی خوبانی
dēsī khūbānī (f.)
an *indigenous* apricot

دفتری کام
daftarī kām (m.)
official work (< **daftar** دفتر, office)

لازمی بات
lāzimī bāt (f.)
essential thing (< **lāzim** لازم , necessary)

Arabic adjectives which happen to end in **ā** (ٰی ، ع ، ا) or **ī** (ی) are unmarked: **ālā** اعلیٰ 'high'; **muttalā** مطّلع , 'informed'; **mubtalā**, مبتلا 'afflicted'; **bāqī** باقی , 'remaining'; **jārī** جاری 'continuing'.

اعلیٰ معیار
ālā mēyār (m.)
a *high* standard

اعلیٰ سطح
ālā satah (f.)
a *high* level

باقی پیسہ
bāqī paisa (m.)
the rest of the money (*remaining* money)

نمائش اگلے ہفتے بھی جاری رہے گی -
numāiś aglē haftē bhī *jārī* rahē gī
The exhibition is *continuing* next week too.

AGREEMENT

303 Agreement in gender and number

Marked adjectives change to agree with nouns in gender and number.

Table 9: Gender and number suffixes of adjectives

	Singular		Plural	
Masculine	بڑا	**baṛā**	بڑے	**baṛē**
	دایاں	**dāyāṁ**	دائیں	**dāēṁ**
Feminine	بڑی	**baṛī**	بڑی	**baṛī**
	دائیں	**dāīṁ**	دائیں	**dāīṁ**

(a) The suffix **-ā** ا (m. sg.) changes to **-ē** ے (m. pl.) or **-ī** ی (f. sg., f. pl.):

بڑا گھوڑا **baṛā ghōṛā**, a big horse
بڑے گھوڑے **baṛē ghōṛē**, big horses
بڑی گھوڑی **baṛī ghōṛī**, a big mare

گہرا پانی **gahrā pānī**, deep water (m.)
گہری نیند **gahrī nīṁd**, deep sleep (f.)

(b) There is only one feminine suffix for both singular and plural.

بڑی گھوڑیاں ***baṛī* ghōṛiyāṁ**, *big* mares

(c) The suffix **-āṁ** اں (m.) changes to **-īṁ** ایں (f.). This adjective group comprises mainly the words **dāyāṁ**, 'right', and **bāyāṁ**, 'left'; and the ordinal numbers. Note the **-y-** in **dāy-**, **bāy-** disappears when the adjective is feminine or masculine plural.

پانچواں باب	**pāṁcvāṁ bāb**, the fifth chapter
پانچویں جلد	**pāṁcvīṁ jild**, the fifth volume
دایاں ہاتھ	**dāyāṁ hāth**, the right hand
دائیں طرف	**dāīṁ taraf**, the right side

304 Agreement in case[1]

An adjective qualifying an oblique noun also becomes oblique.

Table 10: Case suffixes of adjectives

	NOMINATIVE		OBLIQUE		VOCATIVE	
MASCULINE	بڑا	**baṛā**	بڑے	**baṛē**	بڑے	**baṛē**
	دایاں	**dāyāṁ**	دائیں	**dāēṁ**	دائیں	**dāēṁ**
FEMININE	بڑی	**baṛī**	بڑی	**baṛī**	بڑی	**baṛī**
	دائیں	**dāīṁ**	دائیں	**dāīṁ**	دائیں	**dāīṁ**

(a) The suffix **-ā** ا (m. sg.) changes to **-ē** ے, and the suffix **-āṁ** اں changes to ایں **-ēṁ**. Note that the **-y-** in **dāy-**, **bāy-** disappears when the adjective is masculine oblique, vocative or feminine.

بڑے گھوڑے کا	**baṛē ghōṛē kā**, of a big horse
دائیں ہاتھ پر	**dāēṁ hāth par**, on the right hand
بڑے ظلم سے	**baṛē zulm sē**, with great cruelty
پانچویں باب میں	**pāṁcvēṁ bāb mēṁ**, in the fifth chapter

(b) Feminine adjectives do not change (they have no special oblique suffix).

بڑی گھوڑی کا	**baṛī ghōṛī kā**, of a big mare
دائیں آنکھ میں	**dāīṁ āṁkh mēṁ**, in the right eye
پانچویں منزل پر	**pāṁcvīṁ manzil par**, on the fifth floor

1 See Chapter 1, footnote 3, for a definition of the term ‘case’ as used in this work.

(c) There are no special oblique plural suffixes for masculine or feminine adjectives.

بڑے گھوڑوں کا	**baṛē ghōṛōṁ kā**, of big horses
بڑی گھوڑیوں کا	**baṛī ghōṛiyōṁ kā**, of big mares

(d) An adjective modifying a vocative noun is in the oblique case.

میرے بیٹے !	**mērē bēṭē!**	My son!
میرے بیٹو !	**mērē bēṭō!**	My sons!
میری بیٹی !	**mērī bēṭī!**	My daughter!
ارے دائیں لڑکے !	**arē dāēṁ laṛkē!**	Hey, you (boy) on the right!

305 Agreement with noun sequences of different gender

If two or more nouns of different genders or numbers are qualified by one adjective (or the adjectival postposition **kā**), the adjective agrees with the noun nearest to it.

میری پتلون ، جوتے اور جراب
***mērī* patlūn** (f.), **jūtē** (m. pl.) **aur jurrāb** (m. pl.)
my trousers, shoes and socks

بڑا پتیلا اور کڑاہی
***baṛā* patīlā** (m.) **aur kaṛāhī** (f.)
a *big* saucepan and frying pan

آپ کی والدہ اور تینوں ماموں
āp *kī* vālida aur tīnōṁ māmūṁ
your mother and all three maternal uncles

306 Attributive and predicative adjectives

Some adjectives can both precede the noun they qualify (attributive use of adjectives), or follow it in a predicate phrase. When adjectives are used attributively they modify or restrict the meaning of the noun.

خطرناک راستہ
***xatarnāk* rāsta**
a *dangerous* road (more than usually hazardous)

مزیدار کھانا
***mazēdār* khānā**
delicious food (which satisfies taste as well as hunger)

When adjectives are used predicatively, they introduce new information about the noun or pronoun they qualify.

وہ راستہ خطرناک تھا ۔
vo rāsta *xatarnāk* thā
That road was *dangerous.*

کھانا مزیدار ہو گا ۔
khānā *mazēdār* hō gā
The food will be *delicious.*

Some Persian and Arabic adjectives can *only* be used predicatively, not attributively. These adjectives occur in phrases with the verb **hōnā**, 'to be' (see §607, 'Denominative verbs'). Some examples are:

معلوم ہونا	**mālūm hōnā**, to be known
پسند ہونا	**pasand hōnā**, to be liked, pleasing
مبتلا ہونا	**mubtalā hōnā**, to be afflicted, to be embroiled

اُس کے گھر کا پتہ مجھے معلوم ہے ۔
us kē ghar kā pata mujhē *mālūm* hai
I know his home address (his home address is *known* to me).

وحید صاحب کو بریانی پسند ہے ۔
vahīd sāhab kō biryānī pasand hai
Vahid likes the rice cooked in broth (the **biryānī** is *pleasing* to Vahid).

بچّی ہیضے میں مبتلا ہو کر مر گئی ۔
baccī haizē mēṁ *mubtalā* hō kar mar gaī
The baby girl caught (became *afflicted* with) cholera and died.

WRONG	معلوم پتہ	**mālūm pata**
WRONG	پسند بریانی	**pasand biryānī**
WRONG	مبتلا بچّی	**mubtalā baccī**

Other Perso-Arabic adjectives may be used attributively:

حسین عورت	**hasīn aurat**, the beautiful woman
مشکل نکتے	**muśkil nuktē**, the difficult points

Some predicative adjectives occur in a construction with **kā** (~ **kē** ~ **kī**):

(کا) شکر گزار ہونا (**kā**) **śukr guzār hōnā**, to be grateful (to)

EXAMPLE

میں آپ کا شکر گزار ہوں ۔
maiṁ āp kā *śukr guzār* hūṁ
I am *grateful* to you.

(کا) پابند ہونا (**kā**) **pāband hōnā**, to be bound by, abide by

EXAMPLE

میں اپنے وعدے کا پابند ہوں ۔
maiṁ apnē vādē kā *pāband* hūṁ
I keep (am *bound* by) my promise.

PRONOUNS USED AS ADJECTIVES

307 Interrogative pronouns

The interrogative pronouns **kyā**, 'what' (§217) and **kaun**, 'who?' (§219) are also used as adjectives.

308 Indefinite pronouns

The indefinite pronouns **kōī**, 'some', 'any' (§221) and **kuch** 'some', 'any' (§222) are also used as adjectives.

SYMMETRICAL y-v-k-j WORD SETS

309 The categories: NEAR - FAR - INTERROGATIVE - RELATIVE

Urdu distinguishes systematically between the categories 'near', 'far', 'interrogative' and 'relative'.

In §201, it is shown that the demonstrative pronoun **ye** refers to something or someone close at hand. The demonstrative pronoun **vo** refers to something or someone further away. This distinction is also maintained in personal pronouns, and in certain adjectives and adverbs describing the quantity, manner, location, direction, or time of something. When interrogatives and relatives are taken into account, there are four categories, expressed in symmetrical sets of words beginning with **y~i~a** (near), **v~u** (far), **k** (interrogative), and **j** (relative). These sets are shown below in Table 11.

The adjective members of this set (excluding **jaisā** and **jitnā**) are described in detail in this chapter. **jaisā** and **jitnā**, along with other relative words (the **j**-set), are discussed in Chapter 11.

Table 11: Symmetrical **y-v-k-j** word sets

	y~i~a ی ا	**v~u** و ا	**k** ک	**j** ج
	NEAR	FAR	INTERROGATIVE	RELATIVE
PRONOUNS				
	یہ **ye**, he/she/it	وہ **vo**, he/she/it	کون **kaun**, who	جو **jō**, who, which
			کیا **kyā**, what	
ADJECTIVES				
	اِتنا **itnā**, this much	اُتنا **utnā**, that much	کتنا **kitnā**, how much	جتنا **jitnā**, as much
	ایسا **aisā**, like this	ویسا **vaisā**, like that	کیسا **kaisā**, how	جیسا **jaisā**, such as
ADVERBS				
	یہاں **yahāṁ**, here	وہاں **vahāṁ**, there	کہاں **kahāṁ**, where	جہاں **jahāṁ**, where
	اِدھر **idhar**, hither	اُدھر **udhar**, thither	کدھر **kidhar**, whither	جدھر **jidhar**, whither
	یوں **yūṁ**, thus	تیوں (**tyūṁ**) so, thus	کیوں **kyōṁ**, why?	جوں **jūṁ**, as
	اب **ab**, now	تب (**tab**, then[2])	کب **kab**, when	جب **jab**, when

2 **tyūṁ** and **tab** are not members of the 'far' category, but surviving members of a nearly vanished category, the t-set, or correlative set.

Pronouns, except for **jō**, are handled in Chapter 2, including demonstrative pronouns (§201), personal pronouns (§202-§212) and interrogative pronouns (§217, §219). **jō** is discussed in §1106-§1107.

The adverb members of the set are discussed in Chapter 4 (Adverbs).

itnā - utnā - kitnā

itnā means 'this much', 'so much'. **utnā** means 'that much', 'so much'. The plurals, **itnē** and **utnē** mean 'this many', 'that many', 'so many'. **kitnā** means 'how much'; the plural **kitnē** means 'how many'. They are all regularly behaving marked adjectives.

All these words may also be used as adverbs (§318), and **itnā** is used idiomatically as a noun (§319).

اِتنی ہلدی کافی ہے -
***itnī* haldī kāfī hai**
This much turmeric is enough.

اِتنے لوگوں کی گنجائش نہیں (ہے) -
***itnē* lōgōṁ kī gunjāiś nahīṁ (hai)**
There isn't room for *so many* people.

آپ کے پاس کتنا کام ہے ؟
āp kē pās *kitnā* kām hai?
How much work do you have?

منشی کے پاس کتنی دستاویزیں ہیں ؟
munśī kē pās *kitnī* dastāvēzēṁ haiṁ?
How many documents/deeds does the clerk have?

aisā - vaisā - kaisā

aisā means 'such', 'like this', 'of this kind'. **vaisā** means 'such', 'like that', 'of that kind'. **kaisā** means 'what kind?', 'how?' They are all regularly behaving marked adjectives.

The masculine oblique singular cases of **aisā**, **vaisā** and **kaisā** can also be used as adverbs of manner, meaning 'like this/that', 'how', 'such as' (§412).

میں ایسا کام نہیں کرنا چاہتا -
maiṁ *aisā* kām nahīṁ karnā cāhtā
I don't want to do *such* a thing (a deed *like this*).

ویسا لباس یہاں نہیں ملتا -
vaisā libās yahāṁ nahīṁ miltā
You can't get *such* clothing here.

وہ کیسا آدمی ہے ؟
vo _kaisā_ ādmī hai?
What kind of person is he?

آپ کی طبیعت کیسی ہے ؟
āp kī tabīat _kaisī_ hai?
How do you feel (lit. *how* is your disposition)?

ADJECTIVE PHRASES FORMED WITH sā AND vālā

310 The adjectival particle sā (~ sē ~ sī)

sā is added to an adjective, noun or pronoun to form an adjectival phrase. **sā** agrees with the noun which the phrase qualifies.

sā added to adjectives

When **sā** follows an adjective, it expresses approximation or diminution.

آج بہت سے لوگ آئے ہیں -
āj _bahut sē_ lōg āē haiṁ
Rather a lot of people have come today.

Compare آج بہت لوگ آئے ہیں -
āj _bahut_ lōg āē haiṁ
A lot of people have come today.

تھوڑی سی چائے دیجئے -
thōṛī sī cāē dījiē
Please give me *a little* tea (**thōṛī cāē** is not idiomatic).

اچھی سی خبر
acchī sī xabar
rather good news, *goodish* news

Compare اچھی خبر
acchī xabar
good news

کالا سا بادل

***kālā sā* bādal**

a *blackish* cloud (not completely black)

Compare کالا بادل

***kālā* bādal**

a *black* cloud

However if **sā** is added to an adjective of size, such as **baṛā**, 'big', or **chōṭā**, 'small'; or to **itnā**, 'this much', 'this many', the adjective is intensified. **sā** also intensifies **zarā**, '(a) little'.

مچّھر چھوٹی سی چیز ہے مگر نقصان بہت کرتی ہے -

macchar *chōṭī sī* cīz hai, magar nuqsān bahut kartī hai

A mosquito is a *very small* thing, but it does a lot of harm.

وہ اِتنی سی چائے میں کتنی زیادہ چینی ڈالتا ہے !

vo *itnī sī* cāē mēṁ kitnī zyāda cīnī ḍāltā hai!

What a lot of sugar he puts in *such a small amount* of tea!

ذرا سی دیر کے لئے -

***zarā sī* dēr kē liē**

for a *very little* while

sā may be added to participles.

وہاں کچھ ہلتا ہوا سا نظر آیا -

vahāṁ kuch *hiltā hūā sā* nazar āyā

I could make out something *moving* there.

sā added to nouns and pronouns

Following a noun or personal pronoun, **sā** is similar to **jaisā**, 'like'. Personal pronouns will be in the oblique case. Nouns may be in the nominative or oblique case, with different nuances in the meaning of **sā**.

اُن سا آدمی رشوت کھائے گا !

***un sā* ādmī riśvat khāē gā!**

Would a man *like him* accept a bribe!

فرشتہ سا اِنسان
***farista* sā insān**
a person *like an angel*

Also

فرشتے سا اِنسان
***fariśtē* sā insān**
an *angelic* person

فرشتہ جیسا اِنسان
***fariśta jaisā* insān**
a person *like an angel*

sā may be added to nominative case demonstrative pronouns (not personal pronouns), to direct attention to a particular object.

وہ سی چوڑیاں دینا ۔
***vo sī* cūṛiyāṁ dēnā**
Give me *those* bangles.

kā sā + noun

kā sā specifies a following noun, similarly to **(kī) tarah kā** + NOUN.

اُس کی سی عینک آپ کو لاہور میں نہیں ملے گی ۔
***us kī sī* ainak āp kō lāhaur mēṁ nahīṁ milē gī**
You won't find glasses *like those* in Lahore.

Compare

اُس طرح کی عینک آپ کو لاہور میں نہیں ملے گی ۔
***us tarah kī* ainak āp kō lāhaur mēṁ nahīṁ milē gī**
You won't find glasses *like those* in Lahore.

kaun + sā

kaun sā expresses 'which' (out of a finite number of possibilities).

کون سا طالب علم غیر حاضر ہے ؟
***kaun sā* tālib ilm γair hāzir hai?**
Which student is absent (in a particular class)?

Compare

کون طالب علم غیر حاضر ہے ؟
***kaun* tālib ilm γair hāzir hai?**
Is *any* student absent? (rhetorical question)

311 The suffix **vālā**

The suffix **vālā** forms adjective and noun phrases. **vālā** may follow an oblique infinitive, oblique noun or an adjective or adverb.

*Oblique infinitive + **vālā***

The construction OBLIQUE INFINITIVE + **vālā** has a range of meanings, and is discussed in detail in §645. **vālā** agrees with the noun it qualifies.

> گیت گانے والی لڑکی کون ہے ؟
> **gīt *gānē vālī* laṛkī kaun hai?**
> Who is the girl *singing* the song?

*Oblique noun + **vālā***

When **vālā** follows an oblique noun, it makes an adjective phrase, which agrees with the noun it qualifies.

> نیلے کرتے والا آدمی کون ہے ؟
> ***nīlē kurtē vālā* ādmī kaun hai?**
> Who is the man *with the blue kurta* (loose shirt)?

> یورپ میں مجسّموں والے باغ بہت ہیں -
> **yūrap mēṁ *mujassamōṁ vālē* bāγ bahut haiṁ**
> In Europe there are many parks *with statues*.

In some cases, the noun may be omitted, leaving the NOUN + **vālā** phrase to function as a noun.

> نیلے کرتے والا کون ہے ؟
> ***nīlē kurtē vālā* kaun hai?**
> Who is *the one with the blue kurta* (loose shirt)?

*Occupational nouns with **vālā***

Occupational nouns formed with **vālā** are very common.

دودھ والا	**dūdh vālā**, milkman (< **dūdh** دودھ , milk)
ڈاک والا	**ḍāk vālā**, postman (< **ḍāk** ڈاک , post)
پان والا	**pān vālā**, seller of betel-leaf (< **pān** پان , betel-leaf)
پولیس والا	**pōlīs vālā**, policeman (< **pōlīs** پولیس , police)

Adjective + **vālā**

In the spoken idiom (but *not* in standard written Urdu), **vālā** sometimes follows an adjective, making an adjective phrase that focuses on an aspect of the noun which is qualified, and excludes nouns which do not possess that aspect. Both the adjective and **vālā** agree with the noun.

ہمارا دفتر اونچی والی عمارت میں ہے۔
hamārā daftar *ūṁcī vālī* imārat mēṁ hai
Our office is in the *tall* building (not one of the low ones).

In the written language, this would be:

ہمارا دفتر اونچی عمارت میں ہے۔
hamārā daftar *ūṁcī* imārat mēṁ hai
Our office is in the *tall* building.

Adverb + **vālā**

vālā also makes adjective phrases from adverbs. (See §409 for the use of oblique adjectives like **nīcē** and **sāmnē** as adverbs.)

کل والی روٹیاں پرندوں کو کھلا دو۔
***kal vālī* rōṭiyāṁ parindōṁ kō khilā dō**
Feed *yesterday's* bread to the birds.

نیچے والا کمرہ خالی ہے۔
***nīcē vālā* kamra xālī hai**
The *downstairs* room is vacant.

REPEATED ADJECTIVES

312 Simple repetition

The doubling of adjectives usually intensifies them, but may also express distributiveness. (For doubled **kyā** see §224.)

ٹھنڈا ٹھنڈا پانی
***ṭhanḍā ṭhanḍā* pānī**
ice-cold water

اِس منڈی میں کسان دور دور سے اپنی پیداوار لاتے ہیں -
is maṇḍī mēṁ kisān *dūr dūr* sē apnī paidāvār lātē haiṁ
Farmers bring their produce from *far and wide* to this market.

Sometimes distributiveness is the dominant sense.

سب اپنے اپنے گھر گئے -
sab *apnē apnē* ghar gaē
Everyone went *to his own* home.

جیلر نے قیدیوں کو دو دو روٹیاں دیں -
jēlar nē qaidiyōṁ kō *dō dō* rōṭiyāṁ dīṁ
The jailer gave *two* pieces of bread to *each* prisoner.

313 Repetition with an echo word

Sometimes the repetition is made with an echo word. The resulting compound is more intensive than the simple word, but the precise meaning must be looked up in a dictionary.

ٹھیک ٹھاک **ṭhīk ṭhāk**, all right, okay (< **ṭhīk** ٹھیک , right)
ڈھیلا ڈھالا **ḍhīlā ḍhālā**, loose, sloppy, baggy (< **ḍhīlā** ڈھیلا , loose)

COMPARISON OF ADJECTIVES

314 Comparison of adjectives with sē

The comparative degree of adjectives is expressed by a phrase consisting of the postposition **sē** سے + ADJECTIVE. The superlative is expressed by **sab sē** سب سے + ADJECTIVE.

ABSOLUTE
یہ زعفران مہنگا ہے -
ye zāfrān *mahemgā* hai
This saffron is *expensive*.

COMPARATIVE
وہ زعفران اِس (زعفران) سے مہنگا ہے -
vo zāfrān *is* (zāfrān) *sē mahemgā* hai
That saffron is *more expensive than* this (saffron).

SUPERLATIVE کشمیری زعفران سب سے مہنگا ہے ۔
kaśmīrī zāfrān *sab sē maheṁgā* hai
Kashmiri saffron is the *most expensive*.

In some contexts the adjective by itself has the force of a comparative.

اگر کہیں رکشہ مل سکے، تو اچّھا ہو ۔
agar kahīṁ rikśa mil sakē, tō *acchā* hō
It would be *better* if (we) could get a rickshaw.

315 Comparison of adjectives with tar, tarīn

The comparative and superlative of some Perso-Arabic adjectives can be formed with the Persian suffixes **tar** تر (comparative) and **tarīn** ترین (superlative). Some of these Perso-Arabic comparatives are used in colloquial spoken Urdu, but most are used in more formal contexts and are found mainly in written Urdu. Additional examples may be found in §1408.

ABSOLUTE یہ تصویر خوبصورت ہے ۔
ye tasvīr *xūbsūrat* hai
This picture is *pretty*.

COMPARATIVE مگر وہ تصویر خوبصورت تر ہے ۔
magar vo tasvīr *xūbsūrat tar* hai
But that picture is *prettier*.

SUPERLATIVE

خوبصورت ترین لڑکی سے شادی کرنے کی اُس کی خواہش پوری نہ ہوئی ۔
***xūbsūrat tarīn* laṛkī sē śādī karnē kī us kī xāhiś pūrī na hūī**
His wish to marry the *prettiest* girl was not fulfilled.

Persian comparatives and superlatives in common use often lose their comparative and superlative force and merely intensify the adjective.

بہتر ہے ۔
***behtar* hai** (< **beh**, good[3])
It's a *very good* idea.

---

3 **beh** بہ 'good' occurs only as a prefix, whereas **behtar** بہتر 'better' and **behtarīn** بہترین 'best' occur as independent words.

میں بہتر اُردو بولنا چاہتا ہوں -
maiṁ *behtar* urdū bōlnā cāhtā hūṁ
I want to speak *better* Urdu.

یہ بہترین گھڑی ہے -
ye *behtarīn* gharī hai
This is the *best* (quality) watch.

اُس نے بدترین گناہ کیا -
us nē *badtarīn* gunāh kiyā (< **bad**, bad[4])
He committed a *very terrible* sin.

اِس جماعت کے زیادہ تر طالب علم ذہین ہیں -
is jamāat kē *zyādatar* tālib ilm zahīn haiṁ (< **zyāda**, more)
Most of the students in (of) this class are intelligent.

316 zyāda, 'more', 'most' and kāfī, 'quite', 'too'

zyāda and **kāfī** are both adjectives and adverbs. Used adverbially, **zyāda** qualifies adjectives to show a sort of comparative degree. **kāfī** means 'enough', but when used adverbially to qualify adjectives it can mean 'quite', 'too'.

زیادہ کام
***zyāda* kām**
more (too much) work

یہ راستہ زیادہ گندا ہے -
ye rāsta *zyāda gandā* hai
This road is *dirtier*.

کافی پیسہ
***kāfī* paisā**
enough money

کافی دیر ہو رہی ہے -
***kāfī* dēr hō rahī hai**
It's getting *quite* late.

317 Superlatives with adjective + sē + adjective

An absolute superlative can be made by by adding the postposition **sē** سے + ADJECTIVE to the absolute form of the same adjective.

وہ اچّھے سے اچّھا مکان ڈھونڈ رہے ہیں -
vo *acchē sē acchā* makān ḍhūṁḍ rahē haiṁ
He is searching for the *most excellent possible* house (better than good).

4 **bad** بد 'bad', occurs only as a prefix, whereas **badtar** بدتر 'worse' and **badtarīn** بدترین 'worst' occur as independent words.

وہ اُن کے لئے بُرے سے بُرا کوٹ خرید کر لایا ۔
vo un kē liē *burē sē burā* kōṭ xarīd kar lāyā
He bought the *worst possible* coat (deliberately) and brought it for him.

ADJECTIVES WITH OTHER GRAMMATICAL FUNCTIONS

318 Adjectives used as adverbs

Some common adverbs of place are actually adjectives in the masculine oblique singular. See §409. A few adjectives can be used adverbially, to modify other adjectives. See §416.

319 Adjectives used as nouns

Many adjectives can also be used as nouns.

مجھے بڑے دیجئے ، چھوٹے نہیں ۔
mujhē *baṛē* dījiē, *chōṭē* nahīṁ
Give me *the big ones*, not *the small ones*.

بڑوں کی قیمت کیا ہے ؟
***baṛōṁ* kī qīmat kyā hai?**
What is the price of *the big ones*?

جاہلوں کی رائے کا کیا فائدہ ؟
***jāhilōṁ* kī rāē kā kyā fāeda?**
What use (is) the advice of *those who are ignorant*?

A few Perso-Arabic loan words, including **naujavān** نوجوان , 'young man'; **ɣairmulkī** غیرملکی , 'foreigner'; **numāinda** نمائندہ , 'representative', and nouns denoting nationality, are classified as both nouns and adjectives.

ایک نوجوان اور دو بوڑھے آ گئے ۔
ēk *naujavān* aur dō *būṛhē* ā gaē
One *young man* and two *old men* came.

غیرملکی امداد کے سلسلے میں کئی غیرملکی یہاں کام کر رہے ہیں ۔
***ɣairmulkī* imdād kē silsilē mēṁ kaī *ɣairmulkī* yahāṁ kām kar rahē haiṁ**
Several *foreigners* are working here in connection with *foreign* aid.

ایرانی سفارت خانے میں کام کرنے والے ایرانی...
īrānī sifārat xānē mēṁ kām karnē vālē _irānī_ ...
The *Iranians* working in the *Iranian* embassy ...

itnā

itnā is used idiomatically as a noun.

itnē mēṁ, *'in the meanwhile'*

اِتنے میں ہم نے ایک دھماکا سنا ۔
***itnē mēṁ* ham nē ēk dhamākā sunā**
In the meanwhile we heard a crash.

itnē par bhī, 'in spite of it (this)'

اِتنے پر بھی بچّہ سوتا رہا ۔
***itnē par bhī* bacca sōtā rahā**
In spite of this the baby went on sleeping.

ADJECTIVES DISCUSSED IN OTHER CHAPTERS

320 Participles used as adjectives

Participles may be used as adjectives. See §901, §907 for detailed discussions.

321 Possessive adjectives

The possessive forms of the pronoun are grammatically adjectives, and agree with the nouns they qualify. They are discussed in §212.

322 The reflexive possessive adjective **apnā**

The reflexive possessive **apnā** اپنا is grammatically an adjective, and agrees with the noun it qualifies. It is discussed in §213.

323 Numbers

Numbers are, of course, adjectives. They are discussed in Chapter 13.

4 ADVERBS

The category of adverbs includes two different groups of words: words which are original (underived) adverbs; and words which are originally other parts of speech, but are used adverbially. Many adjectives are inflected to masculine oblique singular and used as adverbs. They may occur more frequently this way than as adjectives. Some nouns occur in adverbial phrases; such nouns are also oblique, and are preceded by an oblique demonstrative.

Adverbs qualify verbs, just as adjectives qualify nouns. Urdu adverbs include:

ADVERBS OF TIME: describe the time when an event or action occurs;
ADVERBS OF PLACE: describe the location where an event or action occurs;
ADVERBS OF MANNER: describe how an event or action occurs;
ADVERBS OF DEGREE: intensify the meaning of the verb in some way;
MODAL ADVERBS: modify a verb or adjective.

SYMMETRICAL y-v-k-j ADVERB SETS

401 The categories: NEAR - FAR - INTERROGATIVE - RELATIVE

Urdu distinguishes systematically between the categories 'near', 'far', 'interrogative' and 'relative'. An overview of symmetrical sets of words beginning with **y~i~a** (near), **v~u** (far), **k** (interrogative), and **j** (relative) is given in Table 11 in §309. In Table 12 on p. 52 contains a comprehensive list of symmetrical adverb sets, including some common adverbial phrases with oblique nouns.

ADVERBS OF TIME

Some simple adverbs of time can be looked up in a dictionary, and need no explanation.

ہمیشہ	**hamēśa**, always
کل	**kal**, tomorrow (with future); yesterday (with past)
اکثر	**aksar**, often

Table 12: Symmetrical **y-v-k-j** adverb sets

y~i~a ی ا NEAR	**v~u** و ا FAR	**k** ک INTERROGATIVE	**j** ج RELATIVE
ADVERBS OF TIME			
اب **ab**, now	تب (**tab**, then)	کب **kab**, when	جب **jab**, when
اِس وقت **is vaqt** at this time	اُس وقت **us vaqt** at that time	کس وقت **kis vaqt** at what time	جس وقت **jis vaqt** at the time that
ADVERBS OF PLACE			
یہاں **yahāṁ**, here	وہاں **vahāṁ**, there	کہاں **kahāṁ**, where	جہاں **jahāṁ**, where
اِس جگہ **is jagah** (in) this place, here	اُس جگہ **us jagah** in that place, there	کس جگہ **kis jagah** in which place, where	جس جگہ **jis jagah** in the place that
اِدھر **idhar**, hither	اُدھر **udhar**, thither	کدھر **kidhar**, whither	جدھر **jidhar**, whither
اِس طرف **is taraf** in this direction	اُس طرف **us taraf** in that direction	کس طرف **kis taraf** in which direction	جس طرف **jis taraf** in the direction which
ADVERBS OF MANNER			
یوں **yūṁ**, thus	تیوں (**tyūṁ**) so, thus	کیوں **kyōṁ**, why?	جوں **jūṁ**, as
اِس طرح **is tarah** this way	اُس طرح **us tarah** that way	کس طرح **kis tarah**, which way?	جس طرح **jis tarah** in the way that

402 ab - tab - kab - jab

This set of adverbs refers to points in close time, distant time, questioned time and relative time.

ab, 'now' refers to the present moment (close time).

اب ٹھیک بارہ بج گئے ہیں -
***ab* ṭhīk bāra baj gaē haiṁ**
Now it is exactly twelve o'clock.

اب سے میں سگریٹ پینا چھوڑ دوں گا -
***ab* sē maiṁ sigrēṭ pīnā chōṛ dūṁ gā**
From *now* on I shall stop smoking.

abhī (**ab** + **hī**) means 'right now', 'still'. See also Table 28 in §1207.

ابھی گھنٹی بج رہی ہے -
***abhī* ghanṭī baj rahī hai**
The bell is ringing *right now* (still ringing).

tab, 'then' is not actually a member of the 'far' category, but a surviving member of a nearly vanished category, the **t**-set, or correlative set. It is still most frequent in correlative clauses (§1112) but has also acquired the function of expressing a point in remote time (past or future). However, **us vaqt** is more commonly used to express remote time (see §403).

تب میں نوجوان تھا -
***tab* maiṁ naujavān thā**
Then I was a young man.

تب تک مکان کی صرف پہلی منزل بن چکی تھی -
***tab* tak makān kī sirf pahlī manzil ban cukī thī**
By *then* only the first floor of the house had (already) been built.

tabhī (**tab** + **hī**) means 'just then', 'only then'. See also Table 28 in §1207.

تبھی گھنٹی بجنے لگی -
***tabhī* ghanṭī bajnē lagī**
Just then the bell began to ring.

kab means 'when?'.

دوسری منزل کب بنے گی ؟
dūsrī manzil *kab* banē gī?
When will the second floor be built?

آپ کب واپس آئیں گے ؟
āp *kab* vāpas āēṁ gē?
When will you return?

kabhī (**kab** + **hī**) means 'ever', 'once'. **kabhī** + **nahīṁ** means 'never'. See also Table 28 in §1207.

کیا آپ نے کبھی دہلی کا سفر کیا ہے ؟
kyā āp nē *kabhī* dehlī kā safar kiyā hai?
Have you *ever* travelled to Delhi?

jab, 'when', 'at the time that' is used in the relative clause of relative-correlative sentences. See §1112.

403 is vaqt - us vaqt - kis vaqt

The noun **vaqt** 'time' (m.), occurs in adverbial phrases, preceded by an oblique singular demonstrative, or the oblique of **kyā** or **jō**. These phrases describe a specific point in time.

is vaqt means 'now', 'at this time', 'at present' (close time).

اِس وقت ملک میں احتساب کی ضرورت ہے -
***is vaqt* mulk mēṁ ehtisāb kī zarūrat hai**
At present there is a need for accountability in the nation.

us vaqt means 'then', 'at that time' (distant time).

اُس وقت میں نو جوان تھا -
***us vaqt* maiṁ nau javān thā**
At that time I was a young man.

اُس وقت تک صرف پہلی منزل بنی تھی -
***us vaqt* tak sirf pahlī manzil banī thī**
By that time only the first floor had been built.

kis vaqt means 'at what time?'.

ڈاکیہ کس وقت آتا ہے ؟
ḍākiya *kis vaqt* ātā hai?
At what time does the postman usually come?

Compare ڈاکیہ کب آئے گا ؟
ḍākiya *kab* āē gā?
When will the postman come (today)?

jis vaqt, 'at the time that' is used in the relative clause of relative-correlative sentences. See §1116.

404 Calendar and clock time

See §1308-§1311.

ADVERBS OF PLACE

Many simple adverbs of place can be looked up in a dictionary, and need no explanation.

باہر	**bāhar**, out, outside
اندر	**andar**, in, inside
قریب	**qarīb**, near
دور	**dūr**, far

405 yahāṁ - vahāṁ - kahāṁ

This set of adverbs describes location in a place. **yahāṁ** means 'here' (near location), **vahāṁ** means 'there' (far location) and **kahāṁ** means 'where' (questioned location).

گاڑی یہاں روک دیجئے ۔
gāṛī *yahāṁ* rōk dījiē
Please stop the car *here*.

ہم وہاں چار بجے تک انتظار کرتے رہے ۔
ham *vahāṁ* cār bajē tak intizār kartē rahē
We went on waiting *there* until four o'clock.

ہوائی اڈا کہاں پڑتا ہے ؟
havāī aḍḍā *kahāṁ* paṛtā hai?
Where is the airport located?

jahāṁ, 'where' is used in relative clauses. See §1110.

406 idhar - udhar - kidhar

This set of adverbs describes movement towards a place. **idhar** means 'hither', 'here', **udhar** means 'thither', 'there' and **kidhar** means 'whither', 'where'. To a certain extent, the adverbs describing location: **yahāṁ**, **vahāṁ** and **kahāṁ** are also used to describe movement, thus acquiring some of the functions of this set.

اِدھر آؤ بیٹے -
idhar āō, bēṭē
Come here, son.

اُدھر سے پولیس والے آ رہے تھے ، اِدھر سے چور بھاگ گیا -
***udhar* sē pōlīs vālē ā rahē thē, *idhar* sē cōr bhāg gayā**
The police came from *that side* (as) the thief fled from *this side.*

وہ اِدھر اُدھر دیکھ رہا تھا -
vo *idhar udhar* dēkh rahā thā
He was looking *this way and that.*

تم کدھر جا رہے ہو ؟
tum *kidhar* jā rahē hō?
Where are you going?

Also تم کہاں جا رہے ہو ؟
tum *kahāṁ* jā rahē hō?
Where are you going?

jidhar, 'where' is used in the relative clause of relative-correlative sentences. See §1111.

407 is jagah - us jagah - kis jagah

The oblique noun **jagah**, 'place' (f.), preceded by an oblique singular demonstrative, or the oblique of **kyā** or **jō**, is sometimes used as an adverb of place, describing the specific location of something.

اِس جگہ زمیندار کا خزانہ گڑا ہوا ہے -
***is jagah* zamīndār kā xizāna gaṛā hūā hai**
In this spot the landlord's treasure has been buried.

کمبخت چابی کس جگہ پڑی ہے ؟
kambaxt cābī *kis jagah* paṛī hai?
Where is that wretched key?

jis jagah, 'in the place that' is used in the relative clause of relative-correlative sentences. See §1110.

408 is taraf - us taraf - kis taraf

The oblique noun **taraf**, 'direction', 'side' (f.), preceded by an oblique singular demonstrative, or the oblique of **kyā** or **jō**, may be used as an adverb of place, describing movement in a direction.

نذیر صاحب کا مکان اِس طرف ہے -
nazīr sāhib kā makān *is taraf* hai
Mr. Nazir's house in *in this direction.*

ڈاک خانہ کس طرف ہے ؟
ḍāk xāna *kis taraf* hai?
In which direction is the post office?

jis taraf, 'in the direction that' is used in the relative clause of relative-correlative sentences. See §1111.

409 Obliques as adverbs of place

Some common adverbs of place are made from (a) adjectives, in the masculine oblique singular case and from (b) nouns, in phrases consisting of an oblique noun preceded by an oblique demonstrative. In many instances, the adverbial use is much more common than use as an adjective or noun.

Adjectives

نیچا ← نیچے	**nīcā**, low → **nīcē**, below
پہلا ← پہلے	**pahlā**, first, previous → **pahlē**, first, previously
دایاں ← دائیں	**dāyāṁ**, right → **dāēṁ**, to the right
بایاں ← بائیں	**bāyāṁ**, left → **bāēṁ**, to the left

Nouns

آگا ← آگے	**āgā**, the front part, beginning → **āgē**, ahead, forward
پیچھا ← پیچھے	**pīchā**, the back part, end → **pīchē**, behind, back
سامنا ← سامنے	**sāmnā**, encounter → **sāmnē**, opposite, across, in front

NOUN اس کہانی کا نہ آگا ہے نہ پیچھا
is kahānī kā na *āgā* hai, na *pīchā*
There is neither a *beginning* nor an *end* to this story (it is rubbish).

ADVERB فوج آگے بڑھ گئی
fauj *āgē* baṛh gaī
The army advanced (moved *forward*).

NOUN فوج کا پیچھا
fauj kā *pīchā*
the *rear* of the army

ADVERB فوج پیچھے ہٹ گئی
fauj *pīchē* haṭ gaī
The army retreated (moved *back*).

ADJECTIVE نیچی دیوار
***nīcī* dīvār**
a *low* wall

ADVERB نیچے آ جاؤ
***nīcē* ā jāō**
Come *down* (stairs).

ADJECTIVE بایاں ہاتھ
***bāyāṁ* hāth**
the *left* hand

ADVERB بائیں مڑ جائیے
***bāēṁ* muṛ jāiyē**
Please turn *left*.

410 Adverbial phrase or compound postposition?

Nouns used as adverbs, such as **taraf**, **jagah**, **sāmnā**, **āgā**, etc. can also occur in compound postpositions. Here they are usually preceded by the possessive **kā** (**kē** ~ **kī**). See §527-§530.

مستری کی جگہ اس کا بیٹا آ گیا ۔
mistrī *kī jagah* us kā bēṭā ā gayā hai
In place of the mechanic, his son has come.

باغ مکان کے پیچھے ہے -
bāγ makān ***kē pīchē*** **hai**
The garden is *behind* the house.

ADVERBS OF MANNER

411 yūṁ - kyōṁ - jūṁ

There is no **v~u** (far) member of this set. A correlative, **tyūṁ**, 'so', 'thus' is used mainly in idioms together with **jūṁ** (see §423, §1120).

yūṁ means 'thus'; **kyōṁ** means 'why?'.

یوں کرو -
yūṁ **karō**
Do it *like this.*

یوں کہئے
yūṁ **kahiē**
in a manner of speaking

منّی کیوں چلّا رہی ہے ؟
munnī kyōṁ cillā rahī hai?
Why is Munni screaming?

412 aisā - vaisā - kaisā - jaisā

aisā, 'like this', **vaisā**, 'like that', **kaisā**, 'how?' and **jaisā**, 'such as' (See Table 11 in §309) are adjectives, but may be used as adverbs of manner, usually in the masculine oblique singular case. As adverbs, **jaisē** and **vaisē** occur in relative-correlative sentences (§1117).

ایسا کرو -
aisā **karō**
Do it *this way.*

ایسے کہئے ...
aisē **kahiē ...**
Put (say) it *this way ...*

ویسے کرو جیسے میں کرتا ہوں -
vaisē **karō jaisē maiṁ kartā hūṁ**
Do (it) *in the same way* I do it.

کتّا گھر میں کیسے گھسا ؟
kuttā ghar mēṁ ***kaisē*** **ghusā?**
How did the dog get into the house?

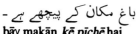

413 is tarah - us tarah - kis tarah - jis tarah

The oblique noun **tarah**, 'kind', 'way' (f.), preceded by an oblique singular demonstrative, or the oblique of **kyā** or **jō**, is sometimes used as an adverb of manner, describing the specific manner of an event or action.

> اِس طرح کرو ۔
> ***is tarah* karō**
> Do it *this way*.

kis tarah means 'in what way', 'how?', but is also used idiomatically, meaning 'how much?'.

> کتّا گھر میں کس طرح گھسا ؟
> **kuttā ghar mēṁ *kis tarah* ghusā?**
> *How* did the dog get into the house?

> پیاز کس طرح ہیں ؟
> **pyāz *kis tarah* haiṁ?**
> *How much* are the onions?

jis tarah, 'in the way that' is used in the relative clause of relative-correlative sentences. See §1119.

414 Adverbial phrases of manner with the postposition sē

The postposition **sē**, added to nouns, forms adverbial phrases of manner.

> سلیم مار کھا کر زور سے چلّایا ۔
> **salīm mār khā kar *zōr sē* cillāyā** (< **zōr**, force + **sē** → loudly, forcefully)
> Salim got a beating, and screamed *loudly*.

> ہم خوشی سے مدد کریں گے ۔
> **ham *xušī sē* madad karēṁ gē** (< **xušī**, happiness + **sē** → gladly)
> We'll *gladly* help.

415 Participles used adverbially

All the participles may be used adverbially. See §902, §908-9 and §913.

ADVERBS OF DEGREE (**416**)

Adverbs of degree intensify the meaning of adjectives they qualify.

bahut, baṛā, zyāda

bahut means 'very'.

وہ بہت ذہین آدمی ہے -
vo *bahut* zahīn admī hai
He is a *very* intelligent man.

The adjective **baṛā**, 'big' can be used adverbially as an intensifier.

وہ بڑا ذہین آدمی ہے -
vo *baṛā* zahīn admī hai
He is a *very* intelligent man.

Compare

وہ بڑا آدمی ہے -
vo *baṛā* admī hai
He is a *big* man.

وہ بڑی نیک عورت ہے -
vo *baṛī* nēk aurat hai
She is a *very* virtuous woman (= **bahut nēk**).

zyāda is both an adjective and an adverb. Used adverbially, it qualifies adjectives to show comparison. See §316 for a more detailed treatment.

یہ راستہ زیادہ گندا ہے -
ye rāsta *zyāda gandā* hai
This road is *dirtier*.

itnā, kitnā

The adjectives **itnā** and **kitnā** (§309) can be used adverbially as intensifiers, meaning 'such', 'what'.

اُس کو اِتنا اچّھا مضمون لکھنے پر انعام ملا -
us kō *itnā* acchā mazmūn likhnē par inām milā
He received a prize for writing *such* a fine essay.

واہ ! کتنی خوبصورت تصویر ہے !
vāh! *kitnī* xūbsūrat tasvīr hai!
What a beautiful picture it is (lit. *how much* beautiful)! [1]

1 **vāh**, an expression of admiration, is untranslatable here.

MODAL ADVERBS

This category includes some very common words.

نہیں ، نہ ، مت	**nahīṁ**, **na**, **mat**, not, do not
شاید	**śāyad**, maybe
ضرور	**zarūr**, certainly
بھی	**bhī**, also, too
پھر	**phir**, again
صرف	**sirf**, only

وہ نہیں جائے گا ۔
vo *nahīṁ* jāē gā
He won't (will *not*) go.

وہ ضرور جائے گا ۔
vo *zarūr* jāē gā
He will *certainly* go.

وہ جائے گا اور واپس آئے گا بھی ۔
vo jāē gā aur vāpas āē gā *bhī*
He will go, and *also* return.

وہ پھر جائے گا ۔
vo *phir* jāē gā
He will go *again*.

417 The negative words nahīṁ, na, mat

nahīṁ makes negative sentences in present tenses, past tenses except the simple past, presumptive tenses and the future. See Table 13, 'Overview of aspect, tense and mood' in §603. Negative words usually come right before the verb phrase. The present auxiliary **hai** is usually dropped.

وہ اِتوار کو نہیں آتا ۔
vo itvār kō *nahīṁ* ātā
He doesn't (does *not*) come on Sundays (dropped **hai**).

وہ اِتوار کو نہیں آتا تھا ۔
vo itvār kō *nahīṁ* ātā thā (Past auxiliary **thā** is kept.)
He didn't (did *not*) use to come on Sundays.

na makes negative sentences in the subjunctive, simple past and conditional tenses. See Table 13. It also makes negative polite requests corresponding to the pronoun **āp**, and sometimes with requests corresponding to the pronoun **tum**.

آج وہ نہ آیا ۔
āj vo *na* āyā
He didn't (did *not*) come today.

وہ پچھلے منگل کو بھی نہ آیا تھا۔
vo pichlē mangal kō bhī *na* āyā thā
He didn't (did *not*) come last Tuesday either.

شاید وہ وقت پر نہ آئے۔
śāyad vo vaqt par *na* āē
Maybe he won't (will *not*) come on time.

کل نہ آئیے ، پرسوں آئیے۔
kal *na* āiyē, parsōṁ āiyē
Please don't (do *not*) come tomorrow; come the day after tomorrow.

سائیکل یہاں نہ چھوڑو۔
sāikal yahāṁ *na* chōṛō
Don't (do *not*) leave the bicycle here.

mat makes negative requests corresponding to the intimate and non-honorific pronouns **tū** and **tum**, and also infinitive-requests.

دیر مت کر ، گھر جا۔
dēr *mat* kar, ghar jā
Don't (do *not*) dawdle; go home (request corresponding to **tū**).

بھائی کو مت چھیڑو۔
bhāī kō *mat* chēṛō
Don't (do *not*) tease (your) brother (request corresponding to **tum**).

اُس دکان سے کچھ مت خریدنا۔
us dukān sē kuch *mat* xarīdnā
Don't (do *not*) buy anything from that shop (infinitive).

418 bhī, 'also', 'too'

bhī functions both as a modal adverb and as an emphatic particle. Its latter function is treated in §1210. The two functions tend to overlap somewhat.

In affirmative sentences, **bhī** may follow any noun, pronoun or verb, adding the meaning 'also', 'too' to the word it follows.

AFFIRMATIVE

مہمان بادشاہی مسجد دیکھنے جائیں گے -
mehmān bādśāhī masjid dēkhnē jāēṁ gē
The guests are going to see the royal mosque.

+ **bhī**

ہم بھی بادشاہی مسجد دیکھیں گے -
ham *bhī* bādśāhī masjid dēkhēṁ gē
We *too* will see the royal mosque.

ہم شاہی قلعہ بھی دیکھیں گے -
ham śāhī qila *bhī* dēkhēṁ gē
We will see the royal fort *too.*

EMPHATIC **bhī**

وہ مسجد دیکھے گا بھی تو کیا ہو گا ؟
vo masjid dēkhē gā *bhī* tō kyā hō gā
Even if he sees the mosque, so what?

419 'both ... and', 'neither ... nor'

bhī ... **bhī** in parallel clauses means 'both ... and'. **nahīṁ** ... **bhī nahīṁ** means 'neither ... nor'.

وہ بادشاہی مسجد بھی دیکھے گا اور قلعہ بھی -
vo bādśāhī masjid *bhī* dēkhē gā aur qila *bhī*
He will see *both* the royal mosque *and* the fort.

وہ بادشاہی مسجد نہیں دیکھے گا اور قلعہ بھی نہیں -
vo bādśāhī masjid *nahīṁ* dēkhē gā aur qila bhī *nahīṁ*
He will *neither* see the royal mosque *nor* the fort.

420 phir, 'again', 'then'

phir means 'again', 'over again', 'then'.

پھر کہئے -
***phir* kahiē**
Please say it *again.*

آپ امتحان میں ناکام ہو گئے ، امتحان پھر دینا چاہئے -
āp imtihān mēṁ nākām hō gaē, imtihān *phir* dēnā cāhiē
You failed the examination (and) should take the examination *over again.*

پہلے درخواست پر مہر لگوا لینا ، پھر یہاں واپس آنا ۔
pahlē darxāst par mohr lagvā lēnā, *phir* yahāṁ vāpas ānā
First get the application stamped, *then* come back here.

ARABIC ADVERBS ENDING IN -an (421)

A group of adverbs borrowed from Arabic ends in اً **-an** (**tanvīn**). See §1511.

عموماً
umūman
commonly, generally

REPEATED ADVERBS

422 Simple repetition

The doubling of adjectives usually intensifies them, but may also express distributiveness.

آہستہ آہستہ بولئے
***āhista āhista* bōliē**
Please speak *very slowly.*

سلیم مار کھا کر زور زور سے چلایا ۔
salīm mār khā kar *zōr zōr sē* cillāyā
Salim got a beating, and screamed *very loudly.*

Sometimes distributiveness is dominant.

اُن کی تلاش میں کہاں کہاں نہیں جانا پڑا !
un kī talāś mēṁ *kahāṁ kahāṁ* nahīṁ jānā paṛā!
How many places I had to look for him (*where-where* didn't I have to go)!

423 Idiomatic repetition

Some doubled adverbs have idiomatic meanings which must be learned individually. These include sequences where the adverb is merely repeated, as well as sequences where two adverbs which are members of the same symmetrical set occur in compounds.

کبھی کبھی	**kabhī kabhī**, now and then
کہیں کہیں	**kahīṁ kahīṁ**, here and there
اِدھر اُدھر	**idhar udhar**, here and there
جوں جوں	**jūṁ jūṁ**, as long as, as far as (§1120)
جوں توں	**jūṁ tūṁ**, somehow or the other (§1120)

INTERROGATIVES AND INDEFINITES USED WITH IRONY

kyā, **kaun**, **kahāṁ**, **kidhar** and **kab** may be used with irony, not as interrogatives, to deny the idea expressed in the sentence.

424 Interrogative adverbs used with irony

اور کہاں جاتی ؟ پوچھتا کون ؟
aur *kahāṁ* jātī? pūchtā *kaun*?
Where else would she go? *No one* cares (asks).[2] (Prem Chand, *Godān*)

425 Indefinite adverbs used with irony

kahīṁ may be delexicalized and used with **agar**, or in place of **agar**, to express improbability.

اگر کہیں رکشہ مل سکے، تو اچّھا ہو۔
agar kahīṁ rikśa mil sakē, tō acchā hō
It would be better if (we) could get a rickshaw (it is improbable).

کہیں آپ کی عینک گم ہو جاتی تو بڑی مشکل ہوتی۔
kahīṁ āp kī ainak gum hō jātī, tō baṛī muśkil hōtī
It would have been a great difficulty if your glasses had been lost.

kahīṁ ... na expresses apprehension. The verb is usually subjunctive and in the compound form. The restriction on the use of the negative with compound verbs (§717) does not apply in the case of **kahīṁ ... na**.

کہیں کوئی نادانی نہ کر بیٹھے۔
kahīṁ kōī nādānī na kar baiṭhē
I just hope he doesn't do something foolish. (Prem Chand, *Godān*)

2 In this sentence, **kahāṁ** is used with its lexical meaning; it is **kaun** which is used sarcastically: 'who asks?—no one.' The verb and pronoun are reversed to show emphasis.

kahīṁ ... tō nahīṁ expresses strong apprehension. The verb is usually in the compound form, but *not* subjunctive. The restriction on the use of the negative with compound verbs does not apply in the case of **kahīṁ tō nahīṁ**.

بس کہیں خراب تو نہیں ہو گئی ؟
bas kahīṁ xarāb tō nahīṁ hō gaī?
I hope the bus hasn't broken down? (If it has we are really in trouble.)

426 Interrogative pronouns used with irony

وہ کیا جانتا تھا کہ اِن میں کیا کھچڑی پک رہی تھی ؟
vo kyā jāntā thā ke in mēṁ kyā khicaṛī pak rahī thī?
How could he know what these two were cooking up between themselves?[3]
(Prem Chand, *Godān*)

ORDER OF MULTIPLE ADVERBS (427)

When a sentence contains two or more adverbs, the adverb of time comes first, followed by the adverb of place and the adverb of manner. If there is more than one adverb of time, the order is YEAR - MONTH - DAY - HOUR.

آپ کل یہاں ضرور آئیے
āp ***kal yahāṁ zarūr*** **āiyē**
Please come *here tomorrow without fail.*

اگلے سال جنوری کی ۱۵ تاریخ کو دس بجے صبح یہاں ضرور آئیے -
aglē sāl janvarī kī pandra tārīx kō das bajē subah (~ **subh**) **yahāṁ zarūr aiyē**
Please come here next year at 10 a.m. on the 15th of January, without fail.

3 'Did he know ... ?—of course not.' **khicaṛī** refers to a dish in which rice and lentils are mixed. Here it means a muddle, mess or conspiracy.

5 POSTPOSITIONS

Postpositions follow nouns or pronouns, and mark (a) grammatical functions, (b) location, movement or extent in space and time. A particular postposition may have *both* grammatical and spatial-temporal functions. Urdu postpositions function similarly to prepositions in European languages. Urdu has only a few prepositions, borrowed from Persian or Arabic (§1404, §1505).

A postposition may consist of a single word (SIMPLE POSTPOSITIONS) or a phrase. Postpositional phrases are of two types: POSTPOSITIONAL SEQUENCES (two postpositions expressing a complex relationship of location and movement), and COMPOUND POSTPOSITIONS.

Whenever a noun is followed by a postposition it occurs in the oblique case (§110). Pronouns also occur in the oblique case before postpositions (§208), except for the first and second person pronouns when preceding the postposition **nē** (§209).

If **bhī**, 'also' or **hī** (emphatic particle) also occur, they normally follow the postposition. (However see §1206 for an exception.)

The commonest postpositions, with their short translations, are:

کا - کے - کی	**kā** (~ **kē** ~ **kī**), of, 's	میں	**mēṁ**, in
کو	**kō**, to	پر	**par**, on, at
نے	**nē** (ergative)	تک	**tak**, till, until
سے	**sē**, from, by		

GRAMMATICAL POSTPOSITIONS

Grammatical postpositions express for the most part grammatical functions, such as possession or marking of objects and subjects.

501 kā ~ kē ~ kī expressing possession

The postposition **kā** (~ **kē** ~ **kī**) shows a possessive relationship between two nouns. It agrees with the noun it qualifies in gender, number and case, like an adjective.

مالیات کا محکمہ	مالیات کے محکمے میں
māliyāt *kā* mahekma	**māliyāt *kē* mahekmē mēṁ**
the Department *of* Finance	in the Department *of* Finance

ماں کی دعا
māṁ *kī* duā
mother*'s* blessing

502 kā marking objects

Some verbs mark objects with **kā**. See §526 for examples of the way that verbs 'take' (collocate with) postpositions.

میں آپ کا شکر گزار ہوں ۔
maiṁ *āp kā* śukr guzār hūṁ
I am grateful *to you*.

سلیم نے جلسے کا بندوبست کیا ۔
salīm nē *jalsē kā* bandobast kiyā
Salim arranged the meeting (did the arrangement *of the meeting*).

503 Inflected kā in compound postpositions

Many compound postpositions are phrases consisting of **kē** ~ **kī** (inflected forms of **kā**) followed by a noun, adjective or adverb. See §527-§531.

NOUN

X کی طرف
X kī taraf < taraf (f.), direction, side, way
in connection with X

ADJECTIVE

X کے مطابق
X kē mutābiq < mutābiq (adj.), conformable, similar
according to X

ADVERB

X کے اوپر
X kē ūpar < ūpar (adv.), above, up, over
above X

504 kō and its alternate forms

Following nouns, **kō** always occurs as a postposition, but following pronouns (including personal, demonstrative, interrogative and relative pronouns, except **āp**), it may be replaced by the suffix **ē** ~ **(h)ēṁ** (§210 and Table 5 in §210).

505 kō marking objects

The indirect object of a verb is marked by **kō**. The indirect object precedes the direct object.

شاہد نے اپنی والدہ کو تار بھیجا

śāhid nē *apnī vālida kō* tār bhējā
Shahid sent a telegram *to his mother.*

بچّی نے مہمان کو پھول پیش کیے ۔

baccī nē *mehmān kō* phūl pēś kiyē
The little girl offered flowers *to the guest.*

kō sometimes marks direct objects. Such objects are either (a) animate direct objects or (b) specified inanimate direct objects. Human objects are normally marked with **kō**, but in certain cases **kō** may be omitted to show that the object is unspecified.[1]

Some verbs take objects marked with **sē** (§515), **kā** (§502) or **par** (§525). See §526 for examples of the way that verbs collocate with postpositions.

Animate direct objects

سلیم کو بلاؤ ۔

***salīm kō* bulāō**
Call *Salim.*

بچّوں کو باغ لے چلو ۔

***baccōṁ kō* bāγ lē calō**
Take *the children* to the park.

کتّے کو مت چھیڑو

***kuttē kō* mat chēṛō**
Don't tease *the dog.*

Specified direct objects

پانی کا نل خراب ہے ، نل والے کو بلاؤ ۔

pānī kā nal xarāb hai, *nal vālē kō* bulāō
The water pipe is broken; call *the plumber.*

اُس صندوق کو خالی کر دو ۔

***us sandūq kō* xālī kar dō**
Empty *that box.*

---

1 Grammarians who treat grammatical postpositions as case-markers define objects marked by **kō** as being in the dative case.

Unspecified direct objects

پانی کا نل خراب ہے ، فوراً نل والا بلاؤ
pānī kā nal xarāb hai, fauran *nal vālā* bulāō!
The water pipe is broken; call *a plumber* at once!

صندوق اوپر لے جاؤ۔
***sandūq* ūpar lē jāō**
Take *the box* upstairs.

506 kō marking subjects

In IMPERSONAL CONSTRUCTIONS (§641) the 'real' or logical subject of the verb is marked by **kō**, and the verb agrees with the logical direct object. It is considered a subject because it may control the reflexive possessive adjective **apnā** (§213), be the subject of a clause with a conjunctive participle (§612), and typically stands in first place in the sentence.[2]

Many impersonal constructions describe the experiencer's subjective state, which has led to the coining of the term EXPERIENCER SUBJECTS. Experiencer subjects tend to occur with the verbs **hōnā**, 'to be', and **ānā**, 'to come' and **lagnā**, 'to be applied'.

اکرم کو سموسے پسند ہیں۔
***akram kō* samōsē pasand haiṁ**
Akram likes samosas.

مجھے اپنا نیا مکان پسند ہے۔
***mujhē* apnā nayā makān pasand hai**
I like my new house.

اُن کو کامیابی کی توقع نہیں۔
***un kō* kāmyābī kī tavaqqō nahīṁ**
He doesn't expect to succeed.

مجھے اُس کا نام یاد نہیں آ رہا۔
***mujhē* us kā nām yād nahīṁ ā rahā**
I don't recall his name.

lagnā *with experiencer subjects*

lagnā has no precise English translation, although it is often defined as 'to be attached', 'to be applied'. In impersonal constructions with experiencer subjects, **lagnā** can mean 'to seem', 'to feel', or 'to catch (an illness)'.

یہ بات سچ نہیں لگتی۔
ye bāt *sac* nahīṁ *lagtī*
This thing does not *seem true*.[3]

2 Grammarians who treat grammatical postpositions as case-markers call subjects marked by **kō** dative subjects.

3 The logical subject is not expressed.

اُن کو میرا جانا بُرا لگا ۔

un kō mērā jānā *burā lagā*
They were displeased by my going (lit. my going *seemed bad* to them).

بچّے کو کھانا دیکھ کر بھوک لگنے لگی ۔

baccē kō khānā dēkh kar *bhūk lagnē lagī*
The child saw the food and *began to feel hungry*.

آپ کو یہ زکام کہاں سے لگ گیا ہے ؟

āp kō ye zukām kahāṁ sē *lag gayā hai*?
How (lit. from where) *did you catch* this cold?

507 kō showing movement in a direction or to a destination

kō occasionally expresses direction of movement in physical space. However in this function it is usually deleted, leaving behind an oblique noun.

چاروں پورب دیس کو چل پڑے ۔

cārōṁ *pūrab dēs kō* cal paṛē (Narang, *Readings*)
All four set off *to an eastern country*.

کیا آپ ڈاک خانے جا رہے ہیں ؟

kyā āp *ḍāk xānē* jā rahē haiṁ? (deleted **kō**)
Are you going *to the post office*?

508 kō after days and dates

kō is commonly used after days and dates, but not after clock time (§1311).

ہفتے کو میں مصروف ہوں ، پیر کو آئیے ۔

***haftē kō* maiṁ masrūf hūṁ, *pīr kō* āiyē**
I am busy *on Saturday*; please come *on Monday*.

پندرہ اگست کو

pandra agast kō
on the 15th of August

وہ دس بجے آئے گا ۔

vo *das bajē* āē gā
He will come *at ten o'clock*.

509 kō following infinitives

kō following an oblique infinitive shows an impending event or purpose (§646).

510 nē marking subjects

nē marks the 'real' or logical subject of transitive verbs in perfective tenses (see §629). The verb agrees with the logical direct object, unless it is marked by **kō**. See §211 for the forms of pronouns used before **nē**.[4]

احمد نے سارے سموسے کھائے ہیں ۔
***ahmad nē* sārē samōsē khāē haiṁ**
Ahmad has eaten all the samosas (agreement with **samōsē**).

Compare احمد سارے سموسے کھائے گا ۔
***ahmad* sārē samōsē khāē gā**
Ahmad will eat all the samosas (agreement with **ahmad**).

SPATIAL-TEMPORAL POSTPOSITIONS

Spatial-temporal postpositions refer to location, movement or extent in space and time. (But these postpositions also have some grammatical functions, particularly **sē**.) They may be divided into two groups: (a) those which may not be followed by a second postposition (**sē**, **tak**), and (b) those which may be followed by **sē** to make postpositional sequences (§533).

511 sē with ablative function

In the following, **sē** shows spatial movement away from something, or elapse of time ('since', 'for').

یہ بس کہاں سے آتی ہے ؟
ye bas *kahāṁ sē* ātī hai?
Where does this bus come *from*?

میں دو دن سے بیمار ہوں ۔
maiṁ *dō din sē* bīmār hūṁ
I have been sick *for two days.*

512 sē marking the instrument

sē may mark the instrument, and is translated as 'with' or 'by'.

قلم سے دستخط کرنا ۔
***qalam sē* dastxat karnā**
Sign (it) *with a pen.*

ہم ریل سے سفر کریں گے ۔
ham *rēl sē* safar karēṁ gē
We will travel *by train.*

4 Grammarians who treat grammatical postpositions as case-markers call subjects marked by **nē** ergative subjects.

sē marks the instrument of verbs expressing incapacity (§635) and involuntary action (§801), as well as causative (Chapter 8) and passive (§634) verbs.

Incapacity

مجھ سے ایسی دوا کھائی نہیں جاتی -
***mujh sē* aisī davā khāī nahīṁ jātī**
I can't possibly take such medicine.

Involuntary action

او ہو ، مجھ سے کیا ہو گیا ؟
ō hō, *mujh sē* kyā hō gayā?
Oh no, what have *I* done (involuntarily)?

Instrument of passive

یہ سڑک مزدوروں سے بنائی جائے گی -
ye saṛak *mazdūrōṁ sē* banāī jāē gī
This road will be built *by labourers.*

Instrument of causative

میں آپ کا کام سلیم سے کرواؤں گا -
maiṁ āp kā kām *salīm sē* karvāūṁ gā
I'll get *Salim* to do your work.

513 sē in comparison of adjectives

The comparison of adjectives with **sē** is discussed in §314 and §317.

514 sē in adverbial phrases

sē is added to nouns to form adverbial phrases of manner. See §414.

احتیاط سے
ehtiyāt sē (< **ehtiyāt**, caution + **sē**)
carefully

515 sē marking objects

Certain verbs require objects marked with **sē**. (See §526 for examples of the way that verbs 'take' (collocate with) postpositions.)

Direct object

ملنا **milnā**, to meet[5]

ادیب رسالے کے مدیر سے ملا ۔
adīb risālē kē *mudīr sē* milā
The writer met *the editor* of the journal.

milnā, 'meet', can also take the object with **kō**, in which case a more coincidental meeting is implied.

آج میں ہمسائے کو بس کے اڈّے پر مل گیا ۔
āj maiṁ *hamsāē kō* bas kē aḍḍē par mil gayā
Today I met *the neighbour* at the bus stop.

پوچھنا **pūchnā**, to ask

کوئی میرے دل سے پوچھے ترے تیرِ نیم کش کو
kōī mērē *dil sē* pūchē tērē tīr-e-nīm kaś kō
Someone should ask my *heart* about your half-released arrow (Ghalib)

Indirect object

کہنا **kahnā**, to say, tell

میں آپ سے کچھ کہنا چاہتی ہوں ۔
maiṁ *āp sē* kuch kahnā cāhtī huṁ
I would like to tell *you* something.

516 sē forming postpositional sequences

sē is added to other spatial-temporal postpositions to make postpositional sequences. See §533.

---

5 **milnā** has another meaning, 'to be available'. In this sense it is intransitive and does not take an object.

517 **tak** showing extent or limit

tak shows that something extends to a specific point in time or space.

چار بجے تک آئیے -
cār bajē tak **āiyē**
Come *by four o'clock* (not later).

اُنہوں نے دور دور تک چور کی تلاش کی -
unhōṁ nē *dūr dūr tak* cōr kī talāś kī
They searched far and wide (*till far and far*) for the thief.

The idiom **X sē lē kar Y tak** shows a complete range 'from X to Y (and everything in between)'.

بیچارہ ۱۹۸۰ سے لے کر ۱۹۹۵ تک قید رہا -
bēcāra *unnīs sau assī sē lē kar unnīs sau pacānavē tak* qaid rahā
The poor man was imprisoned *from 1980 to 1995.*

518 **tak** as an emphatic particle

tak is sometimes used as an particle meaning 'even'. It is more emphatic than **bhī**. In this usage it is not a postposition, and the noun (or pronoun) is not in the oblique case.

نو جوان کیا بوڑھے تک خوشی منا رہے ہیں -
naujavān kyā, *būṛhē tak* xuśī manā rahē haiṁ
Even the elders are celebrating, not to mention the young people.

519 **mēṁ** with locative function

mēṁ expresses location in or at a point in space or time. Such location may be concrete or quite abstract.

کمرے میں	**kamrē mēṁ**, in the room
شیشے میں	**śīśē mēṁ**, in a mirror
دو دن میں	**dō din mēṁ**, in two days
صنعتی شعبے میں	**sanatī śōbē mēṁ**, in the industrial sector
گھر میں	**ghar mēṁ**, at home
اُنگلی میں انگوٹھی	**uṁglī mēṁ angūṭhī**, the ring on the finger

ہم ابھی راستے میں ہیں -
ham abhī *rāstē mēṁ* haiṁ
We are *on the way* now.

دونوں میں گہری دوستی ہے -
***dōnōṁ mēṁ* gehrī dōstī hai**
There is deep friendship *between* (*both of*) *them*.

mēṁ can show transformation from one state to another.

پری نے چوہیوں کو سفید گھوڑوں میں بدل دیا -
parī nē cūhiyōṁ kō *safēd ghōṛōṁ mēṁ* badal diyā
The fairy changed the mice *into white horses*.

mēṁ is used with **lagnā**, 'to be applied' to express 'to cost' and 'to take time'.

اِس کام میں پانچ سو روپئے لگے -
is kām *mēṁ* pāṁc sau rūpaē *lagē*
This work *cost* five hundred rupees.

وہاں جانے میں کتنے دن لگے ؟
vahāṁ jānē *mēṁ* kitnē din *lagē*?
How many days *did it take* to go there?

520 Infinitives followed by mēṁ

Infinitives used as verbal nouns (§639) may be followed by **mēṁ**, with idiomatic meanings.

پرانے شہر جانے میں آدھا گھنٹا لگتا ہے -
purānē śahr jānē *mēṁ* ādhā ghanṭā *lagtā hai*
It *takes* half an hour to go to the old city.

یہ کھانا کھانے میں آسان ہے مگر ہضم کرنے میں مشکل -
ye khānā *khānē mēṁ* āsān hai magar *hazm karnē mēṁ* muśkil
This food is easy *to eat* but hard *to digest*.

521 par with locative function

par expresses location on something which has a surface ('on'), next to something in space, or upon or immediately after a point in time ('at', 'in'). **par** has a variant form **pe** پہ , occurring in colloquial speech and poetry.

راستے پر	**rāstē par**, on the road
میز پر	**mēz par**, on the table
دروازے پر	**darvāzē par**, at the door
وقت پر	**vaqt par**, in (on) time

par occurs in a few contexts where **mēṁ** might be expected. This may reflect former spatial realities. Formerly a shop was a stall, not a room, and customers stood on the threshold.

دکان پر	**dukān par**, in the shop

پانچ بج کر تیرہ منٹ پر شدید زلزلہ آیا ۔
***pāṁc baj kar tēra minaṭ par* śadīd zalzala āyā**
At thirteen minutes after five a violent earthquake occurred.

آپ کی درخواست پر ہم اپنے نصاب کی نقل بھیج رہے ہیں ۔
***āp kī darxāst par* ham apnē nisāb kī naql bhēj rahē haiṁ**
At your request I am sending a copy of our curriculum.

وہ کمرہ ہزار روپئے مہینے پر مل سکتا تھا ۔
vo kamra *hazār rūpaē* mahīnē *par* mil saktā thā
That room used to be available *at a thousand rupees* a month.

522 **par** showing movement to a destination

par may express movement to a destination.

میں کام پر چلا ۔
maiṁ *kām par* calā
I went *to work.*

وہ مہم پر روانہ ہو گیا ۔
vo *muhim par* ravāna hō gayē
He left *on an expedition*.

523 **par** following oblique infinitives

Infinitives used as verbal nouns (§639) may be followed by **par**. This usage is similar to **par** expressing location immediately after a point in time (§521).

حلیم کھانے پر ہی مجھے اُس کا مزہ معلوم ہوا ۔
halīm *khānē par* hī mujhē us kā maza mālūm hūā
Only *on eating* **halīm** did I discover its delicious taste.

524 Oblique infinitive + **par bhī**

See §1213.

525 **par** marking objects

A few verbs require objects marked with **par**. (See §526 for examples of the way that verbs collocate with postpositions.)

گاؤں والے بزرگوں پر اعتبار کرتے ہیں -
gāōṁ vālē *buzurgōṁ par* ētibār kartē haiṁ
The villagers rely *on the elders.*

اُن کی بات پر مجھے ہنسی آ گئی -
un kī *bāt par* mujhē haṁsī ā gaī
What he said made me laugh (laughter came to me *at what he said*).

526 Collocations of verbs with postpositions

Different verbs collocate (occur together with) different postpositions in sentences. These collocations are lexical properties of the verb, that is to say, part of the way in which meaning is encoded in the verb. (In English too, different verbs take different prepositions.) VERB + POSTPOSITION collocations must be learned along with the individual verbs.

(a) Some verbs require no postposition with inanimate direct objects, or if the object is human, or specified, it is marked with **kō** (§505).

کریم نے تار بھیجا
karīm nē *tār* bhējā
Karim sent a *telegram* to his mother.

کریم نے چوکیدار کو بھیجا
karīm nē *caukīdār kō* bhējā
Karim sent the *watchman.*

(b) Some verbs take objects with **kā** (§502).

x کا انتظار کرنا   **X kā intizār karnā**, to wait for X

ہم آپ کا انتظار کریں گے -
ham *āp kā intizār* karēṁ gē
We will wait *for you*.

(c) Some take objects with **sē** (§515).

X سے لڑنا **X sē laṛnā**, to quarrel, fight with X

مرغا مرغے سے لڑا ۔
murγā ***murγē sē*** **laṛā**
The cock fought *with the cock* (in a cockfight).

(d) A few verbs take objects with **par** (§525).

X پر غصّہ آنا **X par γussa ānā**, to get angry at X

بچّوں کی شرارت پر غصّہ کرنا مناسب نہیں ہے ۔
baccōṁ kī ***śarārat par*** **γussa karnā munāsib nahīṁ hai**
It is not appropriate to get angry *at the mischief* of children.

The denominative verbs (§607) formed from **madad**, 'help' illustrate the way in which postpositions contribute to nuancing of meaning in verbs.

X کی مدد کرنا **X kī madad karnā**, to help X

وہ غریبوں کی مدد کرتی ہے ۔
vo γarībōṁ kī madad kartī hai
She helps the poor.

X کو مدد دینا **X kō madad dēnā**, to help X, give help to X

مشکل وقت پر اُنہوں نے مجھے مدد دی ۔
muśkil vaqt par unhōṁ nē mujhē madad dī
He helped me at a difficult time.

X کو مدد ملنا **X kō madad milnā**, X to receive help

بند کے متاثرین کو حکومت سے مدد ملی تھی ۔
band kē mutāsirīn kō hukūmat sē madad milī thī
Those affected by the dam received help from the government.

X سے مدد لینا **X sē madad lēnā**, to get, take help from X

وہ یہ کام اکیلا نہیں کر سکتا ، کسی کی مدد لینا پڑے گی ۔
vo ye kām akēlā nahīṁ kar saktā, kisī kī madad lēnā paṛē gī
He can't do this job alone; (he) must get help from someone.

COMPOUND POSTPOSITIONS

Compound postpositions are postpositional phrases consisting of inflected **kā** + a noun, adjective, adverb or more complex construction. There are a great many such postpositions. Some of the most common are presented here, listed according to the six main structural types to which they belong. The order of the elements in some postpositional phrases is reversible (with or without minor changes in phrase structure or agreement). Those phrases are marked with an asterisk (*) and amplified where necessary by footnotes.

527 kā + oblique noun + postposition

kā is inflected to **kē** or **kī**, agreeing with the noun in gender and case.

(**kī**) **vajah sē**, because of/on account of < وجہ **vajah** (f.), reason, cause

kē sabab sē, because of < سبب **sabab** (m.), cause, reason

* **kē zariē** (**sē**), by means of[6] < ذریعہ **zarīa** (m.), means

* **kē taur par**, as, by way of[7] < طور **taur** (m.), manner, way

kē muqābilē mēṁ, in comparison with < مقابلہ **muqābila** (m.), comparison

آپ یہ کام کس کی وجہ سے کر رہے ہیں؟—امّاں کے حکم کی وجہ سے۔
āp ye kām *kis kī vajah sē* kar rahē haiṁ?—ammāṁ kē *hukm kī vajah sē*
On whose account are you doing this work?—*On account of* mother's order.

Compare the meaning of **kis vajah sē** (without **kī**):

آپ یہ کام کس وجہ سے کر رہے ہیں؟—لازمی ہے۔
āp ye kām *kis vajah sē* kar rahē haiṁ?—lāzimī hai
Why are you doing this work?—It's essential.

تحفے کے طور پر
tohfē *kē taur par*
as a gift

6 Also occurs reversed as **bazarīa-e-X** (with the Persian preposition **ba**). See §531.

7 Also occurs reversed as **bataur-e-X**. See §531 for an example.

528 kā + oblique noun

kā is inflected to **kē** or **kī**, agreeing with the noun in gender and case.

kē sāth, with < ساتھ **sāth** (m. & adv.), company
kē xilāf, against, contrary to[8] < خلاف **xilāf** (m. & adj.), opposition
kē vāstē, for, in order to < واسطہ **vāsta** (m.), connection, reason
kī taraf, towards < طرف **taraf** (f.), direction, way, side
kī jagah, in place of < جگہ **jagah** (f.), place
* **kē ilāva**, in addition to, besides[9] < علاوہ **ilāva** ~ **alāva** (m.), superaddition

لڑکا دوستوں کے ساتھ کھیل رہا ہے ۔
laṛkā dōstōṁ *kē sāth* khēl rahā hai
The boy is playing *with* friends.

یہ قانون کے خلاف ہے ۔
ye qānūn *kē xilāf* hai
This is *against* the law.

مستری کی جگہ اُس کا بیٹا آ گیا ہے ۔
mistrī *kī jagah* us kā bēṭā ā gayā hai
In place of the mechanic, his son has come.

اِن وسائل کے علاوہ ~ علاوہ اِن وسائل کے
in vasāel *kē ilāva* ~ *ilāva* in vasāel *kē*
in addition to these resources

529 kā + oblique adjective

kā is inflected to **kē**, agreeing with the oblique adjective.

* **kē mutaalliq**, about < متعلق **mutaalliq**, connected with
kē mutābiq, according to < مطابق **mutābiq**, conformable, similar
kē barābar, equal to, similar to < برابر **barābar**, even, level, equal

8 Also occurs as **kē bar xilāf**, and with **izāfat** as **xilāf-e-X** (§532). **xilāf** as an independent noun rarely occurs in modern Urdu.

9 Occurs also as **ilāva X kē**. **ilāva** does not take the oblique singular suffix (although **kē** shows the oblique case).

اپنے خاندان کے متعلق کچھ بتائیے -
apnē xāndān *kē mutaalliq* kuch batāiyē
Tell something *about* your family.

جمیلہ کا قد اپنے بھائی کے برابر ہے -
jamīla kā qad apnē bhāī *kē barābar* hai
Jamila's height is *equal to* her brother's.

530 kā + adverb

kā is inflected to **kē**.

kē bād, after < بعد **bād**, afterwards, later
kē pīchē, behind, after < پیچھے **pīchē**, behind, after
kē ūpar, above < اوپر **ūpar**, above, up, over
kē pās, near; shows possession < پاس **pās** (adv. & m.), near; side
* **kē sivā**, except for[10] < سوا **sivā**, apart from

وہ خورشید صاحب کے بعد کمرے میں آیا -
vo xuršīd sāhib *kē bād* kamrē mēṁ āyā
He came into the room *after* Mr. Khurshid.

وہ خورشید صاحب کے پیچھے کمرے میں آیا -
vo xuršīd sāhib *kē pīchē* kamrē mēṁ āyā
He came into the room *behind* Mr. Khurshid.

اُن کی دکان گھر کے پاس ہے -
un kī dukān ghar *kē pās* hai
Their shop is *near* the house.

531 (kā) + Persian preposition + oblique noun

kā is inflected to **kē** or **kī**, agreeing with the noun in gender and case.

---

10 Also occurs as **sivā-e-X kē**. Its inclusion among the adverbs is no more than a matter of convenience, since it only occurs as a postposition.

* **kē baɣair**, without < **ba**, with, by + غیر **ɣair** (m.), stranger
* **kī bajāē**, instead of[11] < **ba**, with, by + جائے **jāē** (f.), place

bazarīa-e-X, by means of X < **ba**, with, by[12] + ذریعہ **zarīa** (m.), means

bataur-e-X, as, by way of X[13] < **ba**, with, by + طور **taur** (m.), manner

* **kē bāvujūd**, in spite of < **bā**, with + وجود **vujūd** (m.), existence

kē bar xilāf, contrary to < **bar**, on, over + خلاف **xilāf** (m.), opposition

kē darmiyān, between, among < **dar**, in + میان **miyān** (m.), the middle

اِن وسائل کے بغیر - بغیر اِن وسائل کے
in vasāel *kē baɣair* ~ *baɣair* in vasāel kē
without these resources

baɣair also occurs with the perfect participle:

بغیر میری بات سمجھے - میری بات سمجھے بغیر
baɣair* mērī bāt samjhē ~ mērī bāt samjhē *baɣair
without having understood what I said (**mērī bāt**)

اِس کمرے کی بجائے - بجائے اِس کمرے کے
is kamrē *kī bajāē* ~ *bajāē* is kamrē *kē*
instead of this room

بطورِ تحفہ
***bataur-e*-tohfa**
as a gift

532 Noun + izāfat

xilāf-e-X, against, contrary to **X**[14] < خلاف **xilāf** (m.), opposition

خلافِ حکم
***xilāf-e*-hukm**
contrary to orders

---

11 **jāē** (properly **jāy**) is an old form of **jā**. When the order is reversed, the postposition **kā** appears in the m. obl. sg. case.

12 Occurs unreversed as **kē zarīa-e-X (sē)**. **kā** is lost when the postposition is reversed.

13 Reversed form of **kē taur par**.

14 Reversed form of **kē xilāf**.

POSTPOSITIONAL SEQUENCES

533 Spatial-temporal postpositions + sē

The postposition **sē** is added to other spatial-temporal postpositions (with the exception of **tak** and **sē** itself) to make postpositional sequences. The first postposition locates an event in space or time, and **sē** expresses further movement beyond that location.

اِن شالوں میں سے ایک چُن لیجئے -
in śālōṁ *mēṁ sē* ēk cun lījiē
Choose one *of* (*out of*) these shawls.

ہوائی جہاز شہر کے اوپر سے گزرا -
havāī jahāz śahar kē *ūpar sē* guzrā
The aeroplane passed *over* the city.

چوہیا پلنگ کے نیچے سے آ نکلی -
cūhiyā palang *kē nīcē sē* ā niklī
The mouse popped *out from under* the bed.

ہم نے دہلی کی طرف سے سفر کیا -
ham nē dehlī *kī taraf sē* safar kiyā
We travelled *via* Delhi.

Compare

ہم نے دہلی کی طرف سفر کیا -
ham nē dehlī *kī taraf* safar kiyā
We travelled *in the direction of* Delhi.

EXPRESSING POSSESSION ('TO HAVE')

Possession may be expressed by **kā** (~ **kē** ~ **kī**), **kē pās** or **kō**, depending on the nature of the possessive relationship.

534 Inalienable possession: kā (~ kē ~ kī)

When possession is of something which one normally or customarily has, such as kin, body parts, reputation, landed property or a home, **kā** (~ **kē** ~ **kī**) is used.

شاہدہ کے دو بھائی ہیں -
śāhida *kē* dō bhāī *haiṁ*
Shahida *has* two brothers.

بیچارے کا صرف ایک پاؤں ہے -
bēcārē *kā* sirf ēk pāōṁ *hai*
The poor fellow *has* only one foot.

ہمارا گھر نہیں ہے -
hamārā* ghar nahīṁ *hai
We *have* no house (home).

اِس تالے کی کوئی چابی نہیں -
is tālē *kī* kōī cābī nahīṁ
This lock *has* no key.

ڈاکٹر صاحب کی بڑی عزّت ہے -
ḍākṭar sāhab *kī* baṛī izzat *hai*
The doctor enjoys (*has*) great respect.

535 Alienable possession: kē pās

When possession concerns (temporary) physical ownership or control of a tangible object, **kē pās** is used.

دھوبی کے پاس سائیکل ہے -
dhōbī *kē pās* sāīkal *hai*
The washerman *has* a bicycle.

ہمارے پاس بہت سے گھر ہیں -
ham*ārē pās* bahut sē ghar *haiṁ*
We have many houses (properties).

536 Intangible possession: kō

When possession concerns something abstract or intangible, impersonal constructions with **kō** are generally used.

Having an illness is expressed with **kō**, however this could equally well be considered a case of an experiencer subject (§506).

اُستاد کو بہت کام ہے -
ustād *kō* bahut kām *hai*
The teacher *has* a lot of work.

کیا آپ کو فرصت ہے ؟
kyā āp *kō* fursat *hai*?
Are you free (do you *have* leisure time)?

مجھے زکام ہے -
mujhē zukām *hai*
I *have* a cold.

6 VERBS

FORMS OF THE VERB

Urdu verbs have four parts, or basic forms: the ROOT, IMPERFECTIVE PARTICIPLE, PERFECTIVE PARTICIPLE, and INFINITIVE. These are elaborated with auxiliaries and suffixes into a complex system of verb tense and aspect (see Table 13 on pages 89-90). The basic form of a verb determines its aspect, whereas the auxiliary (or in the future tense, the future suffix) determines its tense.

601 Root

The verb root is the form to which SUFFIXES are added. A useful rule of thumb states that the root is that part of the verb which remains when the infinitival suffix نا **-nā** is removed. The formation of infinitives is regular.

جانا **jānā**, to go	→	جا **jā**, go
کرنا **karnā**, to do	→	کر **kar**, do
دینا **dēnā**, to give	→	دے **dē**, give
سننا **sunnā**, to hear, to listen	→	سن **sun**, hear, listen

Double transitive and causative STEMS are formed by the addition of the increment, **-ā** (**-lā**) to the root (§803). Double causative stems are formed by the addition of the increment **-vā** (~ **-lvā**) to the root (§811). To inflect a verb, it is not necessary to know whether one is dealing with a verb root or a derived stem, as verbal constructions are formed from roots and stems in the same manner. One must remember that the derived stem of a root is a different verb from the root, and has a different meaning.

سن **sun**, hear, listen	→	سنا **sunā**, tell (§805)
کر **kar**, do	→	کرا **karā**, cause to be done (§810)
دے **dē**, give	→	دلا **dilā**, cause to be given (§810)
سن **sun**, hear, listen	→	سنوا **sunvā**, cause to tell (§811)
کر **kar**, do	→	کروا **karvā**, cause to do (§811)

The subjunctive (§608), request forms (§610), future (§611), conjunctive participle (§612) and continuous tenses (§614-§617) are formed from the verb root (or stem). The verb root is also used with the modal verbs **saknā**, 'to be able' to show ability (§618); and with **cuknā**, 'to be finished' to show completion (§620).

602 Infinitive

The infinitive is the form of a verb which is given in dictionaries. It has the suffix **-nā**, and may be inflected like a masculine noun.

سننا **sunnā** (v.t.) to hear, to listen

کرنا **karnā** (v.t.) to do, to act, to perform

The infinitive is used as a verbal noun (§639), as a request form (§610) and in infinitival constructions showing necessity, advisability, obligation, imminence, the agent, permission, purpose, and negative assertion (§642-§650).

603 Imperfective participle

The imperfective participle is formed from the root by the addition of the present suffix **-tā** (~ **-tē** ~ **-tī**), which is inflected like an adjective to agree with nouns or pronouns in gender and number.

سننا **sunnā**, to hear, listen	→	سنتا **suntā**, hearing, listening
کرنا **karnā**, to do	→	کرتا **kartā**, doing
کرانا **karānā**, to cause to be done	→	کراتا **karātā**, causing to be done

Forms of the imperfective participle

سننا **sunnā**, to hear

	SINGULAR		PLURAL	
MASCULINE	سنتا	**suntā**	سنتے	**suntē**
FEMININE	سنتی	**suntī**	(سنتیں	**suntīṁ**)

The feminine plural suffix **-tīṁ** occurs in the habitual present when the auxiliary is dropped in negative sentences: **suntīṁ**, **kartīṁ**.

The imperfective participle is a verbal adjective. It may be used as an adjective (§901), but its most important function is contribution of the aspect of *incompleteness* to the tense system. Imperfective tenses describe actions or states which are not completed. Most imperfective tenses are *habitual*: they describe actions or states which occur generally or regularly. They include the habitual present (§623), habitual past (§624), habitual conditional (§625), and habitual presumptive (§625). The simple irrealis (§622) is identical with the imperfective participle. The imperfective participle is used in sequences with **rahnā** to show continuation (§626) and **jānā** to show progression (§627).

Table 13: Overview of Aspect, Tense and Mood
(The form of the negative is shown in parentheses after the forms.)

Infinitive	
ānā, 'to come'	
Basic form of verb	ROOT **ā**
Simple constructions	
	SUBJUNCTIVE **(agar) vo āē** (+ **na**) (if) he comes; he might come
	FUTURE **vo āē gā** (+ **nahīṁ**) he will come
Aspect	CONTINUOUS TENSES (DURATIVE ASPECT)
Complex constructions	
Present	CONTINUOUS PRESENT **vo ā rahā hai** (+ **nahīṁ**) he is coming
Past	CONTINUOUS PAST **vo ā rahā thā** (+ **nahīṁ**) he was coming
Conditional	CONTINUOUS CONDITIONAL **(agar) vo ā rahā hō** (+ **na**) (if) he is coming
Presumptive	CONTINUOUS PRESUMPTIVE **vo ā rahā hō gā** (+ **nahīṁ**) he must be coming
Irrealis (Unfulfilled conditions)	CONTINUOUS IRREALIS **(agar) vo ā rahā hōtā** (+ **na**) (if) he were coming

IMPERFECTIVE PARTICIPLE
ātā

IRREALIS
(agar) vo ātā (+ **na**)
(if) he had come

HABITUAL TENSES
(IMPERFECTIVE ASPECT)

HABITUAL PRESENT
vo ātā hai (+ **nahīṁ**)
he comes

HABITUAL PAST
vo ātā thā (+ **nahīṁ**)
he used to come

HABITUAL CONDITIONAL
(agar) vo ātā hō (+ **na**)
(if) he comes

HABITUAL PRESUMPTIVE
vo ātā hō gā (+ **nahīṁ**)
he must come

HABITUAL IRREALIS
(agar) vo ātā hōtā (+ **na**)
(if) he came (regularly).

PERFECTIVE PARTICIPLE
āyā

SIMPLE PAST
vo āyā (+ **na**, **nahīṁ**)
he came

PUNCTUAL/PAST TENSES
(PERFECTIVE ASPECT)

IMMEDIATE PAST
vo āyā hai (+ **nahīṁ**)
he has come

REMOTE PAST
vo āyā thā (+ **nahīṁ**)
he had come; he came.

CONDITIONAL PAST
(agar) vo āyā hō (+ **na**)
(if) he has come

PRESUMPTIVE PAST
vo āyā hō gā (+ **nahīṁ**)
he must have come

PAST IRREALIS
(agar) vo āyā hōtā (+ **na**)
(if) he had come

604 Perfective participle

The perfective participle is formed from the root by the addition of the past suffix **-ā** (~ **-ē** ~ **-ī** ~ **-īṁ**), which is inflected like an adjective to agree with nouns or pronouns in gender and number.

سننا **sunnā**, to hear, listen → سنا **sunā**, heard

کرانا **karānā**, to cause to be done → کرایا **karāyā**, caused to be done

Forms of the perfective participle

سننا **sunnā**, to hear

	Singular		Plural	
Masculine	سنا	**sunā**	سنے	**sunē**
Feminine	سنی	**sunī**	سنیں	**sunīṁ**

When the m. sg. and f. sg. forms -**ā** and -**ī** of the past suffix are added to roots ending in vowels, the root vowel and the suffix vowel combine as follows:

ā + **ā** → **āyā**	**khā**, eat	→	کھایا **khāyā**, eaten (m. sg.)
a + **ā** → **ayā**	**ga** < **jā**, go	→	گیا **gayā**, gone (m. sg.)
ō + **ā** → **ōyā**	**sō**, sleep	→	سویا **sōyā**, slept (m. sg.)
ī + **ā** → **iyā**	**pī**, drink	→	پیا **piyā**, drank (m. sg.)
ī + **ī** → **ī**	**pī**, drink	→	پی **pī**, drank (f. sg.)
i + **ī** → **ī**	**di** < **dē**, give	→	دی **dī**, gave (f. sg.)

Five verbs have irregular perfective stems, as shown in Table 14 on p. 92.

The perfective participle is a verbal adjective. It may be used as an adjective (§907), but its most important function is contribution of the aspect of *completeness* to the tense system. Perfective tenses describe actions or states which are completed. They are also *punctual*: they describe actions or states occurring once. They include the immediate past (§631), remote past (§632), conditional past (§633), and presumptive past (§633). The simple past (§630) is identical with the perfective participle. The perfective participle is used in sequences with **jānā**, 'to go' to form the passive (§634) and with **karnā**, 'to do' to show habit (§636).

Table 14: Irregular perfective participles

Root		Perfective stem		Perfective participle	
		M. SG.	M. PL.	F. SG.	F. PL.
ہو	ہو	ہوا	ہوئے	ہوئی	ہوئیں
hō, be	**hū-** [1]	**hūā**	**hūē**	**hūī**	**hūīṁ**
جا	گ	گیا	گئے	گئی	گئیں
jā, go	**ga-**	**gayā**	**gaē**	**gaī**	**gaīṁ**
کر	کِ	کیا	کیے	کی	کیں
kar, do	**ki-**	**kiyā**	**kiyē**	**kī**	**kīṁ**
دے	دِ	دیا	دیے	دی	دیں
dē, give	**di-**	**diyā**	**diyē**	**dī**	**dīṁ**
لے	لِ	لیا	لیے	لی	لیں
lē, take	**li-**	**liyā**	**liyē**	**lī**	**līṁ**

THE VERB **hōnā**, 'TO BE'

605 The conjugation of **hōnā**

Table 15 shows the present, past and future conjugations of the verb **hōnā**. (For information about the pronouns in the table, see §202-§204.)

Table 15: The present, past, subjunctive and future forms of **hōnā**

Present tense of **hōnā**

SINGULAR			
1st person	میں ہوں	**maiṁ hūṁ**	I am. (m.f.)
2nd person	تو ہے	**tū hai**	You are. (m.f.)
3rd person	وہ ہے	**vo hai**	He, she, it is.
PLURAL			
1st person	ہم ہیں	**ham haiṁ**	We are. (m.f.)
2nd person	تم ہو	**tum hō**	You are. (m.f.)
	آپ ہیں	**āp haiṁ**	You are. (m.f.)
3rd person	وہ ہیں	**vo haiṁ**	They are. (m.f.)

1 Phonetically, the perfective stem has a short vowel: [**hu**]. It is spelled with a long vowel: **hū-**.

The present forms of **hōnā** agree with the subject noun or pronoun in person and number. Negatives are made with **nahīṁ** (§417). In unemphatic negative sentences, present forms of **hōnā** are dropped. (**ye mērī ṭōpī nahīṁ hai** 'This is not my hat' → **ye mērī ṭōpī nahīṁ**.)

Past tense of **hōnā**

SINGULAR

1st person	میں تھا – تھی	**maiṁ thā** (m.) ~ **thī** (f.)	I was.
2nd person	تو تھا – تھی	**tū thā** (m.) ~ **thī** (f.)	You were.
3rd person	وہ تھا – تھی	**vo thā** (m.) ~ **thī** (f.)	He, she, it was.

PLURAL

1st person	ہم تھے – تھیں	**ham thē** (m.) ~ **thīṁ** (f.)	We were.
2nd person	تم تھے – تھیں	**tum thē** (m.) ~ **thīṁ** (f.)	You were.
	آپ تھے – تھیں	**āp thē** (m.) ~ **thīṁ** (f.)	You were.
3rd person	وہ تھے – تھیں	**vo thē** (m.) ~ **thīṁ** (f.)	They were.

The past tense forms of **hōnā** are adjectival, and agree with the noun or pronoun in gender and number. The negative used with the past of **hōnā** is **nahīṁ** (and occasionally **na**) (§417).

Subjunctive mood of **hōnā**

SINGULAR

1st person	میں ہوں	**maiṁ hūṁ**	I may/should be. (m.f.)
2nd person	تو ہو	**tū hō**	You may/should be. (m.f.)
3rd person	وہ ہو	**vo hō**	He, she, it may/should be.

PLURAL

1st person	ہم ہوں	**ham hōṁ**	We may/should be. (m.f.)
2nd person	تم ہو	**tum hō**	You may/should be. (m.f.)
	آپ ہوں	**āp hōṁ**	You may/should be. (m.f.)
3rd person	وہ ہوں	**vo hōṁ**	They may/should be. (m.f.)

The subjunctive forms of **hōnā** agree with the subject noun or pronoun in person and number. Negatives are made with **na** (§417). The first person singular forms of the subjunctive and of the present are identical; the context provides the information necessary to distinguish them.

Future tense of **hōnā**

SINGULAR

1st person	میں ہوں گا	**maiṁ hūṁ gā**	I will be. (m.)
	میں ہوں گی	**maiṁ hūṁ gī**	I will be. (f.)
2nd person	تو ہو گا	**tū hō gā**	You will be. (m.)
	تو ہو گی	**tū hō gī**	You will be. (f.)
3rd person	وہ ہو گا	**vo hō gā**	He, it will be. (m.)
	وہ ہو گی	**vo hō gī**	She, it will be. (f.)

PLURAL

1st person	ہم ہوں گے	**ham hōṁ gē**	We will be. (m.)
	ہم ہوں گی	**ham hōṁ gī**	We will be. (f.)
2nd person	تم ہو گے	**tum hō gē**	You will be. (m.)
	تم ہو گی	**tum hō gī**	You will be. (f.)
	آپ ہوں گے	**āp hōṁ gē**	You will be. (m.)
	آپ ہوں گی	**āp hōṁ gī**	You will be. (f.)
3rd person	وہ ہوں گے	**vo hōṁ gē**	They will be. (m.)
	وہ ہوں گی	**vo hōṁ gī**	They will be. (f.)

The future tense of **hōnā** is formed by adding the future suffix **gā** (~ **gē** ~ **gē**)[2] to the subjunctive forms. Although it is a suffix, it is written as a separate word in Urdu. The future suffix is adjectival, and agrees with the noun or pronoun in gender and number. The form of the negative used is **nahīṁ** (§417). The future tense of **hōnā** expresses both future and presumption.

Examples

آج میں دفتر میں نہیں (ہوں) -
āj maiṁ daftar mēṁ nahīṁ (*hūṁ*)
Today I *am* not in the office.

کل موسم اچّھا تھا لیکن آج اچّھا نہیں -
kal mausam acchā *thā* lēkin āj acchā *nahīṁ*
The weather *was* fine yesterday but today (it) *isn't* fine.

2 The future suffix is a contraction of **gaā** (= **gayā**, the perfective participle of **jānā**). Compare the English 'I am going to be.'

اگر موسم اچّھا ہو ہم سیر کریں گے -
agar mausam acchā *hō*, ham sair karēṁ gē
If the weather *is* good, we will go for a walk.

ریڈیو سے سنا ہے کہ کل موسم اچّھا ہو گا -
rēḍiyō sē sunā hai ke kal mausam acchā *hō gā*
I've heard on the radio that the weather *will be* fine tomorrow.

میری چیزیں یہیں تھیں مگر اب نہیں (ہیں) -
mērī cīzēṁ yahīṁ *thīṁ*, magar ab *nahīṁ* (*haiṁ*)
My things *were* right here, but now they *aren't*.

آپ کی چیزیں محفوظ ہیں - وہ الماری میں ہوں گی -
āp kī cīzēṁ mahfūz *haiṁ*. vo almārī mēṁ *hōṁ gī*
Your things *are* safe. They *must be* in the cabinet.

606 hōnā as an auxiliary verb

In the Urdu verbal system, the tense of the auxiliary verb **hōnā** determines the tense of the verbal construction (Table 13 on pages 89-90).

(a) Present tenses (continuous present, habitual present and immediate past) are formed with the present tense of the auxiliary.

(b) Past tenses (continuous past, habitual past and remote past) are formed with the past tense of the auxiliary.

(c) Conditional tenses (continuous conditional, habitual conditional and conditional past) are formed with the subjunctive mood of the auxiliary.

(d) Presumptive tenses (continuous presumptive, habitual presumptive and presumptive past) are formed with the future tense of the auxiliary.

DENOMINATIVE VERBS (607)

Denominative verbs are verb phrases consisting of a noun or adjective plus an inflected verb. They are very frequent in Urdu, which has borrowed Perso-Arabic nouns, adjectives and derived verbal elements, such as Arabic participles (§1501-§1502) and Persian present and past stems (§1406) extensively. An Urdu verb is added to these loans, most frequently **karnā** (but **dēnā**, 'to give', **lēnā**, 'to take', **bāṁdhnā**, 'to tie', **nikālnā**, 'to take out', **lagānā**, 'to apply', **uṭhānā**, 'to raise' and **rakhnā**, 'to put' also occur). English borrowings are assimilated in the same way.

The intransitive of denominative verbs is formed by substituting a semantically appropriate intransitive verb, such as **hōnā** for **karnā** (see §807 for examples).

When the phrase is not formed with **karnā**, it is essential to check the dictionary to find the intransitive. Denominative verbs are listed under the noun or adjective which forms the head of the phrase.

The inflected verbs in denominative verbs collocate with (take) different postpositions in sentences (§527). These collocations must be learned along with the individual verbs.

x کی عزّت کرنا	**X kī izzat karnā**, to honour X
→ x کی عزّت ہونا	**X kī izzat hōnā**, X to be honoured
x کی سمگلنگ کرنا	**X kī samagling karnā**, to smuggle X
→ x کی سمگلنگ ہونا	**X kī samagling hōnā**, X to be smuggled
x کو عزّت دینا	**X kō izzat dēnā**, to show respect to X
→ x کو y سے عزّت ملنا	**X kō Y sē izzat milnā**, X to be honoured by Y
x کو شکست دینا	**X kō śikast dēnā**, to defeat X
→ شکست کھانا	**śikast khānā**, to be defeated
x کا مہر باندھنا	**X kā mehr bāṁdhnā**, to agree to a dowry of X
x کی ذمہ داری لینا	**X kī zimmēdārī lēnā**, to take responsibility for X

Also:

x کی ذمہ داری اُٹھانا	**X kī zimmēdārī uṭhānā**, to take responsibility for X
جلوس نکالنا	**julūs nikālnā**, to parade, parade in protest

VERB FORMS BASED ON THE VERB ROOT

608 Subjunctive

A verb is used in the subjunctive mood when it describes an action or state which is uncertain in some way, or which is contingent on something else. Hence the subjunctive is often used in conditional sentences and subordinate (dependent) clauses. Certain conjunctions, adverbs and phrases require the subjunctive.

The subjunctive is not a tense. When translating it, the context of the whole sentence, including the tense of the verb in the main clause, must be considered.

Table 16: Forms of the subjunctive

karnā *'to do'*

Singular			
1st person	میں کروں	**maiṁ karūṁ**	I may do. (m.f.)
2nd person	تو کرے	**tū karē**	You may do. (m.f.)
3rd person	وہ کرے	**vo karē**	He, she, it may do. (m.f.)
Plural			
1st person	ہم کریں	**ham karēṁ**	We may do. (m.f.)
2nd person	تم کرو	**tum karō**	You may do. (m.f.)
	آپ کریں	**āp karēṁ**	You may do. (m.f.)
3rd person	وہ کریں	**vo karēṁ**	They may do. (m.f.)

The verbs **hōnā**, 'to be' (§605), **dēnā**, 'to give' and **lēnā**, 'to take' are irregular.

dēnā, *'to give'*

Singular			
1st person	میں دوں	**maiṁ dūṁ**	I may give. (m.f.)
2nd person	تو دے	**tū dē**	You may give. (m.f.)
3rd person	وہ دے	**vo dē**	He, she, it may give.
Plural			
1st person	ہم دیں	**ham dēṁ**	We may give. (m.f.)
2nd person	تم دو	**tum dō**	You may give. (m.f.)
	آپ دیں	**āp dēṁ**	You may give. (m.f.)
3rd person	وہ دیں	**vo dēṁ**	They may give. (m.f.)

lēnā, *'to take'*

Singular			
1st person	میں لوں	**maiṁ lūṁ**	I may take. (m.f.)
2nd person	تو لے	**tū lē**	You may take. (m.f.)
3rd person	وہ لے	**vo lē**	He, etc., may take.
Plural			
1st person	ہم لیں	**ham lēṁ**	We may take. (m.f.)
2nd person	تم لو	**tum lō**	You may take. (m.f.)
	آپ لیں	**āp lēṁ**	You may take. (m.f.)
3rd person	وہ لیں	**vo lēṁ**	They may take. (m.f.)

The forms of the subjunctive agree with the subject noun or pronoun in person and number. Note that subjunctive suffixes do not show gender. The form of the negative used with the subjunctive is **na** (§417).

The subjunctive in main clauses

The subjunctive is used in main clauses: (a) in asking for permission or advice, (b) in making a wish or expressing a preference, (c) in expressing encouragement, (d) in making an indirect command, (e) as one form of request, (f) following **śāyad**,[3] 'maybe', and **kāś (ke)**,[4] 'if only', and (g) in questions expressing doubt or uncertainty.

کیا میں اندر آؤں ؟ — ضرور ، آئیے آئیے -
kyā maiṁ andar *āūṁ*?—zarūr, āiyē āiyē!
May I *come* in?—Certainly, come in, come in!

آئیے ، کھانا کھائیں -
āiyē, khānā *khāēṁ*
Come; let's eat.

حامد سے کہو کہ مت چیخے -
hāmid sē kahō ke mat *cīxē*
Tell Hamid not to *shout*.

بائیں طرف چلیں -
bāīṁ taraf *calēṁ*
Please *drive* on the left.

شاید آج شام کو چاند نظر آئے
śāyad āj śām kō cāṁd *nazar āē*
Maybe this evening the moon *will be visible* (sighted).

کاش آج چاند نظر آئے ، کل عید ہو گی !
kāś āj cāṁd *nazar āē*, kal īd hō gī!
If only the moon *is sighted* tonight, tomorrow will be Eid!

Because the subjunctive may express a wish, when using it to express the possibility of an *undesirable* event, the subjunctive verb is often put in the negative. This is an exception to the restriction on the negative with compound verbs (§717).

---

3 **śāyad** may also be followed by a verb in the simple past, referring to a completed event: **śāyad vo aisī davā na khā sakā**, 'Maybe he couldn't take such medicine.'

4 **kāś** may also introduce clauses in the irrealis: **kāś āp baṭvā na bhūltē**, 'I wish you had not forgotten (your) wallet.'

اتنا بھاری صندوق اوپر نہ رکھو، کہیں گر نہ جائے!
itnā bhārī sandūq ūpar na rakhō, kahīṁ *gir na jāē*!
Don't put such a heavy box up (on a rack), lest it *fall*!

The subjunctive in subordinate clauses

Not all subordinate clauses have verbs in the subjunctive. However subordinate clauses are dependent clauses, and so inherently contingent. Certain conjunctions and impersonal expressions having to do with contingent situations introduce subordinate clauses with verbs in the subjunctive. They may be called SUBORDINATING EXPRESSIONS.

agar, 'if', **ke**, 'that' may introduce clauses containing the subjunctive.

jab tak + NEGATIVE, 'until', 'unless' introduces a relative subordinate clause (§1114) which may contain a subjunctive.

tā ke, 'so that', **baśartēke**, 'on condition that' (§1228) always introduce clauses with the subjunctive.

Subordinating expressions: impersonal constructions

The following impersonal expressions introduce subordinate clauses which contain subjunctive verbs.

ممکن ہے کہ	**mumkin hai ke**, it's possible that ...
چاہئے کہ	**cāhiē ke**, it's needed that ...
ضروری ہے کہ	**zarūrī hai ke**, it's necessary that ...
مناسب ہے کہ	**munāsib hai ke**, it's appropriate that ...
خدا کرے کہ	**xudā karē ke**, God grant that ...
ایسا نہ ہو کہ	**aisā na hō ke**, lest (it should not be such that) ...

Subordinating expressions: personal constructions

The following verbs introduce subordinate clauses which function as direct objects of main clauses, and which contain verbs in the subjunctive.

فرض کرنا (کہ)	**farz karnā (ke)**, to suppose (that)
مجبور ہونا کہ	**majbūr hōnā ke**, to be compelled, obliged to
چاہنا کہ	**cāhnā ke**, to want (to)
(X کا) دل چاہنا کہ	**(X kā) dil cāhnā ke**, (X) to feel like
کوشش کرنا کہ	**kōśiś karnā ke** (in requests), to try (to)

NOTE: many subordinating expressions may also introduce the irrealis. See §609, 'Unfulfilled wishes, conjecture and regret'.

Examples

ممکن ہے کہ مجھے وظیفہ نہ ملے ۔
mumkin hai ke* mujhē vazīfa *na milē
It's possible that I *might not get* the scholarship.

چاہئے کہ ہم اندھیرا ہونے سے پہلے گھر پہنچیں ۔
cāhiē ke* ham andhērā hōnē sē pahlē ghar *pahuṁcēṁ
We *ought to reach* home before dark.

ضروری ہے کہ آج ہی پیسہ ادا کر دوں ۔
zarūrī hai ke* āj hī paisa *adā kar dūṁ
It's necessary that (I) *pay* the money today.

خدا کرے کہ نجمہ کو وظیفہ مل جائے !
***xudā karē ke* najma kō vazīfa *mil jāē*!**
May God grant that Najma *gets* the scholarship!

آج ہی خریدو ، ایسا نہ ہو کہ کل نہ ملے !
āj hī xarīdō, *aisā na hō ke* kal *na milē*!
Buy it today, *lest it be unavailable* tomorrow!

حکومت مجبور ہے کہ لوڈشیڈنگ میں اضافہ کرے ۔
hukūmat *majbūr hai ke* lōḍśēḍing mēṁ *izāfa karē*
The government *is compelled to increase* the power cuts.

فرض کیجئے کہ اِس سال انتخابات ہوں ...
***farz kījiē ke* is sāl intixābāt *hōṁ* ...**
Suppose there *are* elections this year ...

ابّا جان چاہتے تھے کہ میں بڑا آدمی بنوں ۔
abbā jān *cāhtē thē* ke maiṁ baṛā ādmī *banūṁ*
Daddy *wanted* me *to become* an important person.

کوشش کرو کہ کسی کو تکلیف نہ دو ۔
kōśiś karō ke* kisī kō taklīf na *dō
Try not to give trouble to anyone.

609 Conditional sentences

CONDITIONAL sentences consist of two clauses. The first, or condition clause, usually begins with **agar** اگر . The second, or result clause, begins with **tō** تو . **agar** is often deleted, **tō** rarely (§1202). **agar** may also be replaced, by **jab** جب (§1112) or **jō** جو (§1106-§1107).

Urdu conditional sentences belong to two basic categories: fulfillable conditions, and unfulfilled conditions (IRREALIS). Unfulfilled conditional sentences, also called 'contrary to fact' sentences, describe conditions which have not been, or cannot be, fulfilled.

Fulfillable conditions

Fulfillable conditions include (a) those that will probably be met, and (b) conditions which are presumed to be met. When the verb in the condition clause is subjunctive, or in one of the imperfective tenses (present or future), the condition remains open-ended. It is possible or even probable that the condition will be met, but it has not happened yet, or it is not yet confirmed. There is still a possibility that the condition will fail.

The verb in the result clause provides the context of the result (a present result, a future result, or a command), and the tense of the sentence.

When the verb in the condition clause is in the simple past, the action in the condition clause is either (a) complete (and the condition will have been met), or (b) the perfective aspect is used to affirm the result (provided the condition is met).[5] Perfective tenses cannot be used in the condition clause if there is little likelihood of the condition being met, or if the action is still continuing.

Possibility/probability: condition in the subjunctive or the future

اگر تیل گرم ہو تو آلو ڈال دو۔

agar tēl gar(a)m *hō* tō ālū *ḍāl dō*

If the oil *is* hot, *put in* the potatoes. (I expect it is hot.)

اگر آپ مریض کا علاج نہ کریں تو وہ مر سکتا ہے۔

agar āp marīz kā *ilāj na karēṁ* tō vo *mar saktā hai*

If you *don't treat* the patient, he *could die*. (I think you might not do so.)

---

5 Compare the following use of a perfective tense to express affirmation: **mālī!—āyā jī**, 'Gardener!—Just coming, sir.' The gardener has not come, but uses the simple past to affirm that he is doing so immediately.

خیر اگر آپ میرے ساتھ رسوا ہوں گی تو کوئی حرج نہیں ۔
xair agar āp mērē sāth rusvā *hōṁ gī* tō kōī harj nahīṁ
Fine, if you *will be* disgraced along with me, then there *is* no harm. (Rusvā, *Umrāō Jān Adā*)

اگر وہ چاند پر قدم رکھے تو اپنے ملک کا جھنڈا کھڑا کر دے گا ۔
agar vo cāṁd par qadam *rakhē* tō apnē mulk kā jhanḍā *khaṛā kar dē gā*
If he *sets* foot on the moon, he *will set up* the flag of his country. (It is possible but unlikely; a simple past verb is not possible.)

Presumed present fact: condition in the present or habitual present

اگر تیل گرم ہے تو آلو ڈال دو ۔
agar tēl gar(a)m *hai* tō ālū *ḍāl dō*
If the oil *is* hot, *put in* the potatoes. (It looks hot now, but check it.)

اگر آپ مریض کا علاج نہیں کرتے ہیں تو وہ مر سکتا ہے ۔
agar āp marīz kā *ilāj nahīṁ kartē haiṁ* tō vo *mar saktā hai*
If you *don't treat* the patient, he *could die*. (You don't seem to be doing so.)

Completed action/affirmation of result: condition in the simple past

اگر آپ نے مریض کا علاج نہ کیا تو وہ مر سکتا ہے ۔
agar āp nē marīz kā *ilāj na kiyā* tō vo *mar saktā hai*
If you *don't treat* the patient, he *could die*. (You have indicated you won't.)

آپ نے محنت کی تو ضرور کامیاب ہوں گے ۔
āp nē *mehnat kī* tō zarūr *kāmyāb hōṁ gē*
If you *work hard* (you) *will* certainly *succeed*. (You have not yet made the effort, but your success is assured if you do.)

Unfulfilled/unfulfillable conditions (irrealis)

When imperfective participles without auxiliaries are used in both the condition clause and the result clause, the sentence describes a failed condition, or a condition which is impossible to meet (irrealis).

اگر وہ چاند پر قدم رکھتا تو اپنے ملک کا جھنڈا کھڑا کر دیتا ۔
agar vo cāṁd par qadam *rakhtā* tō apnē mulk kā jhanḍā *khaṛā kar dētā*
If he *had set* foot on the moon, he *would have set up* the flag of his country. (He failed to get into the space programme.)

اگر آپ مریض کا علاج نہ کرتے تو وہ مر جاتا ۔
agar āp marīz kā *ilāj na kartē* tō vo *mar jātā*
If you *hadn't treated* the patient, he *would have died.* (You treated him.)

اگر آپ دروازے میں تالا لگاتے تو چور کیسے اندر آتا ؟
agar āp darvāzē mēṁ *tālā lagātē* tō cōr kaisē *andar ātā*?
If you *had locked* the door, how could the thief *have got in*? (He got in.)

اگر اور جیتے رہتے یہی انتظار ہوتا
agar aur *jītē rahtē*, yahī intizār *hōtā*
If I *were to live* longer, it *would only be* to wait like this (Ghalib)

When the condition clause ends in **thā** (~ **thē** ~ **thī**) or a verb in the remote past, the condition has also failed, but the sentence suggests that there is scope for discussion on the subject.

اگر آپ نے دروازے میں تالا لگایا تھا تو چور کیسے اندر آ گیا ؟
agar āp nē darvāzē mēṁ *tālā lagāyā thā* tō cōr kaisē *andar ā gayā*?
If you *had locked* the door, how *did* the thief *get in*? (For the sake of argument, I accept your assertion, nevertheless the thief did get in.)

Unfulfilled wishes, conjecture and regret (irrealis)

Conjunctions, impersonal expressions and verbs which normally require the subjunctive may take the imperfective participle to show IRREALIS (conjecture, regret, etc.). Irrealis may also be used in place of the subjunctive to wish for something impossible.

فرض کیجئے کہ آپ چاند پر قدم رکھتے ...
farz kījiē ke āp cāṁd par qadam *rakhtē* ...
Suppose you *were to set* (*had set*) foot on the moon ...

چاہئے تھا کہ میں دروازے میں تالا لگاتا ۔
cāhiē thā ke maiṁ darvāzē mēṁ *tālā lagātā*
I should *have locked* the door.

کاش آپ بٹوا نہ بھولتے ۔
kāś āp baṭvā *na bhūltē*
I wish you *had not forgotten* (your) wallet.

Complex conditional sentences

Precise distinctions of aspect can be expressed in conditional sentences (both fulfillable and irrealis). See §617 (continuous conditional, continuous irrealis), §625 (habitual conditional, habitual irrealis), and §633 (conditional past, past irrealis).

610 Request forms

*Request forms corresponding to **tū**, **tum** and **āp***

There are three basic levels of request forms in Urdu, corresponding to the three second person pronouns **tū**, **tum** and **āp**. See §203 for a discussion of these pronouns.

The use of compound verbs (Chapter 7) with the vector verbs **dēnā** and **lēnā** is very common with request forms, but particularly with the mid- or **tum**-level forms, where they point to the reciprocal transactions which take place in the solidary relationships where **tum** is often used.

Lower level request forms corresponding to **tū** consist of the verb root alone.

کھانا کھا بیٹے ۔
khānā *khā*, bēṭē
Eat (your) food, son.

سو جا منّے سو جا ۔
sō jā* munnē, *sō jā
Go to sleep, baby, *go to sleep*.

Mid-level request forms corresponding to **tum** consist of the verb root with the suffix **-ō** (identical to second person plural (**tum**-level) subjunctive forms). They are used towards persons addressed with the pronoun **tum**.

کھانا کھا لو ۔
khānā *khā lō*
Eat (your) food.

اب سو جاؤ ، دیر ہو گئی ہے ۔
ab *sō jāō*, dēr hō gaī hai
Go to sleep now; it is late.

آپ بازار جاتے وقت مجھے ساتھ لے چلو نا !
āp bāzār jātē vaqt mujhē sāth *lē calō* nā!
When you go to the market do *take* me along!

Polite request forms corresponding to **āp** consist of the verb root with the suffix **-iē** (~ **-iyē**) for most verbs. **-iyē** is added to most roots ending in long vowels; **-iē** is added to roots ending in consonants.

Four verbs have irregular stems, as shown in Table 17 on p. 105.

چلئے
caliē
Please walk.

جائیے
jāiyē
Please go.

Table 17: Irregular request forms

Root	Polite request stem		Polite request form	
kar, do	کیج	**kīj-**	کیجئے	**kījiē**
dē, give	دیج	**dīj-**	دیجئے	**dījiē**
lē, give	لیج	**līj-**	لیجئے	**lījiē**
pī, drink	پیج	**pīj-**	پیجئے	**pījiē**

Examples

اب کھانا کھائیے – اب کھانا کھا لیجئے
ab khānā *khāiyē* ~ ab khānā *khā lījiē*
Please eat (food) now.

آپ بازار جاتے وقت مجھے ساتھ لے چلئے -
āp bāzār jātē vaqt mujhē sāth *lē caliē*
When you go to the market please *take* me along.

Courteous formal requests may be made by suffixing **gā** to an **āp** level request.

یہاں بیٹھئے گا ، ڈاکٹر صاحب ابھی آنے والے ہیں -
yahāṁ *baiṭhiē gā*, ḍākṭar sāhib abhī ānē vālē haiṁ
Please sit here, the doctor is on his way now.

Other request forms

The infinitive may be used as a request that is neutral with respect to honorific levels (§203). It is appropriate for neutral requests or impersonal instructions.

چوک سے بائیں مڑنا اور سو میٹر آگے چلنا -
cauk sē bāēṁ *muṛnā* aur sau mīṭar āgē *calnā*
Turn left at the crossroads and *walk* a hundred metres further.

پانی پینے کے قابل بنانے کے لئے اُسے پانچ منٹ تک اُبالنا -
pānī pīnē kē qābil banānē kē liē usē pāṁc minaṭ tak *ubālnā*
To make water fit to drink, *boil* it for five minutes.

The subjunctive, (§608, p. 103) may be used as a request form.

صرف تازہ پھل اور سبزیاں خریدیں -
sirf tāza phal aur sabziyāṁ *xarīdēṁ*
Buy only fresh fruit and vegetables.

دھونے سے پہلے ہر پتّے کو الگ کریں ۔
dhōnē sē pahlē har pattē kō *alag karēṁ*
Before washing, *separate* every leaf.

It is appropriate to make formal polite requests to strangers of equal or superior status (persons addressed with **āp** or an honorific title) using verb phrases with **taśrīf**, 'one's honourable self'. (See §1603 for more examples.)

تشریف لانا
taśrīf lānā
to bring one's honourable self (= **ānā**, to come)

آئیے ، تشریف لائیے ، میں آپ کی کیا خدمت کر سکتا ہوں ؟
āiyē, *taśrīf lāiyē*, maiṁ āp kī kyā xidmat kar saktā hūṁ?
Come in, *come in;* how can I help you?

کھانا تیّار ہے ، تشریف لائیے ، کھانا کھائیے ۔
khānā tayyār hai, *taśrīf lāiyē*, khānā khāiyē
The food is ready; *please come* and eat.

تشریف رکھنا
taśrīf rakhnā
to place one's honourable self (= **baiṭhnā**, to sit, **maujūd hōnā**, to be present)

جناب یہاں تشریف رکھئے ۔
janāb, yahāṁ *taśrīf rakhiē*
Sir, *please sit* here.

611 Future tense

The future tense (Table 18 on p. 107) is formed by adding the future suffix **gā** گا (~ **gē** گے ~ **gī** گی) to the subjunctive forms of a verb. The future suffix is adjectival, and agrees with the noun or pronoun in gender and number. Agreement in person, as well as number, is shown by the verb's subjunctive base. The form of the negative used is **nahīṁ** (§417).

The verbs **hōnā**, 'to be' (§605), **dēnā**, 'to give'; and **lēnā**, 'to take' are irregular.

Presumption is expressed by adding the future of **hōnā** to continuous (§617), habitual (§625) or past (§633) tense verbs.

Table 18: Forms of the future

***karnā**, 'to do'*

SINGULAR

1st person	میں کروں گا	**maiṁ karūṁ gā**	I will do. (m.)
	میں کروں گی	**maiṁ karūṁ gī**	I will do. (f.)
2nd person	تو کرے گا	**tū karē gā**	You will do. (m.)
	تو کرے گی	**tū karē gī**	You will do. (f.)
3rd person	وہ کرے گا	**vo karē gā**	He, it will do. (m.)
	وہ کرے گی	**vo karē gī**	She, it will do. (f.)

PLURAL

1st person	ہم کریں گے	**ham karēṁ gē**	We will do. (m.)
	ہم کریں گی	**ham karēṁ gī**	We will do. (f.)
2nd person	تم کرو گے	**tum karō gē**	You will do. (m.)
	تم کرو گی	**tum karō gī**	You will do. (f.)
	آپ کریں گے	**āp karēṁ gē**	You will do. (m.)
	آپ کریں گی	**āp karēṁ gī**	You will do. (f.)
3rd person	وہ کریں گے	**vo karēṁ gē**	They will do. (m.)
	وہ کریں گی	**vo karēṁ gī**	They will do. (f.)

***dēnā**, 'to give'*

SINGULAR

1st person	میں دوں گا	**maiṁ dūṁ gā**	I will give. (m.)
	میں دوں گی	**maiṁ dūṁ gī**	I will give. (f.)
2nd person	تو دے گا	**tū dē gā**	You will give. (m.)
	تو دے گی	**tū dē gī**	You will give. (f.)
3rd person	وہ دے گا	**vo dē gā**	He, it will give. (m.)
	وہ دے گی	**vo dē gī**	She, it will give. (f.)

PLURAL

1st person	ہم دیں گے	**ham dēṁ gē**	We will give. (m.)
	ہم دیں گی	**ham dēṁ gī**	We will give. (f.)

2nd person	تم دو گے	**tum dō gē**	You will give. (m.)
	تم دو گی	**tum dō gī**	You will give. (f.)
	آپ دیں گے	**āp dēṁ gē**	You will give. (m.)
	آپ دیں گی	**āp dēṁ gī**	You will give. (f.)
3rd person	وہ دیں گے	**vo dēṁ gē**	They will give. (m.)
	وہ دیں گی	**vo dēṁ gī**	They will give. (f.)

Examples

کراچی جانے والی ریل گاڑی ساڑھے نو بجے چھُٹے گی ۔
karācī jānē vālī rēl gāṛī sāṛhē nau bajē *chuṭē gī*
The train going to Karachi *will leave* at 9:30.

ہم ہر مشکل میں جیتیں گے ۔
ham har muśkil mēṁ *jītēṁ gē*
We *will win* in every difficulty.

اگلے سال میں ہندوستان جاؤں گا ۔
aglē sāl maiṁ hindūstān *jāūṁ gā*
Next year I *will go* to India.

میں آپ کے وعدے پر بھروسا کروں گی ۔
maiṁ āp kē vādē par *bharōsā karūṁ gī*
I *will rely* on your promise.

612 Conjunctive participles

Form and function of conjunctive participles

The root of **karnā**, **kar** is added to the root of any verb to make a CONJUNCTIVE PARTICIPLE. Conjunctive participles transform two separate but related clauses into a single sentence which shows two actions or events happening in succession. The two clauses must have (a) the same subject, and (b) verbs in the same tense.

The form of the negative used with conjunctive participles is **na** (§417), however negative conjunctive participles are uncommon.

میں گھر جاؤں گا اور آرام کروں گا ۔
maiṁ ghar *jāūṁ gā* aur ārām karūṁ gā
I *will go* home and I will rest.

→ میں گھر جاکر آرام کروں گا ۔
mai ghar *jā kar* ārām karūṁ gā
I *will go* home *and* rest (*having gone* home, I will rest).

سلیمہ نے پڑھا اور امتحان دیا ۔
salīma nē *paṛhā* aur imtihān diyā
Salima *studied* and took the examination.

→ سلیمہ نے پڑھ کر امتحان دیا ۔
salīma nē *paṛh kar* imtihān diyā
Salima *studied and* took the examination.

The sequential order of the two actions becomes unambiguous when the conjunctive participle replaces the first verb: 'I will rest after I go home.' 'Salima studied before taking the examination.'

Alternate form root + kē of conjunctive participles

The conjunctive participle of **karnā** itself is ROOT + **kē**.

میں کام کروں گا اور آرام کروں گا ۔
maiṁ *kām karūṁ gā* aur ārām karūṁ gā
I *will work* and I will rest.

→ میں کام کر کے آرام کروں گا ۔
maiṁ *kām kar kē* ārām karūṁ gā
I *will work and* (*then*) I will rest.

The alternate form root + **kē** is often used to form conjunctive participles with other verbs as well (although conjunctive participles with **kar** are the written standard, and more common, usage).

پڑھ کے آرام کرو !
***paṛh kē* ārām karō!**
Study before you rest!

Short absolutives

The verb root alone may function like a conjunctive participle (the SHORT ABSOLUTIVE). Short absolutives are incorrect in modern standard Urdu,[6] but may

6 In Hindi, when the first action in some way causes the second action, **kar** may be omitted. This usage is not allowed in standard Urdu.

nevertheless be found in texts, particularly older ones.

پانی اِتنا تھا کہ سب کچھ بہا لے گیا ۔
pānī itnā thā ke sab kuch bahā lē gayā
There was so much water that it carried everything away.

Idiomatic phrases with ***kar***

kar is added to **xās**, 'special' to form the phrase خاص کر **xās kar**, 'particularly' (with the same meaning as **xās taur par**). **kyōṁ kar** means 'how?'.

ایسا کیوں کر ہوا ؟
aisā kyōṁ kar hūā?
How did it happen like this?

Conjunctive participles in sentences with impersonal constructions

When the second clause is an impersonal construction, the clauses may appear to have different subjects:

وہاں جا کے اچّھے سموسے ملیں گے ۔
vahāṁ *jā kē* acchē samōsē milēṁ gē
(We) *will go* there *and* get good samosas.

The subject of the first clause is an omitted pronoun (**ham**), whereas the subject of the second appears to be **samōsē**. But **samōsē milēṁ gē** is an impersonal construction, and the verb agrees with the direct object, **samōsē**, while the real subject of the second clause is an omitted **ham kō**. (See §506, §641.)

← ہم وہاں جائیں گے اور ہم کو اچّھے سموسے ملیں گے ۔
***ham* vahāṁ jāēṁ gē aur *ham kō* acchē samōsē milēṁ gē**
We will go there and *we* will get good samosas.

Mixed transitivity with conjunctive participles

The verb in the main clause (below, the second verb) is the sentence verb, and determines the transitivity of the sentence. If the main verb is transitive, the subject is followed by **nē** if the verb tense is perfective (§629). If the main verb is intransitive, the entire sentence is treated as intransitive, and **nē** is not used.

میں پڑھ کر گھر گیا ۔
maiṁ *paṛh kar* ghar gayā
Having studied, I went home.

میں نے گھر جا کر پڑھا ۔
maiṁ nē ghar *jā kar* paṛhā
Having gone home, I studied.

613 Repeated roots in conjunctive participles

When the verb root in a conjunctive participle is repeated, the action of the verb is repeated, takes a period of time or occurs continuously.

اُس نے پیسے گن گن کر اپنے بٹوے میں رکھے -
us nē paisē *gin gin kar* apnē baṭvē mēṁ rakhē
He *counted* the money *very carefully* before putting it in his bag.

کروٹیں بدل بدل کر اور آنسو بہا بہا کر ساری رات کاٹی -
karvaṭēṁ *badal badal kar* aur āṁsū *bahā bahā kar* sārī rāt kāṭī
He spent the entire night tossing and turning (*changing* positions) and *shedding* tears. (Narang, *Readings*)

614 Continuous tenses

Continuous tenses have DURATIVE aspect: they describe actions or states which are incomplete and in progress. They have the following structure:

VERB ROOT + **rahā** ~ **rahī** ~ **rahē** + inflected AUXILIARY VERB

rahā is the perfective participle of **rahnā**, 'to stay', 'remain'. It is delexicalized (has lost its original meaning) and functions as the continuous participle. It agrees with the subject noun or pronoun in gender and number, like an adjective.

For an overview of continuous tenses, see Table 13 on pages 89-90. For the auxiliary verb **hōnā**, see §605-§606.

615 Continuous present

The continuous present tense (Table 19, on p. 112) describes actions or states which are incomplete and in progress at the time of speaking. The present tense of the auxiliary is used, and the verb agrees with the subject.

The form of the negative is **nahīṁ** (§417), although negative sentences in the present continuous tense are rare. If a negative present continuous does occur, the auxiliary may be dropped.

Examples

بھائی ابھی گھر آ رہا ہے -
bhāī abhī ghar *ā rahā hai*
Brother *is coming* home now.

Table 19: Continuous present tense of **karnā**

SINGULAR

1st person	میں کر رہا ہوں	**maiṁ kar rahā hūṁ**	I am doing. (m.)
	میں کر رہی ہوں	**maiṁ kar rahī hūṁ**	I am doing. (f.)
2nd person	تو کر رہا ہے	**tū kar rahā hai**	You are doing. (m.)
	تو کر رہی ہے	**tū kar rahī hai**	You are doing. (f.)
3rd person	وہ کر رہا ہے	**vo kar rahā hai**	He, it is doing. (m.)
	وہ کر رہی ہے	**vo kar rahī hai**	She, it is doing. (f.)

PLURAL

1st person	ہم کر رہے ہیں	**ham kar rahē haiṁ**	We are doing. (m.)
	ہم کر رہی ہیں	**ham kar rahī haiṁ**	We are doing. (f.)
2nd person	تم کر رہے ہو	**tum kar rahē hō**	You are doing. (m.)
	تم کر رہی ہو	**tum kar rahī hō**	You are doing. (f.)
	آپ کر رہے ہیں	**āp kar rahē haiṁ**	You are doing. (m.)
	آپ کر رہی ہیں	**āp kar rahī haiṁ**	You are doing. (f.)
3rd person	وہ کر رہے ہیں	**vo kar rahē haiṁ**	They are doing. (m.)
	وہ کر رہی ہیں	**vo kar rahī haiṁ**	They are doing. (f.)

(Examples)

فریدہ آج کل امتحان کے لئے پڑھ رہی ہے -
farīda āj kal imtihān kē liē *paṛh rahī hai*
Farida *is studying* for exams these days.

افضل اور فریدہ چائے پی رہے ہیں -
afzal aur farīda cāē *pī rahē haiṁ*
Afzal and Farida *are drinking* tea.

چابی ہر جگہ ڈھونڈی ، مگر نہیں مل رہی -
cābī har jagah ḍhūṁḍī, magar nahīṁ *mil rahī*
I looked for the key everywhere, but (I *am*) not *finding* it.

Continuous tenses do not occur with **rahnā**, 'to remain' as a sentence verb; the habitual present is used instead.

میں لاہور میں دو سال سے رہتی ہوں -
maiṁ lāhaur mēṁ dō sāl sē *rahtī hūṁ*
I *have been living* in Lahore for two years.

The continuous present is also used to describe a future action which has already begun, or which is considered as begun.

ٹھیک ہے ، رکھ دو ، میں آپ کے پاس آ رہا ہوں -
ṭhīk hai, rakh dō, maiṁ āp kē pās *ā rahā hūṁ*
Okay, put down (the receiver), I *am on my way* to you.

616 Continuous past

The continuous past tense describes actions or states which were incomplete and in progress at a point in the past. The past tense of the auxiliary is used. The verb agrees with the subject. The form of the negative is **nahīṁ** (§417).

Table 20: Continuous past tense of **karnā**

SINGULAR			
1st person	میں کر رہا تھا	**maiṁ kar rahā thā**	I was doing. (m.)
	میں کر رہی تھی	**maiṁ kar rahī thī**	I was doing. (f.)
2nd person	تو کر رہا تھا	**tū kar rahā thā**	You were doing. (m.)
	تو کر رہی تھی	**tū kar rahī thī**	You were doing. (f.)
3rd person	وہ کر رہا تھا	**vo kar rahā thā**	He, it was doing. (m.)
	وہ کر رہی تھی	**vo kar rahī thī**	She, it was doing. (f.)
PLURAL			
1st person	ہم کر رہے تھے	**ham kar rahē thē**	We were doing. (m.)
	ہم کر رہی تھیں	**ham kar rahī thīṁ**	We were doing. (f.)
2nd person	تم کر رہے تھے	**tum kar rahē thē**	You were doing. (m.)
	تم کر رہی تھیں	**tum kar rahī thīṁ**	You were doing. (f.)
	آپ کر رہے تھے	**āp kar rahē thē**	You were doing. (m.)
	آپ کر رہی تھیں	**āp kar rahī thīṁ**	You were doing. (f.)
3rd person	وہ کر رہے تھے	**vo kar rahē thē**	They were doing. (m.)
	وہ کر رہی تھیں	**vo kar rahī thīṁ**	They were doing (f.)

Examples

بھائی کل گھر آ رہا تھا جب بس خراب ہو گئی -
bhāī kal ghar *ā rahā thā*, jab bas xarāb hō gaī
Brother *was coming* home yesterday, when the bus broke down.

فریدہ اُن دنوں امتحان کے لئے پڑھ رہی تھی -
farīda un dinōṁ imtihān kē liē *paṛh rahī thī*
Farida *was studying* for exams (during) those days.

افضل اور فریدہ چائے پی رہے تھے -
afzal aur farīda cāē *pī rahē thē*
Afzal and Farida *were drinking* tea.

جب گھر میں آگ لگی تب ہم سو رہے تھے -
jab ghar mēṁ āg lagī, tab ham *sō rahē thē*
At the time the fire broke out in the house, we *were sleeping.*

With the stative verb **baiṭhnā**, 'to sit' the continuous tenses refer to the act of sitting, and not to the state of being seated.

میں بیٹھ رہی تھی کہ کرسی کا پایہ ٹوٹ گیا -
maiṁ *baiṭh rahī thī*, ke kursī kā pāya ṭūṭ gayā
I *was just sitting down* when the leg of the chair broke.

میں بیٹھی ہوئی تھی جب کرسی کا پایہ ٹوٹ گیا -
maiṁ *baiṭhī hūī thī*, jab kursī kā pāya ṭūṭ gayā
I *was seated* when the leg of the chair broke.

617 Other continuous tenses

The CONTINUOUS CONDITIONAL tense is used to describe incomplete, continuing actions or states which *may* be happening at the time of speaking. The subjunctive auxiliary is used, and the verb agrees with the subject. The clause is introduced by words like **śāyad**, **agar**, **mumkin hai**, etc. (§608). The form of the negative is **na** (§417), as is always the case with subjunctive verbs.

شاید بھائی اِسی وقت گھر آ رہا ہو -
śāyad bhāī isī vaqt ghar *ā rahā hō*
Maybe brother *is coming* home right now.

اگر نسرین کام کر رہی ہو اُسے تکلیف نہ دو۔
agar nasrīn *kām kar rahī hō*, usē taklīf na dō
If Nasrin *is working*, don't bother her.

The CONTINUOUS PRESUMPTIVE TENSE is used to describe incomplete, continuing actions or states which one presumes to be happening at the time of speaking. The future tense of the auxiliary is used, and the verb agrees with the subject.

پانچ بج گئے ، بھائی اِس وقت گھر آ رہا ہو گا۔
pāṁc baj gaē, bhāī is vaqt ghar *ā rahā hō gā*
It's five o'clock; brother *must be coming* home now.

نسرین اِس سلسلے میں کام کر رہی ہو گی۔
nasrīn is silsilē mēṁ *kām kar rahī hō gī*
Nasrin *must be working* in this connection.

The CONTINUOUS IRREALIS is used to describe unrealized continuous actions or states. The imperfective participle of **hōnā** is the auxiliary, and the verb agrees with the subject.

اگر وہ آ رہا ہوتا تو اُس کا خط مل گیا ہوتا۔
agar vo *ā rahā hōtā*, tō us kā xat mil gayā hōtā
If he *were coming* (on the way), we would have received his letter.

618 Root + **saknā** (ability, possibility)

The modal verb **saknā** shows the ability to perform an action, or the possibility of an event occurring. The verb phrase has the structure:

VERB ROOT + inflected form of **saknā**

saknā, which is intransitive, determines the grammar of the sentence; in perfective tenses, **saknā** agrees with the subject and **nē** is not used even if the verb root belongs to a transitive verb. The tense of **saknā** determines the form of the negative (negatives are shown in Table 13 on pages 89-90).

میرا بچّہ چل سکتا ہے۔
mērā bacca cal *saktā hai*
My child *can* walk.

وحید بیمار ہے ، کل کی دعوت میں نہیں آ سکے گا۔
vahīd bīmār hai, kal kī dāvat mēṁ *nahīṁ* ā *sakē gā*
Wahid is sick; he *won't be able* to come to tomorrow's party.

میں یہ دوا نہیں کھا سکا ، کڑوی ہے -
maiṁ ye davā *nahīṁ* khā *sakā*, kaṛvī hai
I *couldn't* take this medicine; it's (too) bitter.

آسمان میں بادل چھا رہے ہیں ، بارش ہو سکتی ہے -
āsmān mēṁ bādal chā rahē haiṁ, bāriś hō *saktī hai*
Clouds are gathering in the sky; it *could* rain.

619 Root + pānā (possibility)

The verb **pānā**, 'to find' may be used as a modal, showing the possibility of an action dependent on circumstances (most often in negative sentences). The verb phrase has the structure:

VERB ROOT + inflected form of **pānā**

Used as a modal, **pānā** is intransitive, and agrees with the subject.

وحید مصروف ہے ، کل کی دعوت میں نہیں آ پائے گا -
vahīd masrūf hai, kal kī dāvat mēṁ nahīṁ ā *pāē gā*
Wahid is busy; he *can't manage* to come to tomorrow's party.

بچّوں نے اِتنا شور مچایا کہ ہم آرام سے فلم نہ دیکھ پائے -
baccōṁ nē itnā śōr macāyā ke ham ārām sē film *na* dēkh *pāē*
The children made so much noise that we couldn't watch the film in peace.

In negative sentences with **pānā**, the oblique infinitive may be used instead of the root, if a second clause follows. The second clause usually contains a verb of motion. In this case, the negative immediately precedes **pānā**.

وہ ایک مچھلی بھی پکڑنے نہ پایا تھا کہ اُس کا پاؤں پھسل گیا -
vo ēk machlī bhī pakaṛnē *na pāyā thā* ke us kā pāōṁ phisal gayā
He *hadn't managed* to catch a single fish, when his foot slipped.

pānā also occurs as a non-modal verb meaning 'to find', 'to get', whereas **saknā** only occurs as a modal. Although intransitive as a modal, **pānā** is transitive when used as a sentence verb.

انجم نے امتحان میں اچّھے نمبر پائے -
anjum nē imtihān mēṁ acchē nambar *pāē*
Anjum *got* good marks (good numbers) in the examination.

620 Root + **cuknā** (completion)

The modal verb **cuknā** shows completion of an action or event prior to a second action or event, which may be expressed in the sentence, or be the event of narration. It usually occurs in perfective tenses. The verb phrase has the structure:

VERB ROOT + inflected form of **cuknā**

cuknā is sometimes translated as 'already', but it usually corresponds to an English pluperfect. **cuknā**, which is intransitive, determines the grammar of the sentence; thus in perfective tenses, **cuknā** agrees with the subject, and **nē** is not used even if the verb root belongs to a transitive verb.

اندھیرا ہونے لگا - چڑیاں اپنا شام کا گیت گا کر خاموش ہو چکی تھیں -
andhērā hōnē lagā. ciṛiyāṁ apnā śām kā gīt gā kar xāmōś *hō cukī thīṁ*
It began to get dark. The birds *had* sung their evening song and *become* silent. (Narang, *Readings*)

ہم گاڑی بیچ چکے تھے جب ملک صاحب نے دریافت کیا -
ham gāṛī *bēc cukē thē* jab malik sāhib nē daryāft kiyā
We *had already sold* the car when Malik Sahib inquired (about it).

621 Compound verbs

Compound verbs are nuanced verb sequences with a structure similar to ROOT + **saknā** or ROOT + **cuknā**:

VERB ROOT + inflected VECTOR VERB

Vector verbs lose their lexical meaning, and contribute various nuances to the meaning of the main verb, as illustrated below. The commonest vector verbs are **jānā**, **dēnā** and **lēnā**. Compound verbs are described in Chapter 7.

یہ خط پڑھیئے -
ye xat paṛhiē
Please read this letter. (non-compound verb)

یہ خط پڑھ دیجئے -
ye xat paṛh dījiē
Please read this letter (to me). (compound verb, vector **dēnā**)

یہ خط پڑھ لیجئے -
ye xat paṛh lījiē
Please read this letter (to yourself). (compound verb, vector **lēnā**)

VERB FORMS BASED ON THE IMPERFECTIVE PARTICIPLE

With the exception of the IRREALIS, verb structures based on the imperfective participle have habitual aspect: they describe actions or states which occur generally or regularly. Imperfective tenses have the following structure:

IMPERFECTIVE PARTICIPLE + inflected AUXILIARY VERB

For an overview of habitual tenses, see Table 13 on pages 89-90. For the auxiliary verb **hōnā**, see §605-§606.

622 Imperfective participles alone

Irrealis

Imperfective participles without auxiliaries are used in both clauses of conditional sentences to describe a failed condition, or a condition which is impossible to meet (§609, 'Unfulfilled/unfulfillable conditions'). The imperfective participle may also be used in place of the subjunctive to show impossible conditions (§609, 'Unfulfilled wishes, conjecture and regret').

Narrative imperfective

The imperfective participle is used without an auxiliary in narration. Passages with verbs in the narrative imperfective typically start with a verb in the habitual past (§624), describing events occurring regularly in the past. As the narrative continues, the auxiliary is dropped, and only the imperfective participle remains.

وہ اکثر سبق رٹنے سے بھاگتے تھے - کھیتوں اور جنگلوں کی سیر کرتے ،
چُرا کر گنّے یا پھل کھاتے ، یا پھر ریل گاڑی کا تماشا دیکھتے -

vo aksar sabaq raṭnē sē *bhāgtē thē*. khētōṁ aur jangalōṁ kī *sair kartē*, curā kar gannē yā phal *khātē*, yā phir rēl gāṛī kā tamāśā *dēkhtē*

He often used to *play hooky* from memorizing (his) lessons. He *would walk* in the fields or forests, steal sugar cane or fruit and *eat* it, or (again) *watch* the splendid sight of a train. (Narang, *Reader*)

623 Habitual present

The habitual present tense (Table 21, on p. 119) describes actions or states which occur generally or regularly in the present. It may also be used to describe a close future event.

The present tense of the auxiliary is used, and the verb agrees with the subject. See §1009 for agreement with mixed subjects. The form of the negative is **nahīṁ** (§417). In negative sentences, the auxiliary may be dropped. The feminine plural suffix **-tīṁ** occurs in the habitual present when the auxiliary is dropped in negative sentences: سنتیں **suntīṁ**, کرتیں **kartīṁ**.

Table 21: Habitual present tense of **karnā**

SINGULAR			
1st person	میں کرتا ہوں	**maiṁ kartā hūṁ**	I do. (m.)
	میں کرتی ہوں	**maiṁ kartī hūṁ**	I do. (f.)
2nd person	تو کرتا ہے	**tū kartā hai**	You do. (m.)
	تو کرتی ہے	**tū kartī hai**	You do. (f.)
3rd person	وہ کرتا ہے	**vo kartā hai**	He, it does. (m.)
	وہ کرتی ہے	**vo kartī hai**	She, it does. (f.)
PLURAL			
1st person	ہم کرتے ہیں	**ham kartē haiṁ**	We do. (m.)
	ہم کرتی ہیں	**ham kartī haiṁ**	We do. (f.)
2nd person	تم کرتے ہو	**tum kartē hō**	You do. (m.)
	تم کرتی ہو	**tum kartī hō**	You do. (f.)
	آپ کرتے ہیں	**āp kartē haiṁ**	You do. (m.)
	آپ کرتی ہیں	**āp kartī haiṁ**	You do. (f.)
3rd person	وہ کرتے ہیں	**vo kartē haiṁ**	They do. (m.)
	وہ کرتی ہیں	**vo kartī haiṁ**	They do. (f.)

Examples

ہم عام طور پر شام کو باغ میں بیٹھتے ہیں ۔
ham ām taur par śām kō bāɣ mēṁ *baiṭhtē haiṁ*
We *generally sit* in the garden in the evening.

یہاں سردیوں میں برف پڑتی ہے ۔
yahāṁ sardiyōṁ mēṁ *baraf paṛtī hai*
It *snows* (*snow falls*) here in the winter.

Compare گرم کپڑے پہنو ، برف پڑ رہی ہے ۔
gar(a)m kapṛē pehnō, *baraf paṛ rahī hai*
Wear warm clothes; it *is snowing*.

یہ بس صدر نہیں جاتی -
ye bas sadar nahīṁ *jātī*
This bus doesn't *go* to the town centre.

ہم فرش پر سوتے ہیں -
ham farś par *sōtē haiṁ*
We *sleep* on the floor.

مچّھر نقصان دہ ہوتے ہیں -
macchar nuqsāndeh *hōtē haiṁ*
Mosquitoes *are* harmful.

Immediate future

مادہ نے نر سے کہا: خبردار، دشمن آتا ہے -
māda nē nar sē kahā: xabardār, duśman *ātā hai*
The female said to the male: watch out, the enemy *approaches.* (*Mazhab-e-Iśq*)

624 Habitual past

The habitual past tense (Table 22, on p. 121) describes actions or states which occurred generally or regularly in the past. The past tense of the auxiliary is used, and the verb agrees with the subject. See §1009 for agreement with mixed subjects. The form of the negative is **nahīṁ** (§417). The habitual past is often translated as 'used to (VERB)', but is also translated 'VERB-ed', 'was/were (VERB)-ing', depending on the context.

With stative verbs (verbs describing a state), such as **baiṭhnā**, 'to sit', **lēṭnā**, 'to lie', **sōnā**, 'to sleep', **rahnā** 'to remain', and **cāhnā**, 'to want' the distinction between past habitual and past continuous states is not very strong.

Examples

بھائی شام کے پانچ بجے گھر آتا تھا، اب چھ بجے آتا ہے -
bhāī śām kē pāṁc bajē ghar *ātā thā*, ab chē bajē ātā hai
Brother *used to come* home at 5 in the evening, now he comes at 6.

گرمیوں میں ہم شام کو باغ میں بیٹھتے تھے -
garmiyōṁ mēṁ ham śām kō bāγ mēṁ *baiṭhtē thē*
In the summer we *sat/used to sit* in the garden in the evening.

Table 22: Habitual past tense of **karnā**

SINGULAR			
1st person	میں کرتا تھا	**maiṁ kartā thā**	I used to do. (m.)
	میں کرتی تھی	**maiṁ kartī thī**	I used to do. (f.)
2nd person	تو کرتا تھا	**tū kartā thā**	You used to do. (m.)
	تو کرتی تھی	**tū kartī thī**	You used to do. (f.)
3rd person	وہ کرتا تھا	**vo kartā thā**	He, it used to do. (m.)
	وہ کرتی تھی	**vo kartī thī**	She, it used to do. (f.)
PLURAL			
1st person	ہم کرتے تھے	**ham kartē thē**	We used to do. (m.)
	ہم کرتی تھیں	**ham kartī thīṁ**	We used to do. (f.)
2nd person	تم کرتے تھے	**tum kartē thē**	You used to do. (m.)
	تم کرتی تھیں	**tum kartī thīṁ**	You used to do. (f.)
	آپ کرتے تھے	**āp kartē thē**	You used to do. (m.)
	آپ کرتی تھیں	**āp kartī thīṁ**	You used to do. (f.)
3rd person	وہ کرتے تھے	**vo kartē thē**	They used to do. (m.)
	وہ کرتی تھیں	**vo kartī thīṁ**	They used to do. (f.)

(Examples)

وہ کسی زمانے میں وزیر ہوتے تھے -
vo kisī zamānē mēṁ vazīr *hōtē thē*
At some previous time he *used to be* a minister.

جب میں دہلی میں تھی تب قرول باغ میں رہتی تھی -
jab maiṁ dehlī mēṁ thī tab qarōl bāɣ mēṁ *rahtī thī*
When I was in Delhi, I *lived* in Karol Bagh.

ہم فرش پر سوتے تھے -
ham farś par *sōtē thē*
We used to sleep/were sleeping on the floor.

The habitual past may be used in narration to describe events occurring regularly in the past. As the narrative continues, the auxiliary is often dropped, and only the imperfective participle remains (narrative imperfective, §622).

625 Other habitual tenses

The HABITUAL CONDITIONAL tense is used to describe actions or states which *may* occur generally or regularly in the present (present possibility). The subjunctive of the auxiliary is used. The clause is introduced by words like **śāyad**, **agar**, **mumkin hai**, etc. The form of the negative used is **na** (§417), as is always the case with subjunctive verbs. The verb agrees with the subject.

شاید منشی روز آتا ہو ، شاید ہر دوسرے دن آتا ہو -
śāyad munśī rōz *ātā hō*, śāyad har dūsrē din *ātā hō*
Maybe the clerk *comes* daily; maybe he *comes* every second day.

ممکن ہے کہ وہ لوگ کسی اور سڑک پر رہتے ہوں -
mumkin hai ke vo lōg kisī aur saṛak par *rahtē hōṁ*
It's possible that those people *live* on some other street.

The HABITUAL PRESUMPTIVE tense is used to describe actions or states which one presumes to occur generally or regularly in the present. The future tense of the auxiliary is used. The verb agrees with the subject.

منشی روز آتا ہو گا -
munśī rōz *ātā hō gā*
The clerk *must come* daily.

وہ لوگ کسی اور سڑک پر رہتے ہوں گے -
vo lōg kisī aur saṛak par *rahtē hōṁ gē*
Those people *must live* on some other street.

The HABITUAL IRREALIS is used to describe unrealized or impossible habitual actions or states. The imperfective participle of **hōnā** is the auxiliary. The verb agrees with the subject.

اگر منشی روز آتا ہوتا تو سارا کام ہو گیا ہوتا -
agar munśī rōz *ātā hōtā*, tō sārā kām hō gayā hōtā
If the clerk *came* daily, all the work would have been done.

626 Imperfective participle + rahnā (iterative)

The imperfective participle occurs in a phrase with an inflected form of **rahnā**, 'to remain', 'to stay', showing continuation or repetition of an action or state. **rahnā**, which is intransitive, determines the grammar of the sentence; thus in perfective tenses, **nē** is not used even if the participle belongs to a transitive verb. Both the participle and **rahnā** agree with the subject. This construction does not occur (a) in the negative, (b) in continuous tenses. With stative verbs, the perfective participle is used instead (§637).

جھیل میں پانی کی سطح کم ہوتی رہتی ہے -
jhīl mēṁ pānī kī satah *kam hōtī rahtī hai*
The water level in the lake *keeps on going down.*

کتّا رات بھر بھونکتا رہا - نیند اُڑ گئی -
kuttā rāt bhar *bhauṁktā rahā.* nīmd uṛ gaī
The dog *went on barking* the whole night. It was impossible to sleep.

The imperfective participle of **jānā** with **rahnā** has the idiomatic meaning 'to be lost' (to remain gone). It usually occurs in a past tense.

ایک مرتبہ جب میری اُنگلی کا ایک چھلا چندا ڈھیری میں جاتا رہا تھا ...
ēk martaba jab mērī unglī kā ēk challā candā ḍhērī mēṁ *jātā rahā thā* ...
Once when a ring on my finger *was lost* in (playing) blind man's buff ...
(Rusvā, *Umrāō Jān Adā*)

627 Imperfective participle + jānā (progression)

The imperfective participle occurs in a phrase with an inflected form of **jānā**, 'to go', showing the (a) deliberate continuation of an action, and (b) the progression of a condition leading to a change. **jānā**, which is intransitive, determines the grammar of the sentence; in perfective tenses, **nē** is not used even if the verb root belongs to a transitive verb. Both the participle and **jānā** agree with the subject.

واہ واہ ! گاتے جائیے
vāh vāh! *gātē jāiyē*!
Bravo, bravo! Please *go on singing*!

اِتنا بھی گاتے نہ جائیے ، دیکھ لیجئے کہ کوئی پسند کر رہا ہے -
itnā bhī *gātē* na *jāiyē*, dēkh lījiē ke kōī pasand kar rahā hai
Don't *go on singing* so long; check whether anyone is enjoying it.

اگر جھیل میں پانی کی سطح کم ہوتی جائے تو جھیل سوکھ جائے گی -
agar jhīl mēṁ pānī kī satah *kam hōtī jāē*, tō jhīl sūkh jāē gī
If the water level in the lake *continues to go down*, the lake will dry up.

628 Imperfective participle used as an adjective

Imperfective participles may be used as adjectives. See §901.

VERB FORMS BASED ON THE PERFECTIVE PARTICIPLE

Verb structures based on the perfective participle have punctual aspect: they describe actions or states which occur once in the past. Perfective tenses have the following structure:

PERFECTIVE PARTICIPLE + inflected AUXILIARY VERB

For an overview of punctual tenses, see Table 13 on pages 89-90. For the auxiliary verb **hōnā**, see §605-§606.

629 Agreement in perfective tenses

Verbs in non-perfective tenses agree with the subject noun or pronoun. (See §1007-§1010 for a detailed discussion of subject-verb agreement.)

انجم کل امتحان دے گی ۔
anjum imtihān *dē gī*
Anjum *will take* the examination.

زاہد کل امتحان دے گا ۔
zāhidimtihān *dē gā*
Zahid *will take* the examination.

In perfective tenses, the agreement pattern depends on whether the verb is intransitive or transitive. (See §801 for a definition of transitivity.) Intransitive verbs agree with the subject. The subject is in the nominative case.

انجم امتحان میں کامیاب ہو گئی ۔
anjum imtihān mēṁ *kāmyāb hō gaī*
Anjum *passed* the the examination.

زاہد امتحان میں کامیاب ہو گیا ۔
zāhid imtihān mēṁ *kāmyāb hō gayā*
Zahid *passed* the the examination.

Transitive verbs agree with nominative direct objects. The subject takes the postposition **nē** (§510).

انجم نے امتحان دیا ۔
anjum nē imtihān *diyā*
Anjum *took* the examination.

زاہد نے امتحان دیا ۔
zāhid nē imtihān *diyā*
Zahid *took* the examination.

The noun preceding **nē** is in the oblique case.

طالب علموں نے امتحان دیا ۔
tālib ilmōṁ nē imtihān *diyā*
The students *took* the examination.

If the object as well is followed by a postposition, most commonly **kō** (§505), the verb is masculine singular. (A postposition always prevents agreement between a noun or pronoun and a verb.)

میں نے کہانی پڑھی -	میں نے اُس کہانی کو نہیں پڑھا -
maiṁ nē kahānī *paṛhī*	**maiṁ nē us kahānī kō nahīṁ *paṛhā***
I *read* the/a story.	I *have* not *read* that story.

First and second person pronouns take the nominative case when followed by **nē**. Third person pronouns take the oblique case, and third person plural pronouns (**ye, vo, jō**) have variant forms (**inhōṁ** اِنہوں , **unhōṁ** اُنہوں , **jinhōṁ** جنہوں) which occur only before **nē**. See Table 6 in §211.

630 Simple past

The perfective participle is used alone, without an auxiliary, in the simple past tense. (See §604 for the forms of the perfective participle.) The simple past shows the completion of a single action or state at a point in the past, without reference to prior or subsequent events. An adverb of time may focus on the time the event happened; an adverb of place may focus on where it happened, or an adverb of manner, how it happened. When the context of the event or action is not the focus, the simple past is typically used in narration.

The simple past is a perfective tense. If the verb is transitive, it agrees with a nominative direct object (§629). If it is intransitive, it agrees with the subject.

Examples

وہ دیر تک وہاں رہا -

vo dēr tak vahāṁ *rahā*

They *stayed* there until (it was) very late.

... اور اُس نے پھرتی سے ہڈیاں جوڑ دیں - دوسرے نے گوشت ، خون اورکھال تیّار کر دی - تیسرا شیر میں جان ڈالنے کے لئے آگے بڑھا - ان پڑھ نے اُسے ٹوکا اور کہا: «ارے ناسمجھ یہ شیر ہے -»

...aur us nē phurtī sē haḍḍiyāṁ *jōṛ dīṁ*. dūsrē nē gōśt, xūn aur khāl *tayyār kar dī*. tīsrā śēr mēṁ jān ḍālnē kē liē *āgē baṛhā*. an-paṛh nē usē *ṭōkā* aur *kahā:* 'arē nāsamajh, ye śēr hai.'

...And he *connected* the bones with dexterity. The second *prepared* the flesh, blood and hide. The third *stepped forward* in order to put life in the tiger. The illiterate one *stopped* him and *said*, 'O fool, this is a tiger.' (Narang, *Readings*)

The form of the negative (§417) is **na**. **nahīṁ** is also used when the focus of the sentence is on the verb, i.e., the verb contains the most important information in the sentence. In the examples below, the focus is marked with italics.

اُنہوں نے ان پڑھ کی بات نہ مانی ۔
unhōṁ nē *an paṛh kī bāt* na mānī
They did not accept *what the uneducated person said.*

آج صبح بس نہیں آئی ۔
āj subah (~ subh) bas *nahīṁ āī*
This morning the bus *did not come.*

The verb **hōnā** has two past forms: the past tense **thā** (~ **thē** ~ **thī** ~ **thīṁ**) and the perfective participle **hūā** (~ **hūē** ~ **hūī** ~ **hūīṁ**). **thā** shows a state, but **hūā** shows a transition.

جنوری میں موسم کافی ٹھنڈا تھا ۔
janvarī mēṁ mausam kāfī ṭhanḍā *thā*
The weather *was* pretty cold in January.

جب موسم ٹھنڈا ہوا تب لوگ گرم کپڑے پہننے لگے ۔
jab mausam ṭhanḍā *hūā* tab lōg gar(a)m kapṛē pehnnē lagē
When the weather *became* cold, people began to wear warm clothes.

631 Immediate past

The immediate past tense, also called the present perfect (Table 23, p. 127) describes an action or state which is completed, but which still affects the present situation. Very often it refers to events which have recently been completed. The present tense of the auxiliary is used and the form of the negative is **nahīṁ**. The immediate past is a perfective tense; if the verb is transitive, it agrees with the direct object unless the object is marked by **kō** (§629). If it is intransitive, it agrees with the subject.

Examples

بارش ہوئی ہے ، سڑک گیلی ہے ۔
***bāriś hūī hai,* saṛak gīlī hai**
It has rained; the street is wet.

کافی عرصے سے بارش نہیں ہوئی ، خاصا نقصان ہو گیا ہے ۔
kāfī arsē sē *bāriś nahīṁ hūī,* xāsā nuqsān *hō gayā hai*
It has not rained for some time (and) considerable loss *has occurred.*

Table 23: Immediate past of **jānā**

SINGULAR			
1st person	میں گیا ہوں	**maiṁ gayā hūṁ**	I have gone. (m.)
	میں گئی ہوں	**maiṁ gaī hūṁ**	I have gone. (f.)
2nd person	تو گیا ہے	**tū gayā hai**	You have gone. (m.)
	تو گئی ہے	**tū gaī hai**	You have gone. (f.)
3rd person	وہ گیا ہے	**vo gayā hai**	He, it has gone. (m.)
	وہ گئی ہے	**vo gaī hai**	She, it has gone. (f.)
PLURAL			
1st person	ہم گئے ہیں	**ham gaē haiṁ**	We have gone. (m.)
	ہم گئی ہیں	**ham gaī haiṁ**	We have gone. (f.)
2nd person	تم گئے ہو	**tum gaē hō**	You have gone. (m.)
	تم گئی ہو	**tum gaī hō**	You have gone. (f.)
	آپ گئے ہیں	**āp gaē haiṁ**	You have gone. (m.)
	آپ گئی ہیں	**āp gaī haiṁ**	You have gone. (f.)
3rd person	وہ گئے ہیں	**vo gaē haiṁ**	They have gone. (m.)
	وہ گئی ہیں	**vo gaī haiṁ**	They have gone. (f.)

If one is not concerned with a connection between the past event and some other event, but only with the fact that something happened (or when, how or where it happened), the simple past is used:

پہاڑوں میں بہت بارش ہوئی -
pahāṛōṁ mēṁ bahut *bāriś hūī*
In the hills *it rained* a lot.

If the past event or action no longer affects the present, but the time it happened (its temporal context) is relevant; or it is connected to a prior event, the remote past is used (§632).

کل بارش ہوئی تھی -
kal bāriś *hūī thī*
It rained yesterday.

STATIVE VERBS are used in the immediate past to express states which commenced with an action or event in the past, and which continue into the present.

نجمہ باغ میں بیٹھی ہے -
najma bāγ mēṁ *baiṭhī hai*
Najma *is sitting* in the garden (she has sat down and is still sitting).

حامد فرش پر لیٹا ہے -
hāmid farś par *lēṭā hai*
Hamid is *lying* on the floor (he has lain down and is still lying).

632 Remote past

The remote past (also called the past perfect; see Table 24, below) shows that an action was completed in the past and no longer affects the current situation. The action may have been completed within a specified period, in the remote past, or prior to a second event. The past tense of the auxiliary is used and the form of the negative is **nahīṁ**. If the verb is intransitive, it agrees with the subject. If it is transitive, it agrees with a nominative direct object (§629).

Table 24: Remote past of jānā

SINGULAR			
1st person	میں گیا تھا	**maiṁ gayā thā**	I went, had gone. (m.)
	میں گئی تھی	**maiṁ gaī thī**	I went, had gone. (f.)
2nd person	تو گیا تھا	**tū gayā thā**	You went, had gone. (m.)
	تو گئی تھی	**tū gaī thī**	You went, had gone. (f.)
3rd person	وہ گیا تھا	**vo gayā thā**	He, it has gone. (m.)
	وہ گئی تھی	**vo gaī thī**	She, it has gone. (f.)
PLURAL			
1st person	ہم گئے تھے	**ham gaē thē**	We went, had gone. (m.)
	ہم گئی تھیں	**ham gaī thīṁ**	We went, had gone. (f.)
2nd person	تم گئے تھے	**tum gaē thē**	You went, had gone. (m.)
	تم گئی تھی	**tum gaī thīṁ**	You went, had gone. (f.)
	آپ گئے تھے	**āp gaē thē**	You went, had gone. (m.)
	آپ گئی تھیں	**āp gaī thīṁ**	You went, had gone. (f.)
3rd person	وہ گئے تھے	**vo gaē thē**	They went, had gone. (m.)
	وہ گئی تھیں	**vo gaī thīṁ**	They went, had gone. (f.)

Examples

۱۹۹۲ میں میں نے لاہور کا سفر کیا تھا -
unnīs sau bānavē mēṁ maiṁ nē lāhaur kā *safar kiyā thā*
In 1992, I *travelled* to Lahore.

بھائی عید پر گھر آیا تھا ، اور اب واپس گیا ہے -
bhāī īd par ghar *āyā thā*, aur ab vāpas gayā hai
Brother *came* home at Eid, and has now gone back.

However, if one wants to say explicitly that something was completed before a second thing happened, it is preferable to use VERB ROOT + **cuknā** in the remote past (§620).

جب بھائی گھر آ چکا تھا ، شادی کی تیّاریاں شروع ہو گئیں -
jab bhāī ghar ā *cukā thā*, śādī kī tayyāriyāṁ śurū hō gaīṁ
When brother *had come* home, preparations for the wedding began.

633 Other punctual tenses

The CONDITIONAL PAST tense is used to describe actions or states which *may* have occurred in the past. The subjunctive of the auxiliary is used. The clause will be introduced by words like **śāyad**, **agar**, **mumkin hai**, etc. (§608). The form of the negative used is **na** (§417). If the verb is intransitive, it agrees with the subject. If it is transitive, it agrees with a nominative direct object (§629).

ممکن ہے کہ اُن لوگوں نے گھر بدلا ہو -
mumkin hai ke un lōgōṁ nē ghar *badlā hō*
It's possible that those people *have moved.*

شاید منشی نہ گیا ہو -
śāyad munśī *na gayā hō*
Maybe the clerk *has not left.*

The PRESUMPTIVE PAST tense is used to describe actions or states which one presumes to have occurred in the past. The future tense of the auxiliary is used. If the verb is intransitive, it agrees with the subject. If it is transitive, it agrees with a nominative direct object (§629).

منشی گھر گیا ہو گا ، دفتر خالی ہے -
munśī ghar *gayā hō gā*, daftar xālī hai
The clerk *must have left;* the office is empty.

اُس نے ضرور آپ کی بات محسوس کی ہو گی ۔
us nē zarūr āp kī bāt *mahsūs kī hō gī*
He certainly *must have been hurt* by what you said.

The PAST IRREALIS is used to describe unrealized or impossible past actions or states. The imperfective participle of **hōnā** is the auxiliary. If the verb is intransitive, it agrees with the subject. If it is transitive, it agrees with a nominative direct object (§629).

اگر اُس نے میری بات محسوس کی ہوتی ، تو ضرور کچھ کہتا ۔
agar us nē mērī bāt *mahsūs kī hōtī*, tō zarūr kuch kahtā
If he *had been hurt* by what I said, he would certainly have said something.

634 Derived passive

Transitive verbs can be passivized by changing them to the construction:

PERFECTIVE PARTICIPLE + inflected form of **jānā**, 'to go'

jānā, which is intransitive, determines the grammar of the sentence; **nē** is not used, and both the participle and **jānā** agree with the subject. Note that the direct object of the original transitive sentence becomes the subject of the passive one.

ACTIVE وہ تعمیر کا کام وقت پر پورا کریں گے ۔
vo tāmīr kā kām vaqt par *pūrā karēṁ gē*
They *will complete* the construction work on time.

→ PASSIVE تعمیر کا کام وقت پر پورا کیا جائے گا ۔
tāmīr kā kām vaqt par *pūrā kiyā jāē gā*
The construction work *will be completed* on time.

ACTIVE اُس نے پھرتی سے ہڈیاں جوڑ دیں ۔
us nē phurtī sē haḍḍiyāṁ *jōṛ dīṁ*
He *connected* the bones with dexterity.

→ PASSIVE ہڈیاں پھرتی سے جوڑ دی گئیں ۔
haḍḍiyāṁ phurtī sē *jōṛ dī gaīṁ*
The bones *were connected* with dexterity.

If the action has an instrument, it is marked by **kē zariē** or **kē hāth** (preferred if the instrument is human), or **sē**.

ACTIVE تعمیر مزدوروں کے ذریعے پوری کی جائے گی ۔
tāmīr mazdūrōṁ kē zariē ***pūrī kī jāē gī***
The construction *will be completed* by the labourers.

→ PASSIVE ہڈیاں جادو کے ذریعے (جادو سے) جوڑ دی گئیں ۔
haḍḍiyāṁ jādū kē zariē (jādū sē) ***jōṛ dī gaīṁ***
The bones *were connected* by means of magic.

635 Incapacity

Both transitive and intransitive verbs may be passivized to show incapacity, usually in negative sentences. The person (or animate creature) who is incapable of the action is expressed as an instrument marked by **sē**. Note that if an intransitive is passivized, there is no subject. The verb is masculine singular by default.

مجھ سے ایک ہی دن میں اِتنا کام نہیں کیا جاتا ۔
mujh sē ēk hī din mēṁ itnā kām ***nahīṁ kiyā jātā***
I *can't possibly do* so much work in just one day.

کیا تم سے ایسے جوتے پہنے ہوئے اِتنی دور چلا جائے گا ؟
kyā tum sē aisē jūtē pahnē hūē itnī dūr ***calā jāē gā?***
Will you *be able to walk* so far wearing such shoes?

When **jānā** is passivized to show incapacity, its regular perfective participle (**jāyā**) is used.

اُس سے آدھا میل بھی جایا نہ گیا ۔
us sē ādhā mīl bhī ***jāyā na gayā***
He *couldn't go* even half a mile.

636 Perfective participle + karnā (habit or practice)

The uninflected (masculine singular) perfective participle occurs in a phrase with an inflected form of **karnā**, 'to do', showing an action that is done as a practice or habitually. It is not used in punctual tenses.

برائے کرم آیا کریں !
barāē karam ***āyā karēṁ!***
Please *keep coming*!

یوں تو اکثر آپ کی آواز سنا کرتی تھی -
yūṁ tō aksar āp kī āvāz *sunā kartī thī*
Well, I often *used to listen to* your voice. (Rusvā, *Umrāō Jān Adā*)

لکھنؤ میں ایسے معاملے دن رات ہوا کرتے ہیں -
lakhnau mēṁ aisē muāmlē din rāt *hūā kartē haiṁ*
These things *go on* night and day in Lucknow. (Rusvā, *Umrāō Jān Adā*)

The regular perfective participle of **jānā** is used in this construction.

میں رکشے سے جایا کرتی تھی -
maiṁ rikśē sē *jāyā kartī thī*
I always *used to go* by rickshaw.

637 Perfective participle + rahnā (continuation)

The perfective participle of STATIVE VERBS occurs in a phrase with an inflected form of **rahnā**, 'to remain', 'to stay', showing the continuation of a state. This is similar to the construction IMPERFECTIVE PARTICIPLE + **rahnā** (§626), which is used with non-stative verbs. **rahnā**, which is intransitive, determines the grammar of the sentence; thus in perfective tenses, **nē** is not used even if the verb root belongs to a transitive verb. Both the participle and **rahnā** agree with the subject.

بھولا سب کچھ دیکھ رہا تھا ، پر چپ ہی سادھے بیٹھا رہا -
bhōlā sab kuch dēkh rahā thā, par *cup hī sādhē baiṭhā rahā*
Bhola was watching everything, but he *went on keeping mum and doing nothing.* (Prem Chand, *Gōdān*)

638 Perfective participle used as an adjective

Perfective participles may be used as adjectives. See §901.

INFINITIVES

The infinitive may be used as a verbal noun (§639) and as a request form (§610). A variety of infinitival constructions is made with verbs, postpositions or the agent suffix **vālā** (§311). These constructions may be divided into two groups: (a) impersonal constructions with nominative case infinitives, and (b) personal constructions with oblique case infinitives plus a postposition or sentence verb. The first group includes three common impersonal constructions showing advisability, necessity and obligation. The second includes six personal constructions showing the agent, impending action, beginning, permission, purpose, and negative assertion.

639 Infinitives as verbal nouns

The infinitive is basically a verbal noun. It may occur in the nominative case as the subject of the sentence or, in the oblique case, be followed by postpositions.

اُس کے ساتھ میرا جانا بھی ایک ضروری بات تھی -
us kē sāth mērā *jānā* bhī ēk zarūrī bāt thī
My *going* with him was also necessary. (Rusvā, *Umrāō Jān Adā*)

پینے کا پانی
***pīnē* kā pānī**
drinking water (water for *drinking*)

The infinitive + **mēṁ** means 'at (VERB)-ing', 'to (VERB)'. See also §520.

ایسا لباس دیکھنے میں خوبصورت ہے -
aisā libās *dēkhnē mēṁ* xūbsūrat hai
Such clothes are beautiful *to look at.*

The infinitive + **sē** means 'from (VERB)-ing', 'to (VERB)'.

گاڑیوں کے آنے جانے سے سڑک پر دھول اُڑتی رہتی ہے -
gāṛiyōṁ kē *ānē jānē sē* saṛak par dhūl uṛtī rahtī hai
There are always clouds of dust in the street *from the traffic* (*coming and going* of cars).

Compound postpositions (§527-532) are also used with infinitives.

گھر چھوڑنے سے پہلے دروازے میں تالا لگا دیں -
ghar *chōṛnē sē pahlē* darvāzē mēṁ tālā lagā dēṁ
Before leaving the house, (you) should lock the door.

اچھا معاشرہ بنانے کے لئے اچّھی تعلیم ضروری ہے -
acchā muāšara *banānē kē liē* acchī tālīm zarūrī hai
In *order to build* a good society, good education is necessary.

The infinitive is also used in the nominative case with **cāhnā**, 'to want', **sīkhnā**, 'to learn', **jānnā**, 'to know (how)', and **ānā**, 'to come', 'to know'. The infinitive optionally agrees with the noun it refers to (**sair**, **sitār** and **gāṛī** in the examples below) like an adjective.

میں سیر کرنا (کرنی) چاہتا ہوں ۔
maiṁ *sair karnā* (~ *karnī*) cāhtā hūṁ
I want *to go for a walk.*

میں ستار بجانا (بجانی) سیکھ رہا ہوں ۔
maiṁ sitār *bajānā* (~ *bajānī*) sīkh rahā hūṁ
I am learning how *to play* the sitar.

وہ گاڑی چلانا (چلانی) جانتا ہے ۔
vo gāṛī *calānā* (~ *calānī*) jāntā hai
He knows how *to drive* a car.

ānā occurs in impersonal constructions (§641), meaning 'to know'.

اُس کو گاڑی چلانا (چلانی) آتا (آتی) ہے ۔
us kō gāṛī calānā (~ calānī) *ātā* (*ātī*) *hai*
He *knows* how to drive a car.

640 Infinitives as request forms

The infinitive may be used as a neutral request form. See §610.

CONSTRUCTIONS WITH NOMINATIVE CASE INFINITIVES

641 Impersonal constructions

Impersonal constructions are sentence types in which the verb agrees with the logical direct object of the sentence, while the 'real' or logical subject of the sentence (if expressed) is marked by the postposition **kō** (§505) or its alternate forms (§210). Impersonal constructions occur very frequently in Urdu. (See §506 for a treatment of 'experiencer' impersonal constructions.)

PERSONAL

میں سیر کرنا (کرنی) چاہتا ہوں ۔
maiṁ* sair karnā (~ karnī) *cāhtā hūṁ
I want to go for a walk.

فاروق پیاز کے پکوڑے پسند کرتا ہے ۔
fārūq* pyāz kē pakōṛē *pasand kartā hai
Faruq likes onion fritters.

IMPERSONAL

مجھے سیر کرنا (کرنی) چاہئے ۔
mujhē* sair karnā (~ karnī) *cāhiē
I should go for a walk (to me the going for a walk *is wanted*).

فاروق کو پیاز کے پکوڑے پسند ہیں ۔
fārūq kō* pyāz kē pakōṛē *pasand haiṁ
Faruq likes onion fritters (fritters *are pleasing* to Faruq).

In the previous example, the agreement between the verb and the direct object (**pakōṛē**) can be seen.

Deletion of the subject is common.

یہ پکوڑے پسند ہیں ۔
ye pakōṛē *pasand haiṁ*
(I) *like* these fritters.

642 Infinitive + hai (necessity)

The impersonal construction INFINITIVE + **hai** shows the necessity of an action. The subject, if expressed, is followed by **kō** (§506) (or its alternate forms [§210]). Transitive infinitives may take objects of their own, in which case they usually agree with those objects in gender and number, like an adjective. (However the force of the agreement weakens in longer sentences, and there are dialects of Urdu in which the infinitives remain masculine singular.) The agreement of **hai** with the object of the infinitive is obligatory.

مجھے درخواست دینی (دینا) ہے ۔
mujhē* darxāst dēnī (~ dēnā) *hai
I have to submit the application.

کل آپ کو درخواست دینی (دینا) تھی ۔
āp kō* kal darxāst dēnī (~ dēnā) *thī
You were supposed to submit the application yesterday.

—Here agreement of the verb is visible because **thī** is marked for gender.

اُسے فوراً درخواست دینی (دینا) ہو گی ۔
usē* fauran darxāst dēnī (~ dēnā) *hō gī
He will have to submit the application right away.

مجھے امتحان کے لئے پڑھنا ہے -
mujhē* imtihān kē liē paṛhnā *hai
I have to study for the examination.

—Here there is no agreement, because **imtihān** is followed by a postposition.

In the everyday Urdu of Pakistan, the logical subject of the sentence may be followed either by **kō** or by **nē**: **maiṁ nē ḍinar pe jānā thā**, 'I was supposed to go (out) to dinner.' In dialects which have this option, the use of **kō** tends to be restricted to external circumstances which are not under the speaker's control, whereas **nē** refers to circumstances permitting internal choice, or neutral circumstances. This usage is not correct in the standard Urdu of Delhi.

In some dialects of Urdu, inanimate subjects do not require **kō**:

مصیبت آنی ہے -
musībat* ānī *hai
Misfortune is bound to strike.

The future or past forms of **hai** may be used to show future or past necessity. While agreement of the infinitive is optional, agreement of the verb is obligatory.

مجھے برتن مانجھنے ہیں -
mujhē* bartan māṁjhnē *haiṁ
I have to wash the dishes.

—**māṁjhnē** and **haiṁ** both agree with **bartan**, which is masculine plural.

تمہیں صبح برتن مانجھنے (مانجھنا) تھے -
tumhēṁ* subah (~ subh) bartan māṁjhnē (~ māṁjhnā) *thē
You were supposed to wash the dishes (this) morning.

The reproach may be softened by omitting the subject. **bartan** will stand first in the sentence.

برتن صبح مانجھنے (مانجھنا) تھے -
bartan subah (~ subh) māṁjhnē (~ māṁjhnā) *thē*
(You) *were supposed to* wash the dishes (this) morning.

The form of the negative is **nahīṁ**. If the sentence is in the present, **hai** may be dropped.

آپ کو فوراً پیسہ واپس نہیں کرنا (ہے) -
***āp kō* fauran paisa vāpas *nahīṁ* karnā (*hai*)**
You don't need to return the money right away.

مجھے فوراً پیسہ واپس نہیں کرنا تھا -
mujhē* fauran paisa vāpas *nahīṁ* karnā *thā
I didn't need to return the money right away.

Compare مجھے فوراً پیسے واپس نہیں کرنے (کرنا) تھے -
mujhē fauran paisē vāpas nahīṁ karnē (~ **karnā**) ***thē***
I didn't need to return the money right away.

643 Infinitive + cāhiē (advisability)

The impersonal construction INFINITIVE + **cāhiē** shows the advisability of an action. The subject, if expressed, is followed by **kō** (§506) (or its alternate forms (§210)). Transitive infinitives may take objects of their own, in which case they usually agree with those objects in gender and number, like an adjective. (However the force of the agreement weakens in longer sentences, and there are dialects of Urdu in which the infinitives remain masculine singular.) The (number) agreement of **cāhiē** with the object of the infinitive is however obligatory.

cāhiē is historically an old passive form meaning 'is wished', 'is necessary'.

مجھے چینی خریدنی (خریدنا) چاہئے -
(***mujhē***) **cīnī xarīdnī** (~ **xarīdnā**) ***cāhiē***
(*I*) *should* buy sugar.

—**xarīdnā** optionally agrees with **cīnī**, which is feminine.

اُسے انڈے خریدنے (خریدنا) چاہئیں -
usē* aṇḍē xarīdnē** (~ **xarīdnā**) ***cāhiēṁ
He should buy eggs.

The past forms of **hai** may be used to show past necessity. While agreement of the infinitive is optional, agreement of the verb is obligatory.

مجھے کل انڈے خریدنے (خریدنا) چاہئے تھے -
(***mujhē***) **kal aṇḍē xarīdnē** (~ **xarīdnā**) ***cāhiē thē***
I should have bought eggs yesterday.

—Note that because **thē** is marked to show the plural, the plural marker for **cāhiē** becomes unnecessary.

تمہیں کل چینی خریدنی (خریدنا) چاہئے تھی -
tumhēṁ* kal cīnī xarīdnī** (~ **xarīdnā**) ***cāhiē thī
You should have bought sugar yesterday.

The preceding reproach can be softened by omitting the subject. **cīnī** will stand first in the sentence.

چینی کل خریدنی (خریدنا) چاہئے تھی -
cīnī kal xarīdnī (~ **xarīdnā**) ***cāhiē thī***
(You) *should have* bought sugar yesterday.

آپ کو امتحان کے لئے پڑھنا چاہئے -
āp kō **imtihān kē liē paṛhnā** ***cāhiē***
You ought to study for the examination.

—Here there is no agreement, because **imtihān** is followed by a postposition.

The form of the negative is **nahīṁ**.

آپ کو ایسی باتیں کرنی (کرنا) نہیں چاہئیں !
āp kō **aisē bātēṁ karnī (karnā)** ***nahīṁ cāhiēṁ*****!**
You shouldn't say such things!

مجھے وقت ضائع کرنا نہیں چاہئے تھا -
mujhē **vaqt zāē karnā** ***nahīṁ cāhiē thā***
I shouldn't have wasted the time.

644 Infinitive + paṛnā (obligation, lack of choice)

The impersonal construction INFINITIVE + an inflected form of **paṛnā** shows lack of choice concerning an action. The subject, if expressed, is followed by **kō** (or its alternate forms). Transitive infinitives may take objects of their own, in which case they usually agree with those objects in gender and number, like an adjective. (However the force of the agreement weakens in longer sentences, and there are dialects of Urdu in which the infinitives remain masculine singular.) The agreement of **paṛnā** with the object of the infinitive is obligatory.

مجھے یہ کڑوی دوا کھانی (کھانا) پڑی ہے -
(***mujhē***) **ye kaṛvī davā khānī** (~ **khānā**) ***paṛī hai***
(*I*) *must* take this bitter medicine.

ہمیں چار میل چلنے (چلنا) پڑیں گے -
(***hamēṁ***) **cār mīl calnē** (~ **calnā**) ***paṛēṁ gē***
(*We*) *must* walk four miles.

تمہیں امتحان کے لئے پڑھنا پڑے گا ، نہیں تو ناکام ہو جاؤ گے -
(*tumhēṁ*) imtihān kē liē paṛhnā *paṛē gā*, nahīṁ tō nākām hō jāō gē
(*You*) *must* study for the examination, otherwise you will fail.

—Here there is no agreement, because **imtihān** is followed by a postposition.

In more complex sentences, the agreement of the infinitive is optional, however agreement of the verb is obligatory (see example below).

The form of the negative depends on the tense of **paṛnā** (see Table 13 on pages 89-90).

مجھے پیسے فوراً واپس کرنا نہ پڑے -
mujhē* paisē fauran vāpas karnā *na paṛē
I wasn't obliged to return the money right away.

CONSTRUCTIONS WITH OBLIQUE CASE INFINITIVES

645 Oblique infinitive + vālā

The construction: OBLIQUE INFINITIVE + **vālā** shows (a) the agent of an action, (b) an imminent action or event. The construction also occurs adjectivally, modifying a noun.

(خط کے) بھیجنے والے کا پتہ کیا ہے ؟
(xat kē) *bhējnē vālē* kā pata kyā hai?
What is the address of *the sender* (of the letter)?

کشتی بھنور میں ڈوبنے والی ہے -
kiśtī bhaṁvar mēṁ *ḍūbnē vālī* hai
The boat is *about to sink* in a whirlpool. (Narang, *Readings*)

کرکٹ کھیلنے والے کھلاڑی خوشی منا رہے ہیں -
karikaṭ *khēlnē vālē* khilāṛī xuśī manā rahē haiṁ
The cricket *players* are celebrating.

The last example is equivalent to a relative construction with **jō**:

جو کرکٹ کھیل رہے تھے وہ خوشی منا رہے ہیں -
***jō* karikaṭ *khēl rahē thē* vo xuśī manā rahē haiṁ**
Those who were playing cricket are celebrating.

646 Oblique infinitive + kō

The construction: OBLIQUE INFINITIVE + **kō** shows (a) an impending action or event (similar to meaning (b) of the OBLIQUE INFINITIVE + **vālā** (§645)), and (b) purpose (similar to OBLIQUE INFINITIVE + **kē liē**).

اِس لڑکی کی شادی ہونے کو ہے -
is laṛkī kī śādī hōnē kō hai
This girl's wedding is *taking place soon.*

Compare اِس لڑکی کی شادی ہونے والی ہے -
is laṛkī kī śādī *hōnē vālī hai*
This girl's wedding *is taking place soon.*

مجھے کچھ کرنے کو دو -
mujhē kuch *karnē kō* dō
Give me something *to do.*

Compare مجھے کچھ کرنے کے لئے دو -
mujhē kuch *karnē kē liē* dō
Give me something *to do.* (PURPOSE)

میں نے سنا ہے کہ ہڑتال ہونے کو ہے -
maiṁ nē sunā hai ke haṛtāl *hōnē kō hai*
I've heard that a strike *is about to begin.*

647 Oblique infinitive + lagnā (commenced event)

The construction: OBLIQUE INFINITIVE + **lagnā** shows the beginning of an action or event. **lagnā**, which is intransitive, determines the grammar of the sentence, and **nē** is not used even if the infinitive belongs to a transitive verb.

کشتی بھنور میں ڈوبنے لگی -
kiśtī bhaṁvar mēṁ *ḍūbnē lagī*
The boat *began to sink* in the whirlpool.

چھتری لے لو ، شاید بارش ہونے لگے -
chatrī lē lō, śāyad *bāriś hōnē lagē*
Take an umbrella; *it might begin to rain.*

OBLIQUE INFINITIVE + **lagnā** describes only the commencement of an action or event, and is neutral with regard to whether an action is intentional.

As a stative verb, **lagnā** occurs in the immediate past to express states which began in the past and continue in the present. For both reasons, this construction often occurs in perfective tenses.

> چھتری لے لو ، بارش ہونے لگی ہے ۔
> **chatrī lē lō, *bāriś hōnē lagī hai***
> Take an umbrella; *it has begun to rain.*

When expressing an intention to begin something in the future, the denominative verb **śurū karnā**, 'to begin' (with the nominative infinitive) is preferable.

> اگلے مہینے سے میں اپنی تنخواہ سے کچھ بچانا شروع کروں گا ۔
> **aglē mahīnē sē maiṁ apnī tanxāh sē kuch bacānā *śurū karūṁ gā***
> As of next month I *shall begin* to save something from my salary.

648 Oblique infinitive + dēnā ('let')

The construction: OBLIQUE INFINITIVE + **dēnā** shows (a) permission to do an action, or the (b) anticipation of an event. **dēnā**, which is transitive, determines the grammar of the sentence, and **nē** is used in perfective tenses even if the infinitive belongs to an intransitive verb.

> ابّا نے مجھے کتاب خریدنے نہ دی ۔
> **abbā nē mujhē kitāb *xarīdnē na dī***
> Daddy *didn't let* me *buy* the book.

> مچّھروں نے مجھے سونے نہیں دیا ۔
> **maccharōṁ nē mujhē *sōnē nahīṁ diyā***
> The mosquitoes *didn't let* me *sleep.*

> میں قرض کا پیسہ ابھی چکا دوں ؟ — رہنے دو بھائی !
> **maiṁ qarz kā paisa abhī cukā dūṁ?—*rahnē dō*, bhāī!**
> Shall I repay the loan now?—Never mind (*let it remain*), brother!

> چھٹیاں آنے دو ، میں آپ کو اپنے گاؤں لے جاؤں گا ۔
> **chuṭṭiyāṁ *ānē dō*, maiṁ āp kō apnē gāōṁ lē jāūṁ gā**
> *Let* the holidays *come;* I'll take you to my village.

649 Oblique infinitive + verb of motion (purpose)

Oblique infinitives may be used with verbs of motion to express purpose. They may be understood as instances of deletion of **kō**, or the compound postposition **kē liē**.

اشرف صاحب آپ سے ملنے آئے ہیں -
aśraf sāhib āp sē *milnē āē haiṁ*
Mr. Ashraf *has come to meet you.*

کیوں نہ آج ہم سنیما دیکھنے جائیں ؟
kyōṁ na āj ham sinēmā *dēkhnē jāēṁ*?
Why don't we *go to see* a film today?

Compare کیوں نہ آج ہم سنیما دیکھنے کے لئے (کو) جائیں ؟
kyōṁ na āj ham sinēmā *dēkhnē kē liē* (*kō*) *jāēṁ*?
Why don't we *go to see* a film today?

650 Oblique infinitive + kā (negative assertion)

The oblique infinitive is used with **nahīṁ** and **kā** (~ **kē** ~ **kī**) to make a strong negative assertion. **kā** replaces the sentence verb, and agrees with the subject.

میں جھوٹ نہیں بولنے کا !
maiṁ jhūṭ *nahīṁ bōlnē kā*!
I *am not going to tell* a lie!

مہنگائی ختم نہیں ہونے کی -
mahemgāī *xatam nahīṁ hōnē kī*
The rise in prices *is never going to stop.*

7 COMPOUND VERBS

Verb sequences consisting of VERB ROOT + INFLECTED VERB have been given various designations, including 'compound verbs', 'intensive verbs', 'compound verbal formations' and 'verb sequences'. In this work they are called 'compound verbs'.[1] Non-compound verbs are referred to as 'simple verbs'.

COMPOUND VERBS AND SIMPLE VERBS

701 The structure of compound verb phrases

The form of the first verb in a compound verb sequence is in most cases the verb root (§601). It is called the main verb. The main verb shows the lexical (original or 'dictionary') meaning of the sequence.

The second verb has been given various names, including 'vector verb', 'intensifying verb', 'compound auxiliary', and 'explicator verb'. In this work it is called the 'vector verb'. The vector verb loses its lexical meaning to a greater or lesser extent, but adds a nuance to the meaning of the sequence. It functions as the sentence verb, that is, it is inflected to show tense and agreement.

SIMPLE VERB	سونا	**sōnā**, to sleep
COMPOUND VERB	سو جانا	**sō jānā**, to fall asleep
SIMPLE VERB	پڑھنا	**paṛhnā**, to read
COMPOUND VERB	پڑھ دینا	**paṛh dēnā**, to read to someone

While one may generalize about the type of nuance contributed by individual vector verbs, the contribution of a vector verb is also affected by the meaning of the main verb. Sometimes the meaning of the compound verb sequence cannot be deduced from the meaning of the main verb and the force of the vector verb, but must be looked up in a dictionary or discovered from usage.

In some cases a compound has become more or less relexicalized, that is, the compound has a new unitary definition which is distinct from the meaning of the simple verb, and cannot be predicted from its components.

---

1 Verb sequences consisting of a noun or adjective plus an inflected verb are referred to as 'denominative verbs' (§607).

Relexicalized compounds

SIMPLE VERB	مارنا	**mārnā**, to beat
COMPOUND VERB	مار ڈالنا	**mār ḍālnā**, to kill
SIMPLE VERB	لینا	**lēnā**, to take
COMPOUND VERB	لے جانا	**lē jānā**, to take away

The class of Urdu vector verbs is small. The nine vector verbs discussed in this chapter cover most compound sequences occurring in texts. For further information, the student may consult the references given in the bibliography.

702 The difference between compound and simple verbs

A simple verb shows only that an action or event takes place. Compound verbs are *nuanced*. They show the unfolding of an action, or provide contextual information. The difference is comparable to the difference between an outline drawing, and a drawing in which the figures are shaded.

*Simple verb (**hōnā**)*

جب موسم ٹھنڈا ہوا تو پرندے اُڑ گئے -
jab mausam ṭhanḍā *hūā*, tō parindē uṛ gaē
When the weather *became* cold, the birds flew away.

*Compound verb (**hō jānā**)*

جنوری میں موسم ٹھنڈا ہو گیا -
janvarī mēṁ mausam ṭhanḍā *hō gayā*
In January the weather *became* cold.

In the above set, the simple verb **hūā** shows only that the weather changed. The compound verb **hō gayā** allows visualization of the the cooling process.

*Simple verb (**paṛhnā**)*

کیا آپ نے خط پڑھا ؟ — جی ہاں میں نے پڑھا -
kyā āp nē xat *paṛhā*?—jī hāṁ, maiṁ nē *paṛhā*
Did you *read* the letter?—Yes, I *read* it.

Compound verbs (***paṛh lēnā, paṛh dēnā***)

میں نے خط پڑھ لیا ۔
maiṁ nē xat *paṛh liyā*
I *finished reading* the letter (to myself).

میں نے وہ خط امّاں کو پڑھ دیا ۔
maiṁ nē vo xat ammāṁ kō *paṛh diyā*
I *read* that letter (*completely*) to mother.

In the first example in the above set, **paṛhā** shows only that the letter has been read. The compound examples show that the process of reading the letter has been completed; in addition, **paṛh liyā** shows that the speaker read it for himself, whereas **paṛh diyā** shows that he has communicated it to another person (by reading it aloud).

The following quotations from Prem Chand's *Gōdān* illustrates how compound verbs add nuances to events, whereas simple verbs merely show the occurrence of the event.

گوبر نے ناؤ ڈبا دی ۔
gōbar nē nāō *ḍubā dī*
Gobar *sank* the boat.

گوبر نے نہیں ڈبائی ۔ ڈبائی اُسی نے ۔
gōbar nē nahīṁ *ḍubāī. ḍubāī* usī nē
Gobar didn't *sink* it; she is the one who *sank* it.

کسی نے ڈبائی ہو ، اب ڈوب ہی گئی ۔
kisī nē *ḍūbāī* hō, ab tō *ḍūb hī gaī*
Whoever *sank* it, now it has really *gone down*.

The simple verb **ḍūbāī**, 'sank' is used when the question concerns only who has caused the sinking (a metaphor for a misfortune). But when the context of the sinking comes into focus, compound verbs are used. **ḍubā dī** (compound with the vector **dēnā**) implies a completed action which begins with Gobar and affects the external environment. **ḍūb ... gaī** (compound with the vector **jānā**) unfolds the event of sinking, from the initial stage where it could possibly have been prevented, to the final stage where it sank beneath the water.

INTRANSITIVE VECTOR VERBS

Intransitive main verbs usually occur with vector verbs which are also intransitive. The most frequent intransitive vector verb is **jānā**. **paṛnā**, **nikalnā**, **baiṭhnā** and **uṭhnā** are also common. When both verbs are intransitive, the compound sequence is intransitive, and the vector verb agrees with the subject in gender and number.

703 The vector verb jānā

جانا **jānā** (which as a sentence verb means 'to go') shows the unfolding of a transitition from one state to a second state. It occurs with verbs of motion and stative verbs; verbs which cannot show completable actions do not occur with **jānā**.

jānā cannot be used as a vector verb with the main verb **jānā**:

WRONG جا جانا **jā jānā**

بیٹھ جائیے !
baiṭh jāiyē!
Please take your seat! (Why are you still standing?)

Compare بیٹھئے
baiṭhiē
Please sit (down). (a routine request)

بات ایک دن کھلنی تھی ، آخر کھل ہی گئی ۔
bāt ēk din khulnī thī, āxir *khul hī gaī*
The matter had to come out (be opened) some day; finally it *did come out.*

میں نے بستر بچھا دیا اور لیٹ گیا ۔
maiṁ nē bistar bichā diyā aur *lēṭ gayā*
I spread out the bedding and *lay down.* (transition)

سامان ہوائی اڈے پر رہ گیا ۔
sāmān havāī aḍḍē par *rah gayā*
The luggage *was left behind* in the airport.

704 The vector verb paṛnā

پڑنا **paṛnā** (which as a sentence verb means 'to fall', 'to befall') shows something which happens involuntarily, suddenly, unexpectedly, or something one is unable to prevent. **paṛnā** occurs only with main verbs which can show sudden actions or events, and does not occur with stative verbs.

کتّے کے بھونکتے ہی بچّی رو پڑی ۔
kuttē kē bhaumktē hī baccī *rō paṛī*
As soon as the dog barked the little girl *burst into tears.*

لڑکا چلتی ریل گاڑی سے گر پڑا ۔
laṛkā caltī rēl gāṛī sē *gir paṛā*
The boy *fell off* the moving train.

جب ابّا جان فوت ہوئے ، گھر کی ذمہ داری میرے سر پر آ پڑی ۔
jab abbā jān faut hūē, ghar kī zimmē dārī mērē sir par *ā paṛī*
When Daddy died, responsibility for the household *fell* (*inevitably*) on me.

705 The vector verb nikalnā

نکلنا **nikalnā** (which as a sentence verb means 'to come out', 'to emerge'), shows suddenness or unexpectedness, but also motion out or away.

کھلے ہوئے پھاٹک میں سے کتّا بھاگ نکلا ۔
khulē hūē phāṭak mēṁ sē kuttā *bhāg niklā*
The dog *scooted away* through the open gate.

چوہیا پلنگ کے نیچے سے آ نکلی ۔
cūhiyā palang kē nīcē sē *ā niklī*
The mouse suddenly *popped out* from under the bed.

NOTE: Some have analysed **ā** in the preceding verb sequence as a short absolutive (conjunctive participle with deleted **kar**); however if **kar** is added to the sequence, the meaning changes: the element of suddenness is lost.

چوہیا پلنگ کے نیچے سے آ کر نکلی ۔
cūhiyā palang kē nīcē sē *ā kar niklī*
Coming out from under the bed, the mouse *emerged.*

706 The vector verb uṭhnā

اُٹھنا **uṭhnā** (which as a sentence verb means 'to rise', 'to get up') connotes an action which happens suddenly, and it intensifies the main verb. It often occurs with verbs like 'speak', 'cry', 'scream', etc. It occurs only with main verbs which can be intensified, and does not occur with stative verbs. If it is used with a transitive main verb, the main verb cannot take an object, and the sequence is treated as intransitive.

درد اِتنا تھا کہ بچّی رو اُٹھی -
dard itnā thā ke baccī *rō uṭhī*
The pain was so severe that the little girl *burst into a wail.*

دیکھو شور نہ مچانا - نہیں تو سارا گاؤں جاگ اُٹھے گا...
dēkhō, śōr na macānā. nahīṁ tō sārā gāōṁ *jāg uṭhē gā* ... (Prem Chand, *Gōdān*)
Look, don't make noises, otherwise the whole village *will wake up* ...

قاضی یہ سن کر چیخ اُٹھا -
qāzī ye sun kar *cīx uṭhā*
When the judge heard it, he *let out a yell.* (Narang, *Readings*)

707 The vector verb baiṭhnā

بیٹھنا **baiṭhnā** (which as a sentence verb means 'to sit') shows an impulsive or involuntary action, and may imply that the speaker disapproves of the action. It may describe an irremediable mistake. The vector **baiṭhnā** is an exception to the rule that intransitive main verbs usually occur with intransitive vector verbs. **baiṭhnā** occurs most frequently with transitive main verbs.

ملازم مالک سے لڑ بیٹھا ، اور نوکری گئی -
mulāzim mālik sē *laṛ baiṭhā,* aur naukarī gaī
The employee *quarrelled* with the boss, and lost his job (lit. The job went).

TRANSITIVE VECTOR VERBS

Normally, transitive verb roots are used with vector verbs which are also transitive. The most common transitive vector verbs are: **dēnā**, and **lēnā**. **ḍālnā** and **rakhnā** also occur. When both verbs are transitive, the compound sequence is transitive; in perfective tenses, the subject takes **nē** (§510), and the vector verb agrees with a nominative direct object in gender and number.

708 The vector verb dēnā

دینا **dēnā** (which as a sentence verb means 'to give') shows the completion of an action, an action which is done for someone else, directed away from the self, or which affects the external environment. In request forms, use of the compound with **dēnā** makes a request slightly more polite.

ایک شیش محل بنا دو گے... مجھے بہت سا سونا چاندی دے دو گے؟
ēk śīś mahal *banā dō gē*... mujhē bahut sā sōnā cāṁdī *dē dō gē*?
Will you *build* a crystal palace ... *will* you *give* me a lot of gold and silver?
(Narang, *Readings*)

یہ پرانے کاغذ پھینک دو۔
ye purānē kāɣaz *phēṁk dō*
Throw these old papers *away*. (direction away from the self)

میں نے لفافہ تمہارے بٹوے میں رکھ دیا ہے۔
maiṁ nē lifāfa tumhārē baṭvē mēṁ *rakh diyā hai*
I *have put* the envelope in your bag. (I have done it *for you*.)

dēnā is used idiomatically with causatives:

موقع پا کر اُس نے بھی سنا دی۔
mauqā pā kar us nē bhī *sunā dī*
He also took the opportunity to *give* (him) *a piece of his mind*.

اُن کی باتوں کو بُھلا دینا اِتنا آسان نہیں۔
un kī bātōṁ kō *bhulā dēnā* itnā āsān nahīṁ
It is not so easy *to put out of mind* what he said.

709 The vector verb lēnā

لینا **lēnā** (which as a sentence verb means 'to take') shows the completion of an action, an action done for the self, on the self, directed towards the self, or coming from the external environment and affecting the self.

میں نے لفافہ اپنے بٹوے میں رکھ لیا۔
maiṁ nē lifāfa apnē baṭvē mēṁ *rakh liyā*
I *put* the envelope in my bag. (I did it *for myself*.)

آپ کتاب رکھ لیجئے
āp kitāb *rakh lījiē*
You please *keep* the book.

Compare کتاب رکھیئے
kitāb *rakhiē*
Please *put* the book *down*.

وہ واپس آ کر اپنی کتاب لے لیں گے ۔
vo vāpas ā kar apnī kitāb ***lē lēm̐ gē***
After he returns he *will take back* his book.

710 The vector verb ḍālnā

ڈالنا **ḍālnā** (which as a sentence verb means 'to put', 'to pour') shows intensity, urgency, completeness, or even violence.

بچّوں نے برف کا آدمی بنا ڈالا ۔
baccōm̐ nē baraf kā ādmī ***banā ḍālā***
The children *made* a snowman (when they got the chance).

اِس موضوع پر میں نے ساری کتابیں پڑھ ڈالی ہیں ۔
is mauzū par maim̐ nē sārī kitābēm̐ ***paṛh ḍālī haim̐***
On this subject, I *have read* all the books *I could find.*

پولیس والے نہ آتے تو ڈاکو اُسے مار ڈالتے ۔
pōlīs vālē na ātē tō ḍākū usē ***mār ḍāltē***
(If) the police had not come, the bandits *would have killed* him.

711 The vector verb rakhnā

رکھنا **rakhnā** (which as a sentence verb means 'to put', 'to place') occurs with the main verbs **dēnā** and **lēnā**, meaning 'to give/take (as a loan)', and with other semantically appropriate main verbs showing an action performed beforehand.

اُس نے اپنا مکان ہمیں دے رکھا ہے ۔
us nē apnā makān hamēm̐ ***dē rakhā hai***
He has *given* us his house (*allowed* us *to use* it).

میں نے نسیم کو جو رقم دے رکھی ہے ، وہ جلد لوٹا دے گا ۔
maim̐ nē nasīm kō jō raqm ***dē rakhī hai,*** **vo jald lauṭā dē gā**
Nasim will soon return the amount which I *have loaned* (him).

نسیم نے مجھ سے دو ہزار روپئے لے رکھے ہیں ۔
nasīm nē mujh sē dō hazār rupaē ***lē rakhē haim̐***
Nasim *has borrowed* two thousand rupees from me.

فاطمہ نے کیا اچّھی ساڑی پہن رکھی تھی ۔
fātima nē kyā acchī sāṛī ***pahn rakhī thī***
What a fine sari Fatima *was wearing.*

مظاہرین کو روکنے کے لئے پولیس نے عمارت کے گرد گھیرا ڈال رکھا تھا۔
muzāhirīn kō rōknē kē liē pōlīs nē imārat kē gird ghērā *ḍāl rakhā thā*
In order to stop the demonstrators, the police *set up* a barricade around the building.

MIXED TRANSITIVITY IN COMPOUND VERBS

Although intransitive main verbs usually occur with intransitive vectors, and transitive main verbs usually occur with transitive vectors, there are exceptions to this rule. The resulting sequences *are always treated as intransitive* (the vector verb agrees with the subject even if it is transitive as a sentence verb).

712 Transitive main verbs with intransitive vectors

The combination of intransitive main verbs with transitive vectors occurs most often with the vectors **jānā** and **baiṭhnā**, but there are other combinations, which can be found in a comprehensive dictionary.

لے جانا	**lē jānā**, to take away
لے چلنا	**lē calnā**, to take someone somewhere
کھا جانا	**khā jānā**, to eat up
کر جانا	**kar jānā**, to accomplish
کر بیٹھنا	**kar baiṭhnā**, to do as a blunder
کر گزرنا	**kar guzarnā**, to do (in spite of obstacles)
سیکھ جانا	**sīkh jānā**, to learn (quickly)

یاسمین کو بھی ساتھ لے چلو تو اچّھا ہو۔
yāsmīn kō bhī sāth *lē calō* tō acchā hō
It would be better if you also *take* Yasmin *along*.

اِس میں تو جان ڈالے گا تو یہ سب کو کھا جائے گا۔
is mēṁ tū jān ḍālē gā tō ye sab kō *khā jāē gā*
If you put life into it, it *will eat up* everyone. (Narang, *Readings*)

کیا (وہ) کسی سے مار پیٹ کر بیٹھا ؟
kyā (vo) kisī sē mār pīṭ *kar baiṭhā*?
Did he go and *get into* a fight with someone? (Prem Chand, *Gōdān*)

وہ نشہ کرنے کے لئے کچھ بھی کر گزرتا ہے -
vo naśa karnē kē liē kuch bhī *kar guzartā hai*
In order to get high, he (an addict) *will do* anything at all.

طالب علم اُردو ایک ہی سال میں سیکھ گئے -
tālib ilm urdū ēk hī sāl mēṁ *sīkh gaē*
The students *learned* Urdu in only a year.

713 Intransitive main verbs with transitive vectors

The combination of intransitive main verbs with transitive vectors occurs mainly with the vector **dēnā**. The three intransitive main verbs which compound with **dēnā** are **calnā**, **haṁsnā** and **rōnā**:

چل دینا	**cal dēnā**, to set off, depart, leave
ہنس دینا	**haṁs dēnā**, to burst into laughter
رو دینا	**rō dēnā**, to burst into tears

NOTE: even though **dēnā**, the vector verb, is transitive, the subject does not take **nē** in past tenses.

ریل گاڑی چل دی -
rēl gāṛī *cal dī*
The train *departed*.

لطیفہ سن کر میں ہنس دیا -
latīfa sun kar maiṁ *haṁs diyā*
On hearing the joke, I *laughed*.

RESTRICTIONS ON OCCURRENCE OF COMPOUND VERBS

714 Constructions based on the verb root or infinitive

Compound verbs are not used with the following:

Continuous tenses (VERB ROOT + **rahā hai**, **rahā thā**, etc., §614)
VERB ROOT + **saknā** (§618)
VERB ROOT + **cuknā** (§620)
OBLIQUE INFINITIVE + **lagnā** (§647)

EXCEPTION: compounds which have been relexicalized sometimes occur with **saknā**, if the simple form does not express the equivalent meaning. But the usage is uncommon.

نوکر مصروف تھا ، سامان نہیں لے جا سکا ۔

naukar masrūf thā, sāmān *nahīṁ lē jā sakā*

The servant was busy (and) *couldn't take away* the things.

715 Participial constructions

Compounds rarely occur in participial constructions, including the conjunctive participle (§612).

EXCEPTION: compounds which have been relexicalized sometimes occur in participial constructions, as the simple form would mean something else. But the usage is not common.

نوکر نے سامان لے جاتے ہوئے کہا ...

naukar nē sāmān *lē jātē hūē* kahā ...

Taking away the things, the servant said ...

نوکر نے کپڑے لے جا کر دھو دیے

naukar nē kapṛē *lē jā kar* dhō diyē

The servant *took away* the clothes *and* washed them.

716 Passive constructions

Compounds of transitive main verbs and the vector verb **dēnā** are occasionally passivized (§634), but it is uncommon for compounds to occur in the passive.

لفافہ آپ کے بٹوے میں رکھ دیا گیا ہے ۔

lifāfa āp kē baṭvē mēṁ *rakh diyā gaya hai*

The envelope *has been put* in your bag.

717 Negative sentences

Compound verbs are rarely used in negative sentences.

کیا آپ نے یہ کام کر لیا ہے ؟

kyā āp nē ye kām *kar liyā hai*?

Have you *done* this work?

جی ہاں میں نے کر لیا ہے ۔

jī hāṁ, maiṁ nē *kar liyā hai*

Yes, I *have done* (it).

جی نہیں میں نے نہیں کیا -
jī nahīṁ, maiṁ nē *nahīṁ kiyā*
No, I *haven't done* (it).

Exceptions

(a) Compounds which have been relexicalized occasionally occur with negatives, as the simple form would mean something else. However it is not common.

کیا نوکر سامان لے گیا ؟ — نہیں لے گیا ، مصروف تھا -
kyā naukar sāmān *lē gayā?—nahīṁ lē gayā*, masrūf thā
Did the servant *take away* the things?—He *didn't take* them *away;* he was busy.

(b) When **kahīṁ** is used with the negative to express apprehension (§425), compounds do occur. The compound is usually split apart, with the negative coming between the main verb and the vector verb.

اِتنا بھاری صندوق اوپر نہ رکھو ، کہیں گر نہ جائے !
itnā bhārī sandūq ūpar na rakhō, *kahīṁ gir na jāē*!
Don't put such a heavy box up (on a rack) *lest it fall*!

کہیں ڈاکو ہمیں مار نہ ڈالیں -
kahīṁ* ḍākū hamēṁ *mār na ḍālēṁ
I only hope the bandits *don't kill us*.

Compounds also occur in clauses beginning with **jab tak** + NEGATIVE (§1114). However, such sentences are not really negative; in the following sentence, the entire phrase **jab tak** + NEGATIVE means 'until', 'unless'. The negative comes between the main verb and the vector verb.

جب تک آپ قرض چکا نہ دیں وہ یہیں دھرنا دے گا -
***jab tak* āp qarz *cukā na dēṁ*, vo yahīṁ dharnā dē gā**
Until you *return* the loan, he will sit right here in protest.

Use of a compound in a negative sentence may show CONTRADICTION. Again, the compound is split apart, and the negative particle (sometimes accompanied by **tō**) comes between the main verb and the vector verb.

میں آپ کی عینک توڑ تو نہیں دوں گا -
maiṁ āp kī ainak *tōṛ tō nahīṁ dūṁ gā*
I'm *not going to break* your glasses (you seem to think I will).

PERFECTIVE PARTICIPLES AS MAIN VERBS

Occasionally the perfective participle (§604) occurs as the main verb in a compound verb sequence instead of the root.

718 Nominative perfective participles as main verbs

Two very common examples of compounds with perfective participles as main verbs are **calā jānā**, 'to leave' and **calā ānā**, 'to come', which have been relexicalized. Both the participle and the vector verb agree with the subject.

اکرم سارا کام کر کے چلا گیا ۔
akram sārā kām kar kē *calā gayā*
Akram *left* after doing all the work.

یہ آپ کا گھر ہے ، جب جی چاہے یہاں چلے آئیے ۔
ye āp kā ghar hai, jab jī cāhē yahāṁ *calē āiyē*
This is your house; *come* here whenever you like.

The nominative perfect participle occurs with other verbs of motion:

قلی بھاگا گیا اور سامان لے آیا ۔
qulī *bhāgā gayā* aur sāmān lē āyā
The porter *ran* and brought the luggage.

719 Oblique perfective participles as main verbs

When the perfective participle occurs in the masculine oblique singular case, the participle shows (a) continuation or progression, often with the vector verb **jānā**; (b) intensification of the verb, and/or (c) imminence.

Continuation/progression

احمد نے ہی ہم کو روکے رکھا ۔
ahmad nē hī ham kō *rōkē rakhā*
It is Ahmad who *delayed* us.

—**rōkē rakhā** shows continuation of the action. **rōk rakhā** does not occur.

وہ بے بسی سے صادق کی طرف دیکھے جا رہا تھا ۔
vo bē basī sē sādiq kī taraf *dēkhē jā rahā thā*
He *went on looking* helplessly at Sadiq.

نمبر گھمائے جائیے ، کبھی تو ملے گا -
nambar *ghūmāē jāiyē,* kabhī tō milē gā
Do go on dialling the number; you will get it sometime.

Intensification

میں تم سے کہے دیتا ہوں ...
maiṁ tum sē *kahē dētā hūṁ* ...
I *warn* you ...
—**kahē dēnā** means 'to warn', whereas **kah dēnā** would mean 'to tell'.

Imminence

میں آپ کو اِس الماری میں چھپائے دیتی ہوں -
maiṁ āp kō is almārī mēṁ *chupāē dētī hūṁ*
I *will hide* you in this wardrobe *right away.* (Narang, *Readings*)

DENOMINATIVE VERBS IN COMPOUND VERB SEQUENCES (720)

Denominative verbs (verb sequences consisting of a noun or adjective plus an inflected verb, §607), may occur in compound verb sequences, especially with the most common vectors **dēnā**, **lēnā** and **jānā**. It is impossible to formulate rules to predict the occurrence of individual denominative verbs with individual vectors, as the semantics of each individual denominative verb must be considered. Actual usage should be learned as it is encountered.

خورشید نے تینوں آدمیوں میں پیسے تقسیم کر دیے -
xūršīd nē tīnōṁ ādmiyōṁ mēṁ paisē *taqsīm kar diyē*
Khurshid *divided* the money among all three men.

خورشید نے پیسوں کا حساب کر لیا -
xūršīd nē paisōṁ kā *hisāb kar liyā*
Khurshid *made an account* of the money (*and kept* it).

لوگ چوک میں جمع ہو گئے -
lōg cauk mēṁ *jama hō gaē*
People *gathered* in the square.

8 INTRANSITIVE, TRANSITIVE AND CAUSATIVE VERBS

INTRANSITIVE AND TRANSITIVE VERBS

801 The difference between transitive and intransitive verbs

Transitive verbs are verbs which may take objects. The object may be deleted, but can still be inferred, or 'understood'. Intransitive verbs do not take objects. The focus in the sentence also differs. In transitive sentences, the focus is on what the doer does. In intransitive sentences, the focus is on the result of what is done.

English translations of Urdu sentences are not reliable as a guide to whether an Urdu verb is transitive or not, because English verbs may often be used both transitively and intransitively, depending on the context (*This shop sells apples* versus *Apples are selling well now*). Compare the following Urdu sentences:

سلیم کا بازو ٹوٹ گیا ۔ (< ٹوٹنا)
salīm kā *bāzū ṭūṭ gayā* (< **ṭūṭnā**, to be broken)
Salim broke his arm (lit. Salim's *arm broke*).

زاہد نے سلیم کو مارا اور اُس کا بازو توڑ دیا ۔ (< توڑنا)
zāhid nē salīm kō mārā aur us kā *bāzū tōṛ diyā* (< **tōṛnā**, to break (something))
Zahid hit Salim and *broke* his *arm*.

English passives are sometimes needed to translate Urdu intransitives:

چمچہ گر گیا ۔ (< گرنا)
camca *gir gayā* (< **girnā**, to fall)
The spoon *fell*; the spoon *was dropped*.

تاج محل بڑی محنت سے بنا ۔ (< بننا)
tāj mahal baṛī mehnat sē *banā* (< **bannā**, to be built)
The Taj Mahal *was built* with great effort.

Unintentional actions are expressed in Urdu with intransitives. The instrument of the action occurs in a postpositional phrase with **sē** (§512):

بچّے سے چمچہ گر گیا ۔ (› گرنا)
baccē sē camca *gir gayā* (< **girnā**, to fall)
The baby dropped the spoon (accidentally).

A transitive verb (with a subject taking **nē**) would express intentional action:

بچّے نے چمچہ گرا دیا ۔ (› گرانا)
baccē nē camca *girā diyā* (< **girānā**, to drop, let fall)
The baby dropped the spoon (deliberately).

802 Agreement of verbs

Intransitive verbs agree with the subject of the sentence, whatever the tense of the verb. Transitive verbs agree with the subject only in non-perfective tenses. In perfective tenses, the subject of transitive verbs is followed by the postposition **nē** (§510). The verb agrees with a nominative direct object (see §629 for a detailed discussion). All causative verbs are considered transitive with respect to subject-verb agreement, and take the subject with **nē** in perfective tenses.

803 The increment -ā

Transitive and intransitive verbs often occur in pairs which are closely related in both meaning and form. Many transitives are formed from intransitives by adding the increment **-ā** ا to the intransitive root (§601) to make a transitive stem. Roots ending in long vowels take the alternate form of the increment, **-lā** لا .[1] Derivation with the increment **-ā** can be summarized as follows:

(a) The increment may be added to an INTRANSITIVE root to derive a TRANSITIVE stem (§804).

(b) The increment may be added to a TRANSITIVE root to derive a DOUBLE TRANSITIVE stem (§805).

(c) The increment may be added to an INTRANSITIVE or a TRANSITIVE root to derive a DIRECT CAUSATIVE stem (§810).

Transitive and causative stems take infinitival, participial and verbal suffixes just like simple verb roots. They are also found under their own spellings in dictionaries, and not under the intransitive form. (Some dictionaries, however, show indirect causative verbs (§811) under the forms from which they are derived.) For most practical purposes, the transitive or causative stem of a derived verb may be treated and referred to as a verb root.

---

1 An alternate form of the increment, و **-ō-** occurs in one case: **bhīgnā** بھیگنا , 'to get wet' → **bhigōnā** بھگونا , 'to soak'.

There are also BASIC TRANSITIVE VERBS, which are not derived from intransitives. Some transitive verbs have no related intransitive form, for example, **karnā** کرنا, 'to do', **sunnā** سننا, 'to hear', **paṛhnā** پڑھنا, 'to read'. In certain other cases, the intransitive form is obviously derived from the transitive, and not vice versa, for example, **sil** سل, 'to be stitched' < **sīnā** سینا, 'to stitch'; **dhul** دُھل < **dhōnā** دھونا, 'to wash'.

Illustrative sets of transitive and intransitive verbs are shown below. Please note that there are numerous irregularities in the derivation process, and it is not possible to formulate rules which predict every case. Each pair must be learned individually.

804 Transitives derived with the increment -ā

The increment **-ā** may be added to an INTRANSITIVE root to derive a TRANSITIVE stem.

Case I

The vowel in the intransitive root is short, and the root ends in a consonant. The increment **-ā** is simply suffixed to the root of the intransitive verb to form the transitive stem.

بننا ← بنانا
bannā, to form, be made → **banānā**, to make

لگنا ← لگانا
lagnā, to stick, be applied → **lagānā**, to apply

چلنا ← چلانا
calnā, to walk, go → **calānā** to run (something), drive

بچنا ← بچانا
bacnā, to escape → **bacānā**, to save

اُٹھنا ← اُٹھانا
uṭhnā, to rise, get up → **uṭhānā** to lift, wake someone

ملنا ← ملانا
milnā, to meet, be available → **milānā**, to connect, mix[2]

2 **milānā** could also be construed as a double transitive verb in the sentence, **us nē mujh sē hāth milāyā**, 'He shook hands with me.'

اِس محلے میں ایک مسجد بن رہی ہے -
is mahallē mēṁ ēk masjid *ban rahī hai*
A mosque *is being built* in this ward.

مزدوروں نے دن رات کام کر کے مسجد بنائی -
mazdūrōṁ nē din rāt kām kar kē masjid *banāī*
The labourers worked day and night to build (and *built*) the mosque.

آج میں بہت سویرے اُٹھا -
āj maiṁ bahut savērē *uṭhā*
I *got up* very early this morning.

چوکیدار سویا تھا ، میں نے اُسے اُٹھا دیا -
caukīdār sōyā thā, maiṁ nē usē *uṭhā diyā*
The watchman was asleep; I *got* him *up*.

اِتّفاق سے عارف صاحب مل گئے -
ittifāq sē ārif sāhib *mil gaē*
By chance Mr. Arif *met* us (was available).

عارف صاحب سے ملا دیجئے -
ārif sāhib sē *milā dījiē*
Please connect (me) with Mr. Arif (on the telephone).

اُس نے دودھ اور چینی ملائی -
us nē dūdh aur cīnī *milāī*
He *mixed* milk and sugar.

Case II

The intransitive root vowel is long, and the root ends in a consonant. The root vowel is shortened, and the increment **-ā** is suffixed to form the transitive stem.

سوکھنا ← سکھانا
sūkhnā, to dry, dry up → **sukhānā**, to dry (something)

بارش کے بعد زمین سوکھ گئی -
bāriś kē bād zamīn *sūkh gaī*
After the rain, the soil *dried out*.

گرمیوں میں دھوپ زمین کو سکھا دیتی ہے -
garmiyōṁ mēṁ dhūp zamīn kō ***sukhā dētī hai***
In the hot season, the sunlight *dries out* the soil.

The verb **bōlnā**, 'to speak', which may take an object, is treated as an intransitive and forms a transitive by shortening the root vowel and adding **-ā**.

بولنا ← بلانا
bōlnā, to speak → **bulānā**, to call

نجمہ فارسی بول سکتی ہے -
Najma fārsī ***bōl*** **saktī hai**
Najma can *speak* Farsi.

نجمہ آپ کو بلا رہی ہے -
Najma āp kō ***bulā rahī hai***
Najma *is calling* you.

Case III

The vowel (or final vowel) in the intransitive root is short, and the root ends in a consonant. The increment **-ā** is infixed or inserted into the verb root of the intransitive verb to form the transitive stem. This lengthens the root vowel and may also change the vowel quality. The final consonant of the root may be softened.

(a) When long **-ā** is added to short **-a-**, long **-ā-** results.

کٹنا ← کاٹنا
kaṭnā, to be cut → **kāṭnā**, to cut, disconnect

مرنا ← مارنا
marnā, to die → **mārnā**, to beat, hit

نکلنا ← نکالنا
nikalnā, to come out, emerge → **nikālnā**, to take out

اُترنا ← اُتارنا
utarnā, to descend, get out → **utārnā**, to bring down, take out

بجلی کٹ گئی -
bijlī ***kaṭ gaī***
The electricity *was disconnected.*

مستری تار کاٹ رہا ہے -
mistrī tār ***kāṭ rahā hai***
The electrician *is cutting* the wire.

پہلے بس سے بچّوں کو اُتارنا ، پھر خود اُترنا ۔
pahlē bas sē baccōṁ kō *utārnā*, phir xud *utarnā*
First *get* the children *out* of the bus, then *get out* yourself.

(b) When long **-ā** is added to short **-u-**, a long **-ō-** results. This rule also affects a few verbs with long **-ū-**.

مڑنا ← موڑنا
muṛnā, to turn → **mōṛnā**, to turn (something)

کُھلنا ← کھولنا
khulnā, to open → **khōlnā**, to open (something)

رُکنا ← روکنا
ruknā, to stop → **rōknā**, to stop (something)

ٹوٹنا ← توڑنا
ṭūṭnā, to be broken → **tōṛnā**,[3] to break (something)

چھوٹنا ← چھوڑنا
chūṭnā, to be released, depart → **chōṛnā**, to leave, abandon

گاڑی مڑ رہی ہے ۔
gāṛī *muṛ rahī hai*
The car *is turning*.

گاڑی بائیں کو موڑ دیجئے ۔
gāṛī bāēṁ kō *mōṛ dījiē*
Please turn the car left.

دکان دس بجے کھلتی ہے ۔
dukān das bajē *khultī hai*
The shop *opens* at 10.

دکاندار دس بجے دکان کھولتا ہے ۔
dukāndār das bajē dukān *khōltā hai*
The shopkeeper *opens* the shop at 10.

(c) When long **-ā** is added to short **-i-**, long **-ē-** results.

بکنا ← بیچنا
biknā, to be sold → **bēcnā**, to sell

چھدنا ← چھیدنا
chidnā, to be pierced → **chēdnā**, to pierce

---

3 Both the initial **ṭ-** of **ṭūṭnā** and the initial **t-** of **tōṛnā** come from an ancient **tr-**, which has developed in different ways.

میلے میں گھربُنا کپڑا بِک رہا ہے -
mēlē mēṁ gharbunā kapṛā *bik rahā hai*
At the fair, handloom cloth *is being sold*.

میلے میں جولاہے گھربُنا کپڑا بیچ رہے ہیں -
mēlē mēṁ jaulāhē gharbunā kapṛā *bēc rahē haiṁ*
At the fair, the weavers *are selling* handloom cloth.

805 Double transitives derived with the increment -ā

The increment **-ā** (~ **-lā**) may be added to some TRANSITIVE roots to derive a DOUBLE TRANSITIVE stem. Double transitive verbs take two objects, a direct object and an indirect object. The transitive roots which make double transitives are semantically reflexive, and occur with the vector verb **lēnā** (§709) when compound.

Case I

The last vowel in the transitive root is short, and the root ends in a consonant. The increment **-ā** is simply suffixed to the root of the transitive verb to form the double transitive stem. If the transitive root has two short syllables, the vowel in the second syllable is elided.

پڑھنا ← پڑھانا
paṛhnā, to read, study → **paṛhānā**, to teach, educate

سننا ← سنانا
sunnā, to hear, listen to → **sunānā**, to tell

پکڑنا ← پکڑانا
pakaṛnā, to catch → **pakṛānā**, to give to hold

سمجھنا ← سمجھانا
samajhnā, to understand → **samjhānā**, to explain

اُستاد صاحب نے ہمیں اُردو پڑھائی -
ustād sāhib nē hamēṁ urdū *paṛhāī*
The teacher *taught* us Urdu (double transitive).

Compare میں نے اُردو پڑھی ہے -
maiṁ nē urdū *paṛhī hai*
I *have studied* Urdu (transitive).

ناہید نے مجھے خبر سنائی -
nāhīd nē mujhē xabar *sunāī*
Nahid *told* me the news (double transitive).

Compare میں نے خبریں سنیں -
maiṁ nē xabarēṁ *sunīṁ*
I *listened* to the news (transitive).

Case II

The transitive root vowel is long, and the root ends in a consonant. The root vowel is shortened, and the increment **-ā** is suffixed to form the double transitive stem.

دیکھنا ← دکھانا
dēkhnā, to see, look at → **dikhānā**, to show

سیکھنا ← سکھانا
sīkhnā, to learn → **sikhānā**, to teach

نسیم نے مجھے تصویر دکھائی -
nasīm nē mujhē tasvīr *dikhāī*
Nasim *showed* me the picture (double transitive).

Compare میں نے تصویر دیکھی -
maiṁ nē tasvīr *dēkhī*
I *looked at* the picture (transitive).

امّاں بچّے کو چلنا سکھا رہی ہے -
ammāṁ baccē kō calnā *sikhā rahī hai*
The mother *is teaching* the baby to walk.

Compare بچّا چلنا سیکھ رہا ہے -
bacca calnā *sīkh rahā hai*
The baby *is learning* to walk.

Case III

This group is the remnant of a formerly larger group of verb roots ending in aspirated voiceless consonants, which took the increment in **-lā**. **kahnā**, 'to say' is now virtually the only member of the group. It forms a double transitive with **-lā**, and is translated by an English passive.

کہنا ← کہلانا
kahnā, to say → **kahlānā**, to be called

یہ پہاڑ ہمالیہ کہلاتے ہیں ۔
ye pahāṛ himālaya *kahlātē haiṁ*
These mountains *are called* the Himalayas.

806 Transitivity with compound verbs

When compound verbs are used, transitive verbs usually take transitive vector verbs, and intransitive verbs usually take intransitive vector verbs (Chapter 7).

807 Transitivity with denominative verbs

Denominative verb phrases, consisting of a noun or adjective plus a verb (§607) often have parallel transitive and intransitive forms made with **karnā** and **hōnā**, respectively.

داخل کرنا — داخل ہونا
dāxil karnā, to enrol – **dāxil hōnā**, to enter, be enrolled

میں نے اپنے بیٹے کو اِس سکول میں داخل کیا ہے ۔
maiṁ nē apnē bēṭē kō is skūl mēṁ *dāxil kiyā hai*
I have entered my son in this school.

میرا بیٹا اِس سال سکول میں داخل ہوا ہے ۔
mērā bēṭā is sāl skūl mēṁ *dāxil huā hai*
My son *has entered* school this year.

جمع کرنا — جمع ہونا
jamā karnā, to collect – **jamā hōnā**, to gather, accumulate

اُس نے جلسے میں بہت لوگ جمع کر لیے ۔
us nē jalsē mēṁ bahut lōg *jamā kar liyē*
He *collected* many people in the public meeting.

لوگ چوک میں جمع ہو گئے ۔
lōg cauk mēṁ *jamā hō gaē*
People *gathered* in the square.

808 Verbs which function both intransitively and transitively

Some verbs function both transitively and intransitively.

بدلنا	**badalnā**
بھرنا	**bharnā**

badalnā, 'to change' and **bharnā**, 'to fill' are intransitive when there is no object, and transitive when there is. When they function as transitives, they take subjects with the postposition **nē** in perfective tenses. The addition of an intransitive or transitive vector verb often makes their status explicit.

منیر نے بہت دنوں سے کپڑے نہیں بدلے ۔
munīr nē bahut dinōṁ sē kapṛē nahīṁ *badlē*
Munir hasn't *changed* his clothes for days (transitive).

موسم بدل گیا ہے ۔
mausam *badal gayā hai*
The weather *has changed* (intransitive, intransitive vector verb).

میں نے بستر کی چادر بدل دی ۔
maiṁ nē bistar kī cādar *badal dī*
I *changed* the cover on the bed (transitive, transitive vector verb).

میں نے بالٹی میں پانی بھر لیا ۔
maiṁ nē bālṭī mēṁ pānī *bhar liyā*
I *filled* the bucket with water (transitive, transitive vector verb).

بالٹی پانی سے بھر گئی ۔
bālṭī pānī sē *bhar gaī*
The bucket *filled up* with water (intransitive, intransitive vector verb).

809 Exceptions: transitives without nē, intransitives with nē

Transitives which do not take nē

There are a few verbs which may take objects, but which do not take subjects with **nē** in perfective tenses.

لے آنا	**lē ānā**, to bring	بھولنا	**bhūlnā**, to forget
لانا	**lānā**, to bring	ملنا	**milnā**, to meet
لے جانا	**lē jānā**, to take away	بولنا	**bōlnā**, to speak, say

The compound verbs **lē ānā** and **lē jānā** have the intransitive verb **ānā**, 'to come' as their vector verb, therefore they do not take **nē**.

> نوکر چائے دانی لے گیا ۔
> **naukar cāēdānī *lē gayā***
> The servant *took away* the teapot.

> وہ ملاقات کا وقت بھول گیا ۔
> **vo mulāqāt kā vaqt *bhūl gayā***
> He *forgot* the time of the appointment.

> میں سچ بولا ۔
> **maiṁ sac *bōlā***
> I *spoke* the truth.

سمجھنا samajhnā

samajhnā, 'to understand' is transitive, but may occur either with or without **nē** in perfective tenses:

> وہ میری بات نہیں سمجھا – اُس نے میری بات نہیں سمجھی
> **vo mērī bāt nahīṁ *samjhā* ~ us nē mērī bāt nahīṁ *samjhī***
> He didn't *understand* what I mean.

The addition of a transitive or intransitive vector verb to **samajhnā** forces the choice, and contributes different nuances of meaning:

> میں آپ کی بات سمجھ گیا ہوں ۔
> **maiṁ āp kī bāt *samajh gayā hūṁ***
> I *follow* your point.

> میں نے بات سمجھ لی ۔
> **maiṁ nē bāt *samajh lī***
> I *have understood* the matter (and will probably deal with it).

The idioms **dikhāī dēnā**, 'to be seen', 'to be visible' and **sunāī dēnā**, 'to be heard', 'to be audible' do not take **nē** even though **dēnā** is a transitive verb. (**dikhāī** and **sunāī** are nominal forms meaning 'coming into view' and 'hearing', respectively. They are translated with English passives.)

مشین کا شور دور تک سنائی دیا ۔
mašīn kā šōr dūr tak ***sunāī diyā***
The noise of the machine *could be heard* a long way.

Intransitives which take ***nē***

A few intransitive verbs may take **nē**:[4]

تھوکنا	**thūknā**, to spit
جھانکنا	**jhāṁknā**, to peep
موتنا	**mūtnā**, to urinate
کھٹکھٹانا	**khaṭkhaṭānā**, to knock

In some cases the presence of a direct object or quasi-direct object in the deep structure may explain the phenomenon.

(دروازہ) کھٹکھٹانا	**(darvāzā) khaṭkhaṭānā**, to knock (on) a door
(اندر) جھانکنا	**(andar) jhāṁknā**, to peep inside

CAUSATIVE VERBS

Causatives describe the causation of a state or action, sometimes by means of an instrument or intermediary agent (a noun or pronoun followed by **sē** سے , **kē zariē** کے ذریعے , or **kē hāth** کے ہاتھ). The instrument is however not always mentioned. Causative verbs may be divided into direct causatives and indirect causatives.

DIRECT CAUSATIVES are derived by adding the increment **-ā** ا (**-lā** لا) to an INTRANSITIVE or a TRANSITIVE root.

INDIRECT CAUSATIVES are formed by prefixing **-v-** to the increment to make **-vā** وا (**-lvā** لوا) (§811). When the instrument is mentioned, the indirect causative is the preferred form.

If a transitive verb already contains the increment **-ā** (because it is itself derived), then the increment cannot be added again. Such verbs have only the indirect causative in **-vā**.

4 Some scholars include additional items in this list, such as **chīṁknā** چھینکنا , 'to sneeze', or **cillānā** چلّانا , 'to shout'. This reflects differing usages in various dialects of Urdu.

810 Direct causatives derived with the increment -ā

Case I

The vowel in the intransitive root is short, and the root ends in a consonant. The increment **-ā** is simply suffixed to the intransitive root to form the direct causative stem. If no intransitive exists, the suffix is added to the transitive root. Occasionally a shortened form of the transitive stem (rather than the intransitive root) is the basic form.

Sometimes there is not much difference in meaning between direct causatives and derived transitives. For example, the verb **girānā** گرانا (from **girnā** گرنا, 'to fall') can be construed as 'to let fall' (direct causative) and 'to drop' (transitive).

کاٹنا ← کٹانا
kaṭnā, to be cut → **kaṭānā**, to have cut

کرنا ← کرانا
karnā, to do → **karānā**, to have done

توڑنا ← تڑانا
tōṛnā, to break (tr.) → **tuṛānā**, to get broken, break loose

زمیندار نے فصل کٹا لی -
zamīndar nē fasal ***kaṭā lī***
The landlord *got* the harvest *cut*.

گائے نے رسّی تڑا لی -
gāē nē rassī ***tuṛā lī***
The cow *broke* the rope.

Case II

The intransitive root vowel is long, and the root ends in a consonant. The root vowel is shortened, and the increment **-ā** is suffixed to form the direct causative stem.

ڈوبنا ← ڈبانا
ḍūbnā, to sink → **ḍubānā**, to sink something, drown someone

بھاگنا ← بھگانا
bhāgnā, to run away → **bhagānā**, to chase away, disperse

بیٹھنا ← بٹھانا
baiṭhnā, to sit → **biṭhānā**, to seat, cause to sit

کسی نے ڈبائی ہو ، اب ڈوب ہی گئی -

kisī nē *ḍubāī hō*, ab tō *ḍūb* hī *gaī*

Whoever *sank* it, now it has really *gone down*. (Prem Chand, *Gōdan*)

پولیس والوں نے بھیڑ کو بھگا دیا - کچھ بھاگے ، مگر کچھ لڑنے لگے -

pōlīs vālōṁ nē bhīṛ kō *bhagā diyā*. kuch *bhagē*, magar kuch laṛnē lagē

The police *dispersed* the crowd. Some *ran away*, but some started to fight.

Case III

The intransitive or transitive root ends in a long vowel. The root vowel is shortened, and the variant form of the increment, **-lā** لا , is suffixed to form the causative stem.[5]

پینا ← پلانا

pīnā, to drink → **pilānā**, to give to drink

رونا ← رلانا

rōnā, to cry (int.) → **rulānā**, to make cry

سونا ← سلانا

sōnā, to sleep (int.) → **sulānā**, to put to sleep

دینا ← دلانا

dēnā, to give (tr.) → **dilānā**, to have given

This rule also predicts direct causatives from the following transitives:

سینا ← سلانا

sīnā, to stitch, sew → **silānā**, to get (something) stitched

دھونا ← دھلانا

dhōnā, to wash → **dhulānā**, to have (something) washed

ماں نے بچّے کو سلا دیا -

māṁ nē baccē kō *sulā diyā*

The mother *put* the baby *to sleep*.

5 Two irregular verbs are: **chūnā** چھونا , 'to touch' (tr.) which forms the causative **chuvānā** چھوانا , 'to cause to be touched'; and **khānā** کھانا , 'to eat' which forms the causative **khilānā** کھلانا , 'to feed', 'give to eat' (perhaps on the analogy of **pīnā** - **pilānā**).

منّی رو رہی ہے ، کس نے رلایا ہے ؟
munnī rō rahī hai, kis nē *rulāyā hai*?
Munni is crying; who has *made* her *cry*?

میں نے قمیص سلائی ہے -
maiṁ nē qamīs *silāī hai*
I *have got* the shirt *stitched.*

مانگنے والے کو ایک روپیہ دلا دو -
māngnē vālē kō ēk rūpaya *dilā dō*
Have someone *give* the beggar a rupee.

811 Indirect causatives formed with the increment -vā

If the increment وا **-vā** (لوا **-lvā**) is substituted for the increment ا **-ā** (لا **-lā**), a INDIRECT CAUSATIVE stem is derived. In other respects, the rules for deriving the indirect causative are the same as those for deriving the direct causative (§810).

Indirect causatives express the causation of a transitive action through an instrument or intermediary agent (a noun or pronoun followed by by **sē** سے , **kē zarīē** کے ذریعے , or **kē hāth** کے ہاتھ). The subject makes the instrument do something to, on or for the object. The instrument may be omitted, but is still implied. English translations must take context into account, and will vary.

Indirect causatives can be made for most Urdu verbs, and some dictionaries do not show them separately, but under the basic form from which they are derived. Indirect causatives cannot be made for intransitives which do not have derived transitives, such as **ānā**, 'to come, **jānā**, 'to go' and **rahnā**, 'to remain'.

Sometimes there is not much difference in meaning between indirect causatives and direct causatives. For example, the causatives **silānā** سلانا and **silvānā** سلوانا both mean 'to get (something) stitched'. In other cases, there is a clear difference; for example, **ḍubānā** ڈبانا means 'to sink something', 'to let or make sink'; **ḍubvānā** ڈبوانا means 'to have (someone) sink something'.

Case I, intransitive root

بننا	**bannā**, to be made
بنوانا	**banvānā**, to cause to make, get made
بکنا	**biknā**, to be sold
بکوانا	**bikvānā**, to cause to sell, get sold

Case I, transitive root

کرنا	**karnā**, to do
کروانا	**karvānā**, to cause to do, get done
توڑنا	**tōṛnā**, to break
تڑوانا	**tuṛvānā**, to cause to break

Case II, intransitive root

ڈوبنا	**ḍūbnā**, to sink
ڈبوانا	**ḍubvānā**, to cause to sink
بیٹھنا	**baiṭhnā**, to sit
بٹھوانا	**biṭhvānā**, to cause to seat

Case III, intransitive root

سونا	**sōnā**, to sleep
سلوانا	**sulvānā**, to cause to put to sleep

Case III, transitive root

دینا	**dēnā**, to give
دلوانا	**dilvānā**, to cause to give

Case IV, causatives of double transitives

دیکھنا	**dēkhnā**, to see, look at
دکھوانا	**dikhvānā**, to cause to show
پڑھنا	**paṛhnā**, to read, study
پڑھوانا	**paṛhvānā**, to cause to read

بادشاہ نے مزدوروں سے قلعہ بنوایا ۔
bādśāh nē mazdūrōṁ sē qila *banvāyā*
The emperor *had* the fort *built* by the labourers.

ہم باغیچہ مالی سے صاف کرواتے ہیں ۔
ham bāγīca mālī sē *sāf karvātē haiṁ*
We *have* the garden *cleaned* by the gardener.

مہمانوں کو بٹھوا دیجئے
mehmānōṁ kō *biṭhvā dījiē*
Please *have* the guests *seated.*

یہ خط اکرم کے ہاتھ بھجوا دوں گی ۔
ye xat akram kē hāth *bhijvā dūṁ gī*
I will send this letter with Akram.

مانگنے والے کو چوکیدار کے ہاتھ ایک روپیہ دلوا دو ۔
māngnē vālē kō caukīdār kē hāth ēk rūpiya *dilvā dō*
Have the watchman *give* the beggar a rupee.

Causatives of double transitives can take an instrument and up to two objects.

اُستاد نے بچّے سے جماعت کو کہانی سنوائی ۔
ustād nē *baccē sē jamāat kō kahānī* sunvāī
The teacher made *the child* tell *the story to the class.*

Compare بچّے نے جماعت کو پوری کہانی سنائی ۔
baccē nē *jamāat kō pūrī kahānī* sunāī
The child told *the whole story to the class.*

عارف صاحب نے سراج سے ہمیں پرانا قلعہ دکھوایا ۔
ārif sāhib nē *sirāj sē hamēṁ purānā qilā* dikhvāyā
Mr. Arif had *Siraj* show *us the old fort.*

Compare سراج نے ہمیں پرانا قلعہ دکھایا ۔
sirāj nē *hamēṁ purānā qilā dikhāyā*
Siraj showed *us the old fort.*

When causatives are taken into account, most verbs make sets of three:

ملنا – ملانا – ملوانا

milnā–milānā–milvānā

to meet, be available–to join, connect, mix–to have (someone) join, connect

اِتّفاق سے عارف صاحب مل گئے۔

ittifāq sē ārif sāhib *mil gaē*

By chance Mr. Arif *met* us (was available).

عارف صاحب سے ملا دیجئے۔

ārif sāhib sē *milā dījiē*

Please *connect* me with Mr. Arif.

میں آپریٹر کے ذریعے آپ کو عارف صاحب سے ملواؤں گی۔

maiṁ āprēṭar kē zarīē āp kō ārif sāhib sē *milvāūṁ gī*

I *will have* the switchboard *connect* you with Mr. Arif.

Some verbs make sets of four:

کٹنا – کاٹنا – کٹانا – کٹوانا

kaṭnā–kāṭnā–kaṭānā–kaṭvānā

to be cut–to cut–to get cut–to have (someone) cut

فصل کٹ گئی۔

fasal *kaṭ gaī*

The harvest *was cut.*

کسان فصل کاٹ رہے ہیں۔

kisān fasal *kāṭ rahē haiṁ*

The farmers *are cutting* the harvest.

زمیندار نے فصل کٹا لی۔

zamīndar nē fasal *kaṭā lī*

The landlord *got* the harvest *cut*.

زمیندار نے فصل مزدوروں سے کٹوا لی۔

zamīndar nē mazdūrōṁ sē fasal *kaṭvā lī*

The landlord *got* the harvest *cut* by the labourers.

812 Causative denominative verbs

Denominative verb phrases consisting of a noun or adjective plus the verb **karnā**, 'to do' (§607) change transitives to causatives by substituting the causative, **karānā**, 'to cause to be done' or the indirect causative, **karvānā**, 'to cause to do'.

سیاستدان نے لوگ جمع کرائے ۔
siyāsatdān nē lōg jamā karāē
The politician *got* (a lot of) people *collected.*

سیاستدان نے کارکنوں سے لوگ جمع کروائے ۔
siyāsatdān nē kārkunōṁ sē lōg *jamā karvāē*
The politician *got* the workers *to collect* the people.

آخر میں نے اپنا بیٹا اِس سکول میں داخل کرایا ۔
āxir maiṁ nē apnā bēṭā is skūl mēṁ *dāxil karāyā*
At last I *got* my son *entered* in this school.

آخر میں نے سفارش کے ذریعے اپنا بیٹا اِس سکول میں داخل کروایا ۔
āxir maiṁ nē sifāriś kē zariē apnā bēṭā is skūl mēṁ *dāxil karvāyā*
At last I *got* my son *entered* in this school by means of intercession.

813 Causative verbs in requests

Causative verbs are sometimes used in requests to soften them, by implying a higher status to the addressee.

یہ چار جوڑے سلوا دیجئے ۔
ye cār jōṛē *silvā dījiē*
Please *get* these four suits *stitched.*

The speaker hopes to influence a busy tailor to do a big job quickly, so flatters the tailor by implying that he has assistants to do the stitching.

ذرا یہ کام جلدی کروا دیجئے ۔
zarā ye kām jaldī *karvā dījiē*
Please *get* this work *done* quickly.

The addressee will do the work himself; the speaker is simply softening the request.

9 PARTICIPLES AS QUALIFIERS

Imperfective and perfective participles may be used adjectivally and adverbially. Matching forms of the perfective participle of **hōnā** (**hūā** ~ **hūē** ~ **hūī**) are often added to make participial phrases. For the forms of the imperfective participle, see §603; for the perfective participle, see §604. When participles are used as qualifiers, they are inflected like adjectives, and the feminine plural forms are not used.

کرتا ہوا - کرتی ہوئی - کرتے ہوئے
kartā hūā ~ **kartī hūī** ~ **kartē hūē**, doing

کیا ہوا - کی ہوئی - کیے ہوئے
kiyā hūā ~ **kī hūī** ~ **kiyē hūē**, done

Conjunctive participles (§612) may be used adverbially (§913).

IMPERFECTIVE PARTICIPLES

The imperfective participle describes actions or states which are incomplete (and often continuing) at the time shown by the main verb.

901 Adjectival use of imperfective participles

An imperfective participle may modify a noun like an adjective. Adjectival participles agree with the noun in number and gender, and usually occur in phrases with **hūā** (~ **hūē** ~ **hūī**). Preceding a noun, adjectival participles are used attributively (§306).

کانپتی ہوئی عورت رونے لگی -
***kāmptī hūī* aurat rōnē lagī**
The *shivering* woman began to cry.

Compare بوڑھی عورت رونے لگی -
***būṛhī* aurat rōnē lagī**
The *old* woman began to cry.

گرتی ہوئی دیواروں کو ایک دھکّا اور دو۔
***girtī hūī* dīvārōṁ kō ēk dhakkā aur dō**
Give another push to the *falling* walls.

Compare پرانی دیواروں کو ایک دھکّا اور دو۔
***purānī* dīvārōṁ kō ēk dhakkā aur dō**
Give another push to the *old* walls.

آپ کو چلتی بس پر چڑھنا نہیں چاہئے تھا۔
āp kō *caltī* bas par caṛhnā nahīṁ cāhiē thā
You should not have tried to get on the *moving* bus.

Following a noun, adjectival participles are used predicatively (§306).

ذاکر بھاگتا ہوا جا رہا تھا۔
zākir *bhāgtā hūā* jā rahā thā
Zakir was going along *at a run.*

ذاکر گیت گاتا ہوا نہا رہا تھا۔
zākir gīt *gātā hūā* nahā rahā thā
Singing a song, Zakir was bathing.

902 Adverbial use of imperfective participles

An imperfective participle (usually in phrases with **hūā** (~ **hūē** ~ **hūī**)) may add a context to the main verb, or show the simultaneity of the two actions, like an adverb. Adverbial participles are masculine oblique singular.

ذاکر گیت گاتے ہوئے نہا رہا تھا۔
zākir gīt *gātē hūē* nahā rahā thā
Zakir *was singing* a song as he bathed.

ذاکر گیت گاتے ہوئے چل رہا تھا۔
zākir gīt *gātē hūē* cal rahā thā
Zakir *was singing* a song as he walked.

An adverbial participle may precede the subject, if it is given more prominence than the main verb.

بھاگتے ہوئے چور سیڑھیوں سے گر پڑا۔
***bhāgtē hūē* cōr sīṛhiyōṁ sē gir paṛā**
While fleeing, the thief fell down the stairs. (adverbial participle)

Compare: بھاگتا ہوا چور سیڑھیوں سے گر پڑا۔
***bhāgtā hūā* cōr sīṛhiyōṁ sē gir paṛā**
The *fleeing* thief fell down the stairs. (adjectival participle)

If the main verb is transitive and the tense is perfective, the subject takes **nē** and the participle is always masculine oblique singular.

ذاکر نے ہنستے ہوئے ہم کو خبر سنائی ۔
zākir nē *hamstē hūē* ham kō xabar sunāī
Smiling, Zakir told us the news.

کتّے نے بھونکتے ہوئے حملہ کیا ۔
kuttē nē *bhaumktē hūē* hamla kiyā
Barking, the dog attacked.

903 Imperfective participle + **vaqt**, 'while (VERB)-ing'

The construction: IMPERFECTIVE PARTICIPLE + **vaqt** (**-tē vaqt**) shows an action or event which occurs simultaneously with the action or event of the main verb. The participle is oblique, and **hūā** (~ **hūē** ~ **hūī**) is not used.

امتحان دیتے وقت نہ بائیں طرف دیکھنا نہ دائیں طرف ۔
imtihān *dētē vaqt* na bāīṁ taraf dēkhnā na dāīṁ taraf
While writing the examination, do not look left nor right.

منیر کے جاتے وقت اکرم خدا حافظ کہنے نہیں آیا ۔
munīr kē *jātē vaqt* akram xudā hāfiz kahnē nahīṁ āyā
When Munir *was leaving*, Akram didn't come to say goodbye.

904 Imperfective participle + **hī**, 'as soon as (VERB)'

The construction: IMPERFECTIVE PARTICIPLE + **hī** (**-tē hī**) shows an action or event which occurs immediately prior to the action or event of the main verb. The participle is oblique, and **hūā** (~ **hūē** ~ **hūī**) is not used.

وہ لندن پہنچتے ہی آپ کو فون کرے گا ۔
vo landan *pahumctē hī* āp kō fōn karē gā
He will call you *as soon as he reaches* London.

If the subject of the participle is not the subject of the main verb, it will be possessive, and will be followed by **kē**.

حامد کے دروازہ کھولتے ہی وہ اُٹھ بیٹھی ۔
hāmid kē darvāza *khōltē hī* vo uṭh baiṭhī
As soon as Hamid *opened* the door, she jumped up.

905 Repeated imperfective participles

Repeated imperfective participles show continuing or repeated action which culminates in the action or event of the main verb. **hūā** (~ **hūē** ~ **hūī**) is not used. The participles are usually masculine oblique singular, especially in the Urdu of Delhi, however (a) if both participle and main verb have the same subject, (b) the subject is in the nominative case, and (c) the participles follow the subject, the participle may agree with the subject. If the verb is a verb of motion, the participles may also agree with the subject when preceding it (see the last example in this section).

میں سمجھاتی سمجھاتی تھک گئی ہوں -
maiṁ *samjhātī samjhātī* thak gaī hūṁ
I have got tired of *explaining* (it) *again and again.*

میں نے سمجھاتے سمجھاتے اُسے منا لیا -
maiṁ nē *samjhātē samjhātē* usē manā liyā
I persuaded him *by explaining* (it) *again and again.*

سمجھاتے سمجھاتے میں تھک گئی ہوں -
***samjhātē samjhātē* maiṁ thak gaī hūṁ**
I have got tired of *explaining* (it) *again and again.*

لکھتے لکھتے وہ ادیب بن گیا -
***likhtē likhtē* vo adīb ban gayā**
By writing regularly, he became a writer.

وہ لکھتے لکھتے ادیب بن گیا -
vo *likhtē likhtē* adīb ban gayā
He became a writer *by writing regularly.*

Repeated oblique imperfective participles may show an action that is not fully accomplished.

وہ گرتے گرتے بچی -
vo *girtē girtē* bacī
She *nearly fell* (but someone caught her).

ڈاکو بھاگتے بھاگتے پکڑا گیا -
ḍākū *bhāgtē bhāgtē* pakṛā gayā
The robber was caught *while attempting to flee.*

Two different, but semantically related words may occur as repeated imperfective participles.

بچّی چیختی چلّاتی اندر آ گئی ۔
baccī *cīxtī cillātī* andar ā gaī
The little girl came inside *screaming and yelling.*

چیختی چلّاتی بچّی اندر آ گئی ۔
***cīxtī cillātī* baccī andar ā gaī**
Screaming and yelling, the little girl came inside.

906 Imperfective participles used as nouns

Adjectives may be used as nouns (§319), and the same is true of participles, although it is not common. Imperfective participles as nouns show an (uncompleted) condition of an omitted noun.

شور مچاتے ہوئے کو چپ کرانا پڑا ۔
***śōr macātē hūē* kō cup karānā paṛā**
The noisemaking (person) had to be told to be quiet.

The more usual way of expressing the above would be:

شور مچانے والے کو چپ کرانا پڑا ۔
***śōr macānē vālē* kō cup karānā paṛā**
The noisemaker had to be told to be quiet.

PERFECTIVE PARTICIPLES

The perfective participle is a verbal adjective. It describes (a) completed actions or processes which result in the condition of the subject or object at the time shown by the main verb, (b) actions completed prior to the action shown by the main verb. Compare the imperfective and perfective participles in the following sets.

Imperfective participle

گرتی ہوئی دیواریں
***girtī hūī* dīvārēṁ**
falling walls

پولیس والوں نے گھر جلتا ہوا پایا ۔
pōlīs vālōṁ nē ghar *jaltā hūā* pāyā
The police found the house *on fire.*

Perfective participle

گری ہوئی دیواریں	پولیس والوں نے گھر جلا ہوا پایا ۔
girī hūī dīvārēṁ	**pōlīs vālōṁ nē ghar jalā hūā pāyā**
toppled walls	The police found the house *burned down.*

907 Adjectival use of perfective participles

A perfective participle may modify a noun like an adjective. Adjectival participles agree with the noun in number and gender, and usually occur in phrases with **hūā** ~ **hūē** ~ **hūī**. Preceding a noun, adjectival participles are used attributively (§306).

پھٹی ہوئی مرزئی	محبت سے بھرے ہوئے لفظ
***phaṭī hūī* mirzaī**	**muhabbat sē *bharē hūē* lafz**
a *torn* quilted coat	words *filled* with love

زمین پر گرے ہوئے تمام کاغذ ہٹا دیجئے ۔
zamīn par *girē hūē* tamām kāɣaz haṭā dījīē
Please remove all the papers (*that have*) *fallen* on the floor.

Following a noun, adjectival participles are used predicatively (§306). If two participles occur in the phrase, **hūā** is dropped.

(a) Qualifying the subject, the participle agrees with it in gender and number.

مرزئی پھٹی ہوئی تھی ۔
mirzaī *phaṭī hūī* thī
The quilted coat was *torn.*

Compare مرزئی پرانی تھی ۔
mirzaī *purānī* thī
The quilted coat was *old.*

آپ کچھ تھکے ہوئے نظر آ رہے ہیں ۔
āp kuch *thakē hūē* nazar ā rahē haiṁ
You look rather *tired.*

(b) Qualifying the object, the participle agrees with objects which are in the nominative case (§109). If the object is marked by **kō**, the participle is masculine singular by default.

آپ نے الماری کھلی (ہوئی) کیوں چھوڑی تھی ؟
āp nē almārī *khulī* (*hūī*) kyōṁ chōṛī thī?
Why did you leave the cupboard *open*?

دروازہ کھلا (ہوا) پا کر چوکیدار نے گھنٹی بجائی -
darvāzā *khulā* (*hūā*) pā kar caukīdār nē ghanṭī bajāī
Finding the door *open*, the watchman rang the bell.

اِن چوڑیوں کو چُھپا ہوا پا کر میں بھونچکی رہ گئی -
in cūṛiyōṁ kō *chupā hūā* pā kar maiṁ bhauṁcakkī rah gaī
Finding these bangles *hidden*, I was astonished.

Stative verbs

Perfective participles of STATIVE VERBS show a continuing state (in the same way that stative verbs are used in the immediate past to show states which commenced with an event in the past, and continue into the present (§631)).

وہ لیٹا ہوا پڑھ رہا تھا -
vo *lēṭā hūā* paṛh rahā thā
He was reading (while) *lying down* (in a lying position).

سوئے ہوئے کتّے کو نہ جگاؤ -
***sōē hūē* kuttē kō na jagāō**
Don't wake a *sleeping* dog.

908 Adverbial use of perfective participles

The perfective participle may be used conjunctively (§612), to describe an action which precedes the action or state of the main verb. They may qualify the subject or the object; the participle often has an object of its own; in every case, they are masculine oblique singular. **hūā** (~ **hūē** ~ **hūī**) is usually dropped.

Qualifying the subject

تم یہ تھیلا لیے کہاں جا رہے ہو ؟
tum ye thailā *liyē* kahāṁ jā rahē hō?
Where are you going with (lit. *taken*) this bag?

Compare تم یہ تھیلا لے کر کہاں جا رہے ہو ؟
tum ye thailā *lē kar* kahāṁ jā rahē hō?
Where are you going with (lit. *having taken*) this bag?

Qualifying the object

فقیر نے کتّے کو راستے میں لیٹے ہوئے دیکھ کر راستہ بدل لیا -
faqīr nē kuttē kō rāstē mēṁ *lēṭē hūē* dēkh kar rāsta badal liyā
The faqir, seeing the dog *lying* on the path, changed the path.

—In the previous example, the use of the oblique participial phrase **lēṭē hūē** implies that the dog lay down on the path before the faqir arrived.

Contrast the following sentence in which a perfective participle is used predicatively, not conjunctively:

میں نے ایک کتّا راستے میں سویا ہوا پایا -
maiṁ nē ēk kuttā rāstē mēṁ *sōyā hūā* pāyā
I found a dog *sleeping* on the path.

—which merely describes the condition of the dog.

In the following sentence, the conjunctive perfective participle is used adverbially.

آپ کو یہاں آئے کتنا عرصہ ہو گیا ہے ؟
āp kō yahāṁ *āē* kitnā arsa hō gayā hai?
How long has it been *since you came* here?

The core sentence, to which the phrase **yahāṁ āē** is added, is an impersonal construction with a subject marked by **kō** (§506):

آپ کو کتنا عرصہ ہو گیا ہے ؟
***āp kō* kitnā arsa hō gayā hai?**
How much time have *you* passed?

909 Adverbial perfective participles in expressions of time

The perfective participles of **hōnā**, 'to be', **jānā**, 'to go', **rahnā**, 'to remain', **caṛhnā**, 'to rise' and **bītnā**, 'to pass' are used adverbially in expressions of time (see also §1311).

پانچ سال ہوئے اُس کی تعلیم پوری ہوئی تھی -
pāṁc sāl *hūē* us kī tālīm pūrī hūī thī
Five years *ago* (five years *having become*) his education was completed.

اِتنی رات گئے شہر میں گھومنا ٹھیک نہیں ۔

itnī rāt *gaē* śahr mēṁ ghūmnā ṭhīk nahīṁ

So late at night (so much night *having gone*), it isn't safe to roam about the city.

مچھیرا کچھ رات رہے اُٹھتا ہے ۔

machērā kuch rāt *rahē* uṭhtā hai

The fisherman gets up very early (some night *having remained*).

تم اِتنا دن چڑھے کیوں سوئے ہوئے ہو ؟

tum itnā din *caṛhē* kyōṁ sōē hūē hō?

Why are you asleep so late (so much day *having risen*)?

910 Repeated perfective participles

Perfective participles may be repeated to show continuing action; however, since perfective participles have the aspect of completeness, the semantics of these sequences are less straightforward than with repeated imperfective participles. If the main verb is in a perfective tense and the subject is in the nominative case (i.e., the verb is intransitive), the participles usually agree with the subject in gender and number. In all other cases the participles are masculine oblique singular. **hūā** (~ **hūē** ~ **hūī**) is not used.

Repeated perfective participles of STATIVE VERBS show a continuing state which began with an event in the past.

یہ کھڑی کھڑی اُسے پکارتی رہی ۔

ye *khaṛī khaṛī* usē pukārtī rahī

She *kept standing* and calling (him). (Prem Chand, *Gōdān*)

The main verb may show culmination:

یہ سیب پڑے پڑے خراب ہو گئے ہیں ۔

ye sēb *paṛē paṛē* xarāb hō gaē haiṁ

These apples *have been lying around so long* they have gone rotten.

Repeated perfective participles of VERBS OF MOTION occur, but are semantically somewhat anomalous, as they show the continuation of a completed action. They suggest motion which is haphazard or frantic.

اکرم بھاگا بھاگا ہمارے گھر آیا ۔

akram *bhāgā bhāgā* hamārē ghar āyā

Akram *rushed frantically* to our house.

Compare اکرم نے بھاگتے بھاگتے بس پکڑ لی -
akram nē *bhāgtē bhāgtē* bas pakaṛ lī
Akram *ran after* the bus and caught it (purposefully, to get away).

سب ڈاکٹر کیوں پریشان اور گھبرائے گھبرائے پھرتے ہیں ؟
sab ḍākṭar kyōṁ parēśān aur *ghabrāē ghabrāē* phirtē haiṁ?
Why are all the doctors running about *worried and panic-stricken*?

Two semantically related perfective participles may be used in the same way as repeated participles, functioning both as adjectives and predicate complements.

پڑھا لکھا آدمی
***paṛhā likhā* ādmī**
an *educated* person (*read written* person)

اُس کی اردو ٹوٹی پھوٹی ہے -
us kī urdū *ṭūṭī phūṭī* hai
His Urdu is *broken.*

The perfective participles of related intransitives and causatives (or transitives and causatives) may be used idiomatically as adjectives.

سلے سلائے کپڑے
***silē silāē* kapṛē**
ready-made clothes (< **silnā**, to be stitched + **silānā**, to get stitched)

سنی سنائی بات
***sunī sunāī* bāt**
hearsay (< **sunnā**, to hear + **sunānā**, to tell)

911 Perfective participles used as nouns

Adjectives may be used as nouns (§319), and the same is true of participles, although it is not common.

پڑھے لکھوں کو ایسا کام نہیں کرنا چاہیے -
***paṛhē likhōṁ* kō aisā kām nahīṁ karnā cāhiyē**
Educated (people) shouldn't do such a thing.

پڑھے بغیر تم کامیاب نہیں ہو سکتے -
***paṛhē* baɣair tum kāmyāb nahīṁ hō saktē**
Without *studying* you cannot succeed (in the examination).

912 Perfective participles in compound verbs

Perfective participles may occur as main verbs in compound verb sequences (§718-§719).

CONJUNCTIVE PARTICIPLES

913 Conjunctive participles used adverbially

Conjunctive participles describe two actions or events which take place in a sequence (§612). Conjunctive participles may be used adverbially.

وہ گھبرا کر بولا ...
vo *ghabrā kar* bōlā ...
He said anxiously (*having become anxious*) ...

They may also function instrumentally:

وہ پان بیچ کر روزی کماتا ہے
vo pān *bēc kar* rōzī kamātā hai
He earns a living by selling (*having sold*) betel leaf preparation.

914 Repeated roots in conjunctive participles

The root in a conjunctive participle may be repeated (see also §613).

باتیں تو ہنس ہنس کے کر رہے تھے -
bātēṁ tō *haṁs haṁs* kē kar rahē thē
He was talking cheerfully (*having smiled-smiled*). (Prem Chand, *Gōdān*)

چلتے ہوئے مڑ مڑ کر وہ ہماری طرف دیکھتی رہی -
caltē hūē *muṛ muṛ* kar vo hamārī taraf dēkhtī rahī
While walking, she *kept turning around* and looking at us *time and again*.

The conjunctive participles of two different but semantically related words may be used adverbially.

سوچ سمجھ کر بات کریں -
***sōc samajh* kar bāt karēṁ**
You should choose your words carefully (having thought-understood).

10 WORD ORDER AND AGREEMENT IN SENTENCES

The following remarks are intended as an overview of Urdu word order and agreement for the student, and not as a comprehensive treatment of Urdu syntax. The subject is also treated in other other sections of this work, to which the reader is referred for information and more examples.

WORD ORDER

1001 Word order in sentences

The basic word order in Urdu sentences is SUBJECT - PREDICATE

گھوڑا + دوڑتا ہے -
ghōṛā + dauṛtā hai
The horse runs.

کتّا + بڑا ہے -
kuttā + baṛā hai
The dog is big.

If there is an object, it comes in between the subject and predicate.

گھوڑا چارا کھاتا ہے -
ghōṛā *cārā* khātā hai.
A horse eats *fodder*.

The unemphatic word order for simple declarative sentences is:

SUBJECT - OBJECT + **kō** - TIME ADVERB - PLACE ADVERB - SIMPLE OBJECT - VERB

ملک صاحب مجھے ہر روز یہاں چائے پلاتے ہیں -
malik sāhib mujhē har rōz yahāṁ cāē pilātē haiṁ
Mr. Malik gives me tea to drink here every day.

میں آپ کو کل اُردو بازار میں ایک اچّھی دکان دکھاؤں گا -
maiṁ āp kō kal urdū bāzār mēṁ ēk acchī dukān dikhāūṁ gā
I will show you a good shop in the Urdu Bazaar tomorrow.

An adverb of time is often given prominence by placing it right after the subject, or even first in the sentence. An adverb of place may also be given prominence by moving it forward in the sentence. The order of the subject, object and verb is rarely changed. If the verb provides the necessary information about the person, number and gender of the speaker, the subject may be omitted.

میں کل آپ کو اُردو بازار میں ایک اچّھی دکان دکھاؤں گا ۔
maiṁ *kal* āp kō urdū bāzār mēṁ ēk acchī dukān dikhāūṁ gā
Tomorrow I will show you a good shop in the Urdu Bazaar.

کل (میں) آپ کو اُردو بازار میں ایک اچّھی دکان دکھاؤں گا ۔
***kal* (maiṁ) āp kō urdū bāzār mēṁ ēk acchī dukān dikhāūṁ gā**
Tomorrow I will show you a good shop in the Urdu Bazaar.

1002 Objects

Indirect objects marked by **kō** or its alternate forms (§210) precede unmarked direct objects. (See §505 for **kō** with objects.)

بچّی نے مہمان کو پھول پیش کیے ۔
baccī nē *mehmān kō* phūl pēś kiyē
The little girl offered flowers *to the guest.*

شاہد نے اپنی والدہ کو تار بھیجا ۔
śāhid nē *apnī vālida kō* tār bhējā
Shahid sent a telegram *to his mother.*

1003 Noun phrases

Adjectives precede nouns which they qualify.

دلچسپ کام
***dilcasp* kām**
interesting work

Adjectives may be preceded by a modifier, such as **bahut**, **sirf** or **zyāda**.

بہت دلچسپ کام
***bahut* dilcasp kām**
very interesting work

صرف گرم چائے پیو
***sirf* garm cāē pīō**
Drink *only* hot tea.

In a sequence of adjectives, possessive adjectives precede other adjectives.

آپ کا دلچسپ کام
***āp kā* dilcasp kām**
your interesting work

ہمارا بڑا گھر
***hamārā* baṛā ghar**
our large house

Numerals, demonstratives and interrogatives follow possessives, but precede other adjectives.

آپ کی وہ بڑی لغت کہاں رکھی ہے ؟
āp kī *vo* baṛī luɣat kahāṁ rakhī hai?
Where is *that* big dictionary of yours kept?

میرے دو بڑے بھائی کراچی میں پڑھتے ہیں ۔
mērē *dō* baṛē bhāī karācī mēṁ paṛhtē haiṁ
My *two* elder brothers study in Karachi.

ملک صاحب کا کون سا رشتہ دار کل آیا تھا ؟
malik sāhib kā *kaun sā* riśtēdār kal āyā thā?
Which of Mr. Malik's relatives came yesterday?

Postpositions (Chapter 5) follow nouns or pronouns, and mark (a) grammatical functions, (b) location, movement or extent in space and time. Whenever a noun is followed by a postposition it occurs in the oblique case (§110). Pronouns also occur in the oblique case before postpositions (§208), except for the first and second person pronouns when preceding the postposition **nē** (§209).

بیرے کو بلاؤ ۔
***bairē kō* bulāō**
Call *the waiter.*

اُس کو بلاؤ ۔
***us kō* bulāō**
Call *him.*

The adverb **bhī**, 'also' or the emphatic particle **hī** normally follow the postposition (§1106). Adverbs are treated under §1004, below.

خانساماں کو بھی بلاؤ ۔
xānsāmāṁ kō *bhī* bulāō
Call the cook *too.*

خانساماں کو ہی بلاؤ ، بیرے کو نہیں ۔
xānsāmāṁ kō *hī* bulāō, bairē kō nahīṁ
Call the cook (*emph.*), not the waiter.

1004 Adverbs

In simple declarative sentences, adverbs of time and adverbs of place come between the subject and the predicate. Adverbs of time precede adverbs of place.

میں ہر روز یہاں کھاتا ہوں ۔
maiṁ *har rōz yahāṁ* khātā hūṁ
I eat *here every day.*

Simple objects follow adverbs.

میں ہر روز یہاں چائے پیتا ہوں ۔
maiṁ har rōz yahāṁ *cāē* pītā hūṁ
I drink *tea* here every day.

In unemphatic sentences, objects followed by **kō** or its alternate forms (§210) precede adverbs of time and place. However the order of adverbs is quite flexible.

ملک صاحب مجھے ہر روز یہاں چائے پلاتے ہیں ۔
malik sāhib *mujhē* har rōz yahāṁ cāē pilātē haiṁ
Mr. Malik gives *me* tea to drink here every day.

ہر روز میں یہاں چائے پیتا ہوں ۔
har rōz maiṁ *yahāṁ* cāē pītā hūṁ
Every day I drink tea *here*.

یہاں میں چائے نہیں پیتا ۔
***yahāṁ* maiṁ cāē nahīṁ pītā**
Here I don't drink tea.

phir (§420) receives prominence in a sentence. It usually precedes an object and may precede the subject. The same is true of adverbs of manner which signal a departure from the usual, such as **pahlē**, 'first', **āxir kār**, 'at last', or **jaldī**, 'quickly'.

میں پہلے خانساماں کو بلاؤں گا ، پھر بیرے کو ۔
maiṁ *pahlē* xānsāmāṁ kō bulāūṁ gā, *phir* bairē kō
I'll call the cook *first, then* the waiter.

آخر کار ذاکر کا خط مل ہی گیا ۔
***āxir kār* zākir kā xat mil hī gayā**
At last, Zakir's letter was received.

The adverb **bhī**, 'also' (§418) or the emphatic particle **hī** (§1105) immediately follow the word they refer to.

وہ بھی بادشاہی مسجد دیکھیں گے ۔
vo *bhī* bādśāhī masjid dēkhēṁ gē
They *too* will see the royal mosque.

وہ بادشاہی مسجد بھی دیکھیں گے -
vo bādśāhī masjid *bhī* dēkhēṁ gē
They will see the royal mosque *too*.

When a sentence contains two or more adverbs, the adverb of time comes first, followed by the adverb of place, and the adverb of manner or modification. If there is more than one adverb of time, the order is YEAR - MONTH - DAY - HOUR. See §427 for examples.

1005 Negative sentences

Negatives (§417) usually come right before the verb phrase. If the phrase contains the present tense auxiliary **hai** (**haiṁ**, **hūṁ**, etc.), the auxiliary is often dropped.

سبزی خور گوشت نہیں کھاتے -
sabzī xōr gōśt *nahīṁ* khātē
Vegetarians *don't* eat meat.

وہ پہلے سبزی خور نہیں تھا -
vo pahlē sabzī xōr *nahīṁ* thā
He was *not* a vegetarian before.

آپ کل یہاں نہ آئیے -
āp kal yahāṁ *na* āiyē
Please *don't* come here tomorrow.

1006 Interrogative sentences

Interrogative words usually come right before the verb.

یہ کیا ہے ؟
ye *kyā* hai?
What is this?

دروازے پر کون ہے ؟
darvāzē par *kaun* hai?
Who is at the door?

آپ چائے کب پیتے ہیں ؟
āp cāē *kab* pītē haiṁ?
When do you drink tea?

آپ چائے کہاں پیتے ہیں ؟
āp cāē *kahāṁ* pītē haiṁ?
Where do you drink tea?

Interrogative adverbs may precede direct objects (although not objects marked by **kō**, or subjects).

آپ کب چائے پیتے ہیں ؟
āp *kab* cāē pītē haiṁ?
When do you drink tea?

The interrogative **kyā**, used to introduce a yes-or-no question (and not in the sense of 'what?'), usually comes at the beginning of the sentence.

کیا آپ سبزی خور ہیں ؟
kyā āp sabzī xōr haiṁ?
Are you a vegetarian?

kyā may also come at the end of short questions, like a tag:

آپ سبزی خور ہیں کیا ؟
āp sabzī xōr haiṁ kyā?
Aren't you a vegetarian?

See also: conditional sentences (§609) and order of clauses in relative-correlative sentences (§1103).

AGREEMENT

1007 Subject-verb agreement

Intransitive verbs agree with subject nouns or pronouns in gender and number (for agreement with transitive verbs, see §1011).

لڑکا دوڑتا ہے	**laṛkā dauṛtā hai**	The boy runs.
لڑکی دوڑتی ہے	**laṛkī dauṛtī hai**	The girl runs.
لڑکا دوڑتا تھا	**laṛkā dauṛtā thā**	The boy used to run.
لڑکے دوڑتے تھے	**laṛkē dauṛtē thē**	The boys used to run.

1008 Verb phrases

Most verb constructions are phrases consisting of a participle and an auxiliary verb. Participles show gender and number (but not person); masculine participles show number, however feminine participles show plural number only when there is no auxiliary verb (either because it is dropped following a negative (§1005), or because no auxiliary occurs in the construction, as in the irrealis (§622) or simple past (§630)). The present tense auxiliary verb shows number and person, but not gender; the past tense auxiliary verb shows number and gender, but not person (§605-§606). So it would be more accurate to say that verb phrases as a whole (not simply verbs) agree with subjects in gender and number.

Verb phrases with participles and auxiliaries

میں دوڑتا ہوں	**maiṁ dauṛtā hūṁ**	I (m.) run.
میں دوڑتی ہوں	**maiṁ dauṛtī hūṁ**	I (f.) run.
تم دوڑتے ہو	**tum dauṛtē hō**	You (m.) run.
تم دوڑتی ہو	**tum dauṛtī hō**	You (f.) run.
ہم دوڑتے ہیں	**ham dauṛtē haiṁ**	We (m.) run.
ہم دوڑتی ہیں	**ham dauṛtī haiṁ**	We (f.) run.
وہ دوڑتا ہے	**vo dauṛtā hai**	He runs.
وہ دوڑتی ہے	**vo dauṛtī hai**	She runs.

Feminine plural participles

ہم نہیں دوڑتیں	**ham nahīṁ dauṛtīṁ**	We (f.) don't run.
ہم دوڑیں	**ham dauṛīṁ**	We (f.) ran.

1009 Agreement with mixed subjects

If the subject of the sentence is a phrase containing two or more inanimate nouns, the verb agrees with the noun nearest to it.

باغ میں پھول ، پودے اور آم کا پیڑ لگا ہوا ہے -
bāγ mēṁ phūl, paudē aur ām kā *pēṛ lagā hūā hai*
Flowers, vegetables and a mango *tree are planted* in the garden.

If the phrase contains two or more animate nouns, the verb is plural.

کتّا اور بلی لڑ رہے تھے -
kuttā aur billī laṛ rahē thē
The dog and cat were fighting.

میرا بھائی اور بہن کھیل رہے ہیں -
mērā bhāī aur bahen khēl rahē haiṁ
My brother and sister are playing.

1010 Agreement with transitive verbs

Transitive verbs agree with the subject only in imperfective tenses. In perfective tenses, transitive verbs agree with nominative direct objects, and subjects take the postposition **nē**. (See §510, §629 for details and examples.)

Perfective intransitive

گھوڑی دوڑی -
ghōṛī dauṛī
The mare ran.

Perfective transitive

گھوڑی نے چارا کھا لیا ہے -
ghōṛī nē *cārā khā liyā hai*
The mare *has eaten fodder.*

1011 Agreement with impersonal verbs

Impersonal verbs of various types, such as **cāhiē** چاہئے , **pasand hōnā** پسند ہونا or some uses of **milnā** ملنا or **paṛnā** پڑنا , also agree with the direct object of the sentence. The subject is followed by the postposition **kō** کو or its alternate forms (§210). (See §641 for a discussion of impersonal constructions and §506 for the postposition **kō** marking subjects.)

مجھے پیسہ چاہئے -
mujhē *paisa cāhiē*
I *need money.*

مجھے دو ہزار روپئے چاہئیں -
mujhē dō hazār *rūpaē cāhiēṁ*
I *need two thousand rupees.*

1012 Mixed transitivity

Mixed transitivity with conjunctive participles

When two separate statements are transformed into a single sentence by means of an conjunctive participle (§612), it may happen that one of the verbs is transitive and the other intransitive. In such a case, the verb in the main clause (usually the second verb) determines the transitivity of the sentence. If the main verb is transitive, the subject of both clauses is followed by **nē** (§510, §629) when the verb is in perfective tenses. If the main verb is intransitive, the entire sentence is treated as intransitive, and **nē** is not used.

میں پڑھ کر گھر گیا -
maiṁ* paṛh kar ghar *gayā
Having studied, *I went* home.

میں نے گھر جا کر پڑھا -
maiṁ nē* ghar jā kar *paṛhā
Having gone home, *I studied.*

Mixed transitivity in compound verbs

In compound verb constructions (Chapter 7) intransitive main verbs usually occur with intransitive vectors, and transitive main verbs with transitive vectors. However, there are exceptions to this rule. The resulting sequences are always treated as intransitive. In other words, both the main verb and the vector verb must be transitive in order for the entire sequence to be treated as transitive. See §712 and §713.

1013 Adjective-noun agreement

Adjectives agree with nouns in gender, number and case (however adjectives have no feminine plural form). See §303-§305.

Nominative

بڑا گھوڑا **baṛā ghōṛā**, (a) *big* horse
بڑی گھوڑی **baṛī ghōṛī**, (a) *big* mare
بڑے گھوڑے **baṛē ghōṛē**, *big* horses

Oblique

بڑے گھوڑے کا **baṛē ghōṛē kā**, of a *big* horse
بڑے گھوڑوں کا **baṛē ghōṛōṁ kā**, of *big* horses

However, only adjectives which have suffixes that inflect to show gender and number (marked adjectives) change to show agreement. Unmarked adjectives do not change. This is discussed in detail in §301-§302.

If two or more nouns are qualified by one adjective, the adjective agrees with the noun nearest to it. See §305.

آپ کی والدہ اور بھائی
āp *kī* *vālda* aur bhāī
your mother and brother

11 RELATIVE-CORRELATIVE SENTENCES

THE STRUCTURE OF RELATIVE SENTENCES

1101 Relative words and their counterparts

Urdu distinguishes systematically between the categories 'near', 'far', 'interrogative' and 'relative'. An overview of symmetrical sets of words beginning with **y~i~a**, 'near', **v~u**, 'far', **k** (interrogative), and **j** (relative) is given in Table 11, §309. Table 25, §1102 lists the relative words in the set along with their corresponding 'far' counterparts. The relative words are used in relative clauses, while the 'far' words are used in correlative clauses.

1102 Structure of relative-correlative sentences

Relative-correlative sentences can be considered as transformed from two simpler sentences.

وہ نیک کام کرے گا۔ وہ پھل پائے گا ۔
***vo* nēk kām karē gā. *vo* phal pāē gā**
He does good deeds. *He* will reap rewards.

→ جو نیک کام کرے گا وہ پھل پائے گا ۔
***jō* nēk kām karē gā vo phal pāē gā**
The one who does good deeds will reap rewards.

وہ شخص رشوت کھاتا ہے ۔ وہ شخص گناہ کرتا ہے ۔
***vo* śaxs riśvat khātā hai. *vo* śaxs gunāh kartā hai**
That person takes bribes. *That person* commits a sin.

→ جو شخص رشوت کھاتا ہے وہ شخص گناہ کرتا ہے ۔
***jō śaxs* riśvat khātā hai, vo gunāh kartā hai**
The person who takes bribes commits a sin.

In the examples above, the relative word **jō**, 'who' introduces the relative clause. The correlative clause is introduced by **vo**, 'he', 'that' (§201, §202). Formerly there was a group of correlative words beginning with **t-**, of which the adverb **tab** is one surviving member. (Other surviving members are **tyūṁ**, which occurs mainly in compounds with **jūṁ**, and not as a correlative word (§1120); and **taisā**, which occurs only in a compound with **jaisā** (§1108).) The 'far' words now function as correlative words (and will be referred to as such in this chapter).

Table 25: Relative (**j**) words and their 'far' (**v ~ u**) counterparts

		j ج RELATIVE		v ~ u وا FAR
PRONOUN				
	جو	**jō**, who, which	وہ	**vo**, he/she/it
ADJECTIVE				
	جو	**jō**, who, which	وہ	**vo**, he/she/it
	جیسا	**jaisā**, such as	ویسا	**vaisā**, like that
	جتنا	**jitnā**, as much	اُتنا	**utnā**, that much
ADVERB				
	جہاں	**jahāṁ**, where	وہاں	**vahāṁ**, there
	جدھر	**jidhar**, whither	اُدھر	**udhar**, thither
	جب	**jab**, when	(تب	**tab**, then)
	جوں	**jūṁ**, as, like	ووں	**vūṁ**, so (obsolete)
	جس جگہ	**jis jagah** in the place that	اُس جگہ	**us jagah** in that place, there
	جس طرف	**jis taraf** (in) the direction that	اُس طرف	**us taraf** in that direction
	جس وقت	**jis vaqt** at the time that	اُس وقت	**us vaqt** at that time
	جس طرح	**jis tarah** in the way that	اُس طرح	**us tarah** that way

The typical relative sentence is characterized by symmetry of both clauses. The clauses may make two statements about a single subject (relative pronoun), locate two subjects in one place or time (relative adverb) or express a similiarity or comparison (relative adjective).

A relative clause with **jō** referring to a human subject can be replaced by a construction of OBLIQUE INFINITIVE + **vālā** (§645):

نیک کام کرنے والا پھل پائے گا ۔
nēk kām *karnē vālā* phal pāē gā
The doer of good deeds will reap rewards.

رشوت کھانے والا شخص گناہ کرتا ہے ۔
riśvat *khānē vālā* śaxs gunāh kartā hai
The person taking bribes commits a sin.

1103 Order of clauses in relative-correlative sentences

The relative clause normally precedes the correlative clause in unemphatic speech. However the order of the clauses can be reversed, with a corresponding shift in focus to the first clause.

وہ پھل پائے گا جو نیک کام کرے گا ۔
vo phal pāē gā *jō* nēk kām karē gā
The one who will reap rewards is he *who* does good deeds.

If **jō** is used adjectivally, qualifying a noun (**jō śaxs**) in the unemphatic sentence, the noun remains in the first clause when the order is reversed.

وہ شخص گناہ کرتا ہے جو رشوت کھاتا ہے ۔
vo śaxs gunāh kartā hai *jō* riśvat khātā hai
That person commits a sin, *who* takes bribes.

The relative clause may also be put inside the correlative clause. English speakers may be tempted to do this because it most nearly corresponds to English usage, but it is the least frequent order in Urdu.

وہ شخص جو رشوت کھاتا ہے گناہ کرتا ہے ۔
vo śaxs *jō* riśvat khātā hai, gunāh kartā hai
The person *who* takes bribes commits a sin.

1104 Stipulative relative clauses

In the following example, the relative clause stipulates the thing which fulfils the condition in the correlative clause.

میں ایسا آدمی رکھوں گا جو ایماندار ہو ۔
maiṁ aisā ādmī rakhūṁ gā *jō* īmāndār hō
I will hire a man *who* is honest.

1105 Correlatives specified by hī

Correlative words are very often made more specific by the addition of the emphatic particle **hī** (§1205).

جو نیک کام کرے گا وہی پھل پائے گا -
jō nēk kām karē gā *vahī* phal pāē gā
It is the one who does good deeds who will reap rewards.

THE RELATIVE PRONOUN jō

A relative-correlative sentence with **jō** is one in which each clause makes a statement about a single subject (identity of subject). The nominative form **jō** is both singular and plural, but there are distinct singular and plural oblique forms.

1106 Nominative form of jō

jō may function as a pronoun or adjectivally, qualifiying a noun. When **jō** comes first in the sentence, it usually qualifies a noun. When the relative clause comes in second place, or is embedded in the correlative clause, **jō** is more often used pronominally. Examples of sentences with the relative pronoun **jō** are given below and in §1102.

جو بات آپ کہہ رہے ہیں وہ بہت اہم ہے -
***jō bāt* āp kah rahē haiṁ, vo bahut aham hai**
The thing (*which*) you are saying is very important.

وہ بات بہت اہم ہے جو آپ کہہ رہے ہیں -
vo bāt bahut aham hai *jō* āp kah rahē haiṁ
The thing that is very important is *what* you are saying.

jō sometimes links juxtaposed contrasting clauses (see also §1230).

وہ جو دولتمند ہے ، غریب آدمی کا دکھ کیا جانے ؟
vo *jō* daulatmand hai, γarīb ādmī kā dukh kyā jānē?
How would he, *who* is rich, understand the suffering of a poor person?

1107 Oblique and plural forms of jō

The oblique and plural forms of **jō** are shown in Table 26, on p. 200. **jō** has a variant oblique plural form which occurs only before **nē**.

Table 26: Oblique and plural forms of **jō**

	NOMINATIVE	OBLIQUE	+ **nē**
SINGULAR	جو **jō**, who, which?	جس **jis**	جس نے **jis nē**
PLURAL	جو **jō**, who, which?	جن **jin**	جنہوں نے **jinhōṁ nē**

Examples

جس بات کا ذکر آپ کر رہے ہیں وہ بہت اہم ہے -
***jis bāt* kā zikr āp kar rahē haiṁ, vo bahut aham hai**
The thing (which) you are mentioning is very important.

جس نے یہ کتاب لکھی ہے وہ ماہرِ تعلیم ہے -
***jis nē* ye kitāb likhī hai, vo māhir-e-tālīm hai**
The one who has written this book is an expert on education.

جنہوں نے حفاظتی ٹیکہ لگوایا وہ ٹھیک رہے -
***jinhōṁ nē* hifāzatī ṭīka lagvāyā, vo ṭhīk rahē**
Those who got a preventive vaccination remained healthy.

The oblique forms of **jō** may take the alternate forms of **kō** (§210).

اُس آدمی کا کیا نام ہے جسے (جس کو) آپ نے بلایا تھا ؟
us ādmī kā kyā nām hai, *jisē* (*jis kō*) āp nē bulāyā thā?
What was the name of the person (*whom*) you invited?

وہ لوگ کتنے بجے آئیں گے جنہیں (جن کو) آپ نے بلایا ہے -
vo lōg kitnē bajē āēṁ gē, *jinhēṁ* (*jin kō*) āp nē bulāyā hai?
When are the people (*whom*) you invited coming?

jis is the form of **jō** used in relative adverbial phrases, which are always oblique (see Table 25, §1102):

جس وقت	**jis vaqt**, at the time that (§1116)
جس جگہ	**jis jagah**, in the place that (§1110)
جس طرف	**jis taraf**, (in) the direction that (§1111)
جس طرح	**jis tarah**, in the way that (§1119)

RELATIVE ADJECTIVES

Relative adjectives express a similarity or comparison between nouns in the relative and correlative clauses. In English they are often translated by words or phrases that describe similarity/comparison: 'such', 'like', 'just like', 'as'. They agree with the noun they qualify.

1108 jaisā

In the nominative case **jaisā** may be used adjectivally, qualifying a noun ('like', 'similar to') or adverbially, qualifying a verb ('as'). The oblique case, **jaisē**, is also used adverbially and is described in §1117.

جیسا قالین آپ کے پاس ہے ویسا ہی مجھے چاہئے
***jaisā* qālīn āp kē pās hai, *vaisā hī* mujhē cāhiē**
I want a carpet *just like* the one you have.

جیسا کرو گے ویسا بھرو گے -
***jaisā* karō gē, vaisā bharō gē**
As you sow, so shall you reap (as you do, so will you fill).

When **jaisā** expresses the equivalency of two things ('two of the same') the correlative word (**vaisā**) may be omitted.

میں آپ کے جیسا قالین چاہتا ہیں -
maiṁ āp kē *jaisā* qālīn cāhtā hūṁ [1]
I want a carpet *like* yours.

وہ بلی شیر جیسی ہے -
vo billī śēr *jaisī* hai
That cat is *like* a tiger.

jaisā-taisā means 'ordinary' and is a euphemism for 'disgraceful'. Some compounds formed with **taisā** are used in idioms.

جیسے کا تیسا
jaisē kā taisā
verbatim, unaltered

جیسے کو تیسا
jaisē kō taisā
tit for tat

[1] The oblique **kē** is hard to explain here, but keeps the sentence apart from **āp kā jaisā qālīn**, which would mean 'a carpet like you'.

جیسے تیسے
jaisē-taisē
by hook or by crook

کمبخت نے جیسے تیسے ویزا لے لیا اور باہر چلا گیا ۔
kambaxt nē *jaisē taisē* vīzā lē liyā aur bāhar calā gayā
The wretch got a visa *by fair means or foul,* and went abroad.

1109 jitnā

jitnā refers to amount or quantity, and is often used in comparisons.

جتنی دھوپ پاکستان میں ہوتی ہے ، یہاں اُتنی نہیں ہوتی ۔
***jitnī* dhūp pākistān mēṁ hōtī hai, yahāṁ *utnī* nahīṁ hōtī**
There is not *as much* sunlight here *as* there is in Pakistan.

In sentences with **jitnā**, the correlative clause more often comes in first place.

شہر میں بیروزگاروں کی تعداد اُتنی نہیں ، جتنی دیہات میں ہے ۔
śahar mēṁ bērōzgārōṁ kī tādād *utnī* nahīṁ, *jitnī* dēhāt mēṁ hai
In the city the number of unemployed is not *as much as* in the countryside.

When the amount or quantity is identical in both clauses, the correlative (**utnā**) may be omitted.

جتنے ملیں ، لے آؤ ۔
***jitnē* milēṁ, lē āō**
Bring *as many as* may be available.

RELATIVE ADVERBS OF PLACE

1110 jahāṁ, jis jagah

jahāṁ and **jis jagah** locate the subjects of the relative and correlative clauses in the same place (symmetry of place). In English this is rendered by words or phrases like: 'where ... there', 'the same place as'.

جہاں صنعتی ترقّی ہوتی ہے وہاں بیروزگاری کم ہوتی ہے ۔
***jahāṁ* sanatī taraqqī hōtī hai, vahāṁ bērōzgārī kam hōtī hai**
Where industrial development exists, there is less unemployment.

The preceding sentence is based on two simple sentences:

وہاں صنعتی ترقّی ہوتی ہے - وہاں بیروزگاری کم ہوتی ہے - ←

vahāṁ **sanatī taraqqī hōtī hai.** ***vahāṁ*** **bērōzgārī kam hōtī hai**

There is industrial development there. *There* is less unemployment there.

جس جگہ آپ کا نیا مکان ہے اُس جگہ باغ ہے نہ ؟

jis jagah **āp kā nayā makān hai,** ***us jagah*** **bāγ hai na?**

There is a park *at the same place* your new house is, isn't there?

1111 jidhar, jis taraf

jidhar and **jis taraf** orient the subjects of the relative and correlative clauses in the same direction (symmetry of direction). This can be translated by words or phrases like 'where', 'the same way (as)'.

جدھر آپ جائیں گے (اُدھر) میں بھی آؤں گی -

jidhar **āp jāēṁ gē (*udhar*) maiṁ bhī āūṁ gī**

I shall go (come) *where* you may go.

جس طرف سے آئے ہیں ، اُس طرف واپس چلیں -

jis taraf **sē āē haiṁ,** ***us taraf*** **vāpas calēṁ**

You should go back *the same way* you came.

The preceding sentence is based on two simple sentences:

(آپ) اُس طرف سے آئے ہیں - (آپ) اُس طرف واپس چلیں - ←

(āp) ***us taraf*** **sē āē haiṁ. (āp)** ***us taraf*** **vāpas calēṁ**

You came from *that way*. You should go back *that way*.

RELATIVE ADVERBS OF TIME

1112 jab

Clauses introduced by **jab** ... **tab** locate the subjects of the relative and correlative clauses at the same or a close time (symmetry of time).

جب بارش ختم ہوئی تب سب لوگ چلے گئے -

jab **bāriś xatm hūī** ***tab*** **sab lōg calē gaē**

When the rain finished, (*only then*) everybody left.

Clauses introduced by **jab** ... **tō** often express a relation of temporal sequentiality.

جب بارش ختم ہوئی تو سب لوگ چلے گئے ۔

***jab* bāriś xatm hūī *tō* sab lōg calē gaē**

When (after) the rain finished, everybody left.

جب ہم پہنچیں گے تو پھاٹک بند ہو چکا ہو گا ۔

***jab* ham pahuṁcēṁ gē, *tō* phāṭak band hō cukā hō gā**

When we arrive, the gate will already be locked.

If the second clause begins with **tō**, **jab** is sometimes deleted in the first clause.

عورت نے باہر آ کر دروازہ کھولا تو بڑھئی نے جُھک کر سلام کیا ۔

aurat nē bāhar ā kar darvāza khōlā *tō* baṛhaī nē jhuk kar salām kiyā

(*When*) the woman came out and opened the door, the carpenter bowed and greeted (her). (Narang, *Readings*)

1113 jab sē, jab tak

The postpositions **sē** and **tak** may be added to **jab** to express duration.

jab sē expresses the duration or extent of time from a specific point ('since').

جب سے حامد شہر گیا تب سے نوکری ڈھونڈ رہا ہے ۔

***jab sē* hāmid śahar gayā, *tab sē* naukarī ḍhūṁḍ rahā hai**

Since Hamid went to the city, (he) has been looking for employment.

The correlative phrase **tab sē** may be omitted, but the sentence is less idiomatic. In that case the pronoun **vo** introduces the correlative clause.

جب سے حامد شہر گیا وہ نوکری ڈھونڈ رہا ہے ۔

***jab sē* hāmid śahar gayā, vo naukarī ḍhūṁḍ rahā hai**

Since Hamid went to the city, he has been looking for employment.

جب سے میرا بیٹا چلا گیا میں گھر میں اکیلی ہوں ۔

***jab sē* mērā bēṭā calā gayā, maiṁ ghar mēṁ akēlī hūṁ**

Since my son left, I am alone in the house.

jab tak expresses the duration or extent of time till a specific point ('as long as'). The correlative phrase is usually omitted.

جب تک ہم جیتے ہیں ، کسی بات کا کھٹکا مت کر ۔

***jab tak* ham jītē haiṁ, kisī bāt kā khaṭkā mat kar**

As long as we're alive, don't be anxious about anything. (Prem Chand, *Gōdān*)

1114 **jab tak** + negative, 'until', 'unless'

jab tak + NEGATIVE, 'until', 'unless' introduces a relative subordinate clause. The negative is not translated in English. The verb in the relative phrase normally matches the tense of the verb in the correlative phrase, but may be subjunctive if the correlative verb is in a non-perfective tense.

جب تک حامد کو نوکری نہیں (نہ) ملے گی وہ ڈھونڈتا رہے گا -
***jab tak* hāmid kō naukarī *nahīṁ* (*na*) milē gī vo ḍhūṁḍtā rahē gā**
Until Hamid gets employment, he will keep looking.
(*As long as* Hamid does *not* get work, he will keep looking.)

جب تک تم مدد نہ کرو میں یہ کام کیسے کر سکتا ہوں ؟
***jab tak* tum madad *na* karō, maiṁ ye kām kaisē kar saktā hūṁ?**
Unless you help, how can I do this job?

1115 **jab ke**, 'while'

Followed by the conjunction **ke**, **jab** expresses simultaneity ('while'). Here **jab** has no relative function; **jab ke** is a coordinating conjunction.

شادی میں تاجو ڈھولک بجاتی تھی جب کہ عورتیں گاتی تھیں -
šādī mēṁ tājō ḍhōlak bajātī thī *jab ke* aurtēṁ gātī thīṁ
In the wedding, Tajo played the drum *while* the women sang.

1116 **jis vaqt**

Clauses introduced by **jis vaqt ... (us vaqt)** locate the subjects of the relative and correlative clauses at precisely the same time.

جس وقت چوری کا پتہ چلا ، اُس وقت چور بھاگ چکا تھا -
***jis vaqt* cōrī kā pata calā, *us vaqt* cōr bhāg cukā thā**
At the time the theft was discovered, the thief had (already) fled.

RELATIVE ADVERBS OF MANNER

Although one might expect relative adverbs of manner to express symmetry of manner, only **jis tarah ... us tarah** clearly shows this. The other relative adverbs of manner, **jaisē** and **jūṁ**, may show similarity ('as', 'like'), but often they function as simple adverbs of manner or even as conjunctions.

1117 jaisē

The oblique case of **jaisā**, **jaisē**, is used alone, without the correlative (**vaisā**), meaning 'like', 'as'.

جیسے آپ نے کہا ، ہمیں اِس کام کو پورا کرنا ہے -
***jaisē* āp nē kahā, hamēṁ is kām kō pūrā karnā hai**
As you said, we must complete this work.

Used adverbially, with the meaning 'as if', 'as though', a correlative is possible, but here it is not the 'far' **vaisā**, but the 'near' **aisā**. Here, **jaisē** functions as a conjunction and not as a relative word.

وہ ایسے چلّایا جیسے کوئی اُسے قتل کر رہا ہے -
vo (*aisē*) cillāyā, *jaisē* kōī usē qatl kar rahā hai
He shouted *as though* someone were killing him.

Compare وہ ایسے چلّایا کہ کوئی اُسے قتل کر رہا ہے -
vo *aisē* cillāyā, *ke* kōī usē qatl kar rahā hai
He shouted *as though* someone were killing him.

1118 jaisē hī

jaisē hī may be used (a) as a relative adverb, meaning 'exactly as', or (b) as a conjunction, meaning 'as soon as'. As a relative adverb, it takes the correlative **vaisē hī**. As a conjunction, it occurs without the correlative.

جمیل جیسے ہی کہیں گے ، تمہیں ویسے ہی کرنا ہے -
jamīl *jaisē hī* kahēṁ gē, tumhēṁ vaisē hī karnā hai
You are to do (it) *exactly as* Jamil tells you.

جیسے ہی دن نکلا گھوڑے سفید چوہیوں میں بدل گئے -
***jaisē hī* din niklā, ghōṛē safēd cūhiyōṁ mēṁ badal gaē**
As soon as the sun rose, the horses changed into white mice.

1119 jis tarah

Clauses introduced by **jis tarah ...** (**us tarah**) show actions or states in the relative and correlative clauses which happen in the same manner (symmetry of manner). The correlative word is often followed by the emphatic particle **hī**.

اُستاد جس طرح سبق پڑھتا تھا ، طالب علم اُسی طرح دوہراتے تھے -
ustād *jis tarah* sabaq paṛhtā thā, tālib ilm *usī tarah* dohrātē thē
The pupils were repeating the lesson *exactly as* the teacher recited it.

1120 jūṁ

jūṁ occuring by itself is obsolete. It occurs followed by **hī**, and in compounds (**jūṁ tyūṁ, jūṁ jūṁ, jūṁ kā tyūṁ**). The 'equivalent' force of these compounds is rather weak. The following examples illustrate the meanings of individual compounds.

جیوں ہی رشیدہ وہاں پہنچی وہ فوت ہو گیا -
***jyūṁ hī* rašīda vahāṁ pahuṁcī vo faut hō gayā**
As soon as Rashida reached there he passed away.

میں نے اُن کے الفاظ جوں کے تیوں لکھ لیے -
maiṁ nē un kē alfāz *jūṁ kē tyūṁ* likh liyē
I wrote down his words *verbatim* (just as they were spoken).

میں نے جوں تیوں ریل گاڑی کا ٹکٹ لے ہی لیا -
maiṁ nē *jūṁ tyūṁ* rēl gāṛī kā ṭikaṭ lē hī liyā
Somehow or another I got the train ticket.

jūṁ jūṁ collocates with the progressive IMPERFECTIVE PARTICIPLE + **jānā** construction (§627):

جوں جوں گھر کے قریب آتا گیا ، میرا اندیشہ بڑھتا گیا -
***jūṁ jūṁ* ghar kē qarīb ātā gayā, mērā andēša baṛhtā gayā**
The closer (*more* close) I came to home, *the more* my anxiety grew.

INDEFINITE COMPOUNDS AND REPEATED RELATIVES

1121 Relative words followed by indefinite words, '-ever'

The relative words **jō**, **jahāṁ** and **jab** may be followed by their indefinite counterparts. The indefinite word adds the meaning '-ever'. These indefinite compounds are similar in meaning to relative words followed by **bhī** (§1122).

jō kōī, 'whoever', 'anyone who'

جو کوئی نیک کام کرے گا پھل پائے گا ۔
***jō kōī* nēk kām karē gā, phal pāē gā**
Whoever does good deeds will reap the reward.

جو کوئی جلدی جانا چاہے اُسے اجازت لینی پڑے گی ۔
***jō kōī* jaldī jānā cāhē, usē ijāzat lēnī paṛē gī**
Anyone who wants to leave early must get permission.

جس کسی کے پاس دفتر کی چابی ہو ، اُسے واپس کر دینی چاہئے ۔
***jis kisī* kē pās daftar kī cābī hō, usē vāpas kar dēnī cāhiē**
Whoever may have a key to the office, (he) should return it.

Modifying a noun, **jō kōī** means 'whatever', 'whichever'.

جو کوئی تجویز میں پیش کرتا ہوں ، وہ اعتراض کرتی ہے ۔
***jō kōī* tajvīz maiṁ pēś kartā hūṁ, vo etirāz kartī hai**
Whatever suggestion I make, she raises an objection.

jō kuch, 'whatever'

جو کچھ میں کرتا ہوں ، وہ اعتراض کرتی ہے ۔
***jō kuch* maiṁ kartā hūṁ, vo etirāz kartī hai**
Whatever I do, she raises an objection.

jahāṁ kahīṁ, 'wherever', 'everywhere'

جہاں کہیں ہم نے دیکھا برف ہی برف دکھائی دی ۔
***jahāṁ kahīṁ* ham nē dēkhā baraf hī baraf dikhāī dī**
Everywhere we looked, nothing but snow could be seen.

jab kabhī, 'whenever'

جب کبھی وہ یہاں آتا ہے ، وہ ہمارے پاس رہتا ہے ۔
***jab kabhī* vo yahāṁ ātā hai, vo hamārē pās rahtā hai**
Whenever he comes here he stays with us.

1122 Relative words followed by **bhī**, '-ever'

When followed by **bhī**, the relative words **jō**, **jahāṁ**, **jab** and **jaisā**, acquire indefinite meanings: 'whoever', 'wherever', 'no matter where', 'whenever', 'no matter when', 'however'. These phrases are similar to compounds of relative words followed by indefinite words (§1121), but are slightly more emphatic.

جو بھی نیک کام کرے گا پھل پائے گا ۔
***jō bhī* nēk kām karē gā, phal pāē gā**
Whoever does good deeds will reap the reward.

تم جہاں بھی جاؤ گے کامیاب ہو گے ۔
tum *jahāṁ bhī* jāō gē kāmyāb hō gē
Wherever you go you will be successful.

جب بھی میں وہاں جاتا ہوں ، دودھ نہیں ملتا ۔
***jab bhī* maiṁ vahāṁ jātā hūṁ, dūdh nahīṁ miltā**
No matter when I go there, milk is not available.

جیسے بھی (جیسا بھی) آپ چاہیں کر سکتے ہیں ۔
***jaisē bhī* (jaisā bhī) āp cāhēṁ, kar saktē haiṁ**
You can do it *however* you wish.

1123 Repeated relative words

Relative pronouns and adverbs may be repeated. The repetition has distributive force, and is in some cases similar to the use of indefinite compounds (§1121).

جو جو عجائب گھر کی سیر کرنا چاہیے ، اپنا نام لکھوا دیں ۔
***jō jō* ajāib ghar kī sair karnā cāhēṁ, apnā nām likhvā dēṁ**
Those who wish to tour the museum, please sign up (get your name written).

Compare جو کوئی عجائب گھر کی سیر کرنا چاہیے...
***jō koī* ajāib ghar kī sair karnā cāhēṁ ...**
Anyone who wishes to tour the museum ...

اُس نے جس جس ملک کا سفر کیا ، وہاں کا قومی لباس جمع کر لیا ۔
us nē *jis jis* mulk kā safar kiyā, vahāṁ kā qaumī libās jamā kar liyā
He collected the national dress from *each* country to *which* he travelled.

جہاں جہاں دیکھا گلاب ہی گلاب تھے ۔
***jahāṁ jahāṁ* dēkhā gulāb hī gulāb thē**
Wherever (we) looked, there was nothing but roses.

12 PARTICLES, INTERJECTIONS AND CONJUNCTIONS

PARTICLES

1201 The contrastive emphatic particle tō

In main clauses, **tō** emphasizes the preceding noun or verb and contrasts it with something else.

وہ اُردو پڑھے گا ۔
vo urdū paṛhē gā
He will study Urdu. (simple statement)

وہ تو اُردو پڑھے گا ۔
***vo tō* urdū paṛhē gā**
He will study Urdu. (Contrast: the other students may not.)

وہ اُردو تو پڑھے گا ۔
vo *urdū tō* paṛhē gā
He will study *Urdu.* (Contrast: he may not study other subjects.)

وہ اُردو پڑھے گا تو لیکن امتحان نہیں دے گا ۔
vo urdū *paṛhē gā tō* lēkin imtihān nahīṁ dē gā
He will *study* Urdu, *of course*, but he won't take the examination.

Sometimes the use of **tō** in main clauses is a prompt for confirmation.

آپ اچّھے تو ہیں ؟
āp acchē *tō* haiṁ?
You are well, *I presume*?

1202 tō introducing result clauses in conditional sentences

tō introduces the result clause of conditional sentences (see §609). **agar**, 'if' may be omitted in the condition clause, but **tō** only rarely, so that many conditional sentences are shown not by **agar**, but by **tō** in the result clause.

اگر فرصت ملی تو (میں) کل آپ کے ساتھ جاؤں گا ۔
agar fursat milī tō (maiṁ) kal āp kē sāth jāūṁ gā
If I get free time, (I) will go with you tomorrow.

کل فرصت ملی تو (میں) آپ کے ساتھ جاؤں گا ۔
kal fursat milī tō (maiṁ) āp kē sāth jāūṁ gā
If I get free time tomorrow, (I) will go with you.

فرصت ملتی تو جاتا ۔
fursat miltī tō jātā
If I had free time, (I) would go.

1203 nahīṁ tō

The phrase **nahīṁ tō**, 'otherwise', links a condition clause consisting of an injunction, and a result clause describing the consequences of failure to obey it.

پڑھو نہیں تو ناکام ہو جاؤ گے !
paṛhō, *nahīṁ tō* nākām hō jāō gē!
Study, *otherwise* you will fail!

tō is sometimes omitted:

چپ رہو نہیں مار کھاؤ گے !
cup rahō, *nahīṁ* mār khāō gē!
Keep quiet, *or* you will get a beating!

1204 tō introducing correlative clauses

tō may introduce the correlative clause in relative sentences beginning with **jab**. See §1112.

1205 The exclusive emphatic particle hī

hī emphasizes the preceding word and excludes something else (which may not be expressed).

احمد قلعہ دیکھنا چاہتا تھا ۔
ahmad qila dēkhnā cāhtā thā
Ahmad wanted to see the fort. (simple statement)

احمد ہی قلعہ دیکھنا چاہتا تھا ، ہم تو ہوٹل واپس آنا چاہتے تھے -
***ahmad hī* qila dēkhnā cāhtā thā, ham tō hōṭal vāpas ānā cāhtē thē**
It is Ahmad who wanted to see the fort; we wanted to return to the hotel.

احمد قلعہ ہی دیکھنا چاہتا تھا ، بادشاہی مسجد نہیں -
ahmad *qila hī* dēkhnā cāhtā thā, bādśāhī masjid nahīṁ
Ahmad wanted to see *the fort*, not the royal mosque.

1206 Sequences of nouns or pronouns + postpositions + hī

If **hī** is added to a noun or pronoun which is followed by a postposition, **hī** usually follows the postposition, but may separate the noun/pronoun and the postposition. This is to some extent a matter of personal style.

احمد نے ہی ہم کو روکے رکھا -
***ahmad nē hī* ham kō rōkē rakhā**
It is Ahmad who delayed us.

احمد ہی نے ہم کو روکے رکھا -
***ahmad hī nē* ham kō rōkē rakhā**
It is Ahmad who delayed us.

The pronouns **maiṁ** and **tū** (which do not take the oblique case before **nē**) may not be separated from **nē** by **hī**.

میں نے ہی یہ کام کیا -
***maiṁ nē hī* ye kām kiyā**
I'm the one who did this work

تو نے ہی میری مدد کی -
***tū nē hī* mērī madad kī**
You are the one who helped me.

The pronouns **āp**, **tum** and **ham** may be separated from **nē** by **hī**. When **tum** and **ham** are oblique, it is preferable however to use the suffixal form of **hī** (§1207).

ہمیں نے دروازہ بند کیا -
***hamīṁ nē* darvāza band kiyā**
We closed the door (preferred).

Also: ہم ہی نے دروازہ بند کیا -
***ham hī nē* darvāza band kiyā**
We closed the door.

1207 hī occurring as a suffix

hī, or its variant forms **ī** ~ **(h)īṁ**, may occur as a suffix with:

(a) the oblique forms of all the pronouns except **āp**;
(b) the nominative forms of **vo** and **ye**;
(c) the adverbs of time **ab**, **tab**, **kab** and **jab**;
(d) the adverbs of place **yahāṁ**, **vahāṁ**, **kahāṁ** and **jahāṁ**.

These bound constructions may not be separated by postpositions. Table 27, p. 213 shows the suffixing of **hī** (~ **ī** ~ -**(h)īṁ**) to certain personal pronouns.

Table 28, p. 214 shows the suffixing of **hī** to certain adverbs. Note that when **hī** is suffixed to the interrogative adverbs **kab** and **kahāṁ**, it makes indefinites.

Table 27: Personal pronouns + bound forms of **hī**

		NOMINATIVE + hī		OBLIQUE + hī	
SINGULAR					
1st person	(میں ہی	**maiṁ hī**, I)	مجھی	**mujhī**
2nd person	(تو ہی	**tū hī**, you)	تجھی	**tujhī**
3rd person	وہی	**vahī**, he, she, it	اُسی	**usī**
	یہی	**yahī**, he, she, it	اِسی	**isī**
PLURAL					
1st person	(ہم ہی	**ham hī**, we)	ہمیں	**hamīṁ**
2nd person	(تم ہی	**tum hī**, you)	تمہیں ~ تمھیں	**tumhīṁ**
	(آپ ہی	**āp hī**, you)	(آپ ہی	**āp hī**)
3rd person	وہی	**vahī**, they	اُنہیں ~ اُنھیں	**unhīṁ**
	یہی	**yahī**, they	اِنہیں ~ اِنھیں	**inhīṁ**

(Items shown in parentheses: **hī** does not occur as a suffix with this pronoun.)

Examples

میں ہی فیصلہ کروں گا ۔
***maiṁ hī* faisalā karūṁ gā**
I'm the one who will make the decision.

مجھی کو فیصلہ کرنا ہے ۔
***mujhī kō* faisalā karnā hai**
I'm the one who has to make the decision.

مجھی پر یہ ذمّہ داری ہے ۔
***mujhī* par ye zimmēdārī hai**
This is *my* responsibility (lit. the responsibility is *on me*).

اُنہیں کو ماننا پڑے گا ۔
***unhīṁ kō* mānnā paṛē gā**
They must comply.

آپ ہی کی حفاظت کی بات ہے ۔
***āp hī kī* hifāzat kī bāt hai**
It is a matter of *your* safety.

Also: آپ کی ہی حفاظت کی بات ہے ۔
āp *kī hī* hifāzat kī bāt hai
It is a matter of *your* safety.

However, if the alternate forms of **kō** (§210) are used, **hī** occurs as a separate word, not as a suffix.

مجھے ہی یہ فیصلہ کرنا ہے ۔
***mujhē hī* ye faisalā karnā hai**
I have to make this decision.

اُنہیں ہی ماننا پڑے گا ۔
***unhēṁ hī* mānnā paṛē gā**
They must comply.

Table 28: Adverbs + bound forms of **hī**

اب **ab**, now	تب **tab**, then	کب **kab**, when	جب **jab**, when
ابھی **abhī**, right now	تبھی **tabhī**, just then	کبھی **kabhī**, ever	جبھی **jabhī**, as soon as
یہاں **yahāṁ**, here	وہاں **vahāṁ**, there	کہاں **kahāṁ**, where	جہاں **jahāṁ**, where
یہیں **yahīṁ**, right here	وہیں **vahīṁ**, right there	کہیں **kahīṁ**, somewhere	جہیں (**jahīṁ**, in the very place where (obsolete)

Examples

کیا آپ نے کبھی اونٹ پر سواری کی ؟
kyā āp nē *kabhī* ūṁṭ par savārī kī?
Have you *ever* ridden on a camel?

کہیں ایک سونے کا محل ہے ۔
***kahīṁ* ēk sōnē kā mahal hai**
Somewhere there is a golden palace.

آپ کی عینک وہیں میز پر رکھی ہے ۔
āp kī ainak *vahīṁ* mēz par rakhī hai
Your glasses are (placed) *right there* on the table.

1208 kahīṁ expressing improbability or apprehension

kahīṁ may be delexicalized and used with **agar**, or in place of **agar**, to express improbability. **kahīṁ ... na** expresses apprehension. See §425.

1209 Oblique imperfect participle + hī, 'as soon as'

OBLIQUE IMPERFECT PARTICIPLE + **hī** means 'as soon as'. See §904.

1210 bhī as inclusive emphatic particle, 'even'

The use of **bhī** as a modal adverb meaning 'also', 'too' is described in §418. Note that whereas **tō** is contrastive and **hī** is exclusive, **bhī** is inclusive.

میں بھی فیصلہ کروں گا ۔
maiṁ *bhī* faisalā karūṁ gā
I'll *also* make a decision.

Compare میں ہی فیصلہ کروں گا ۔
***maiṁ hī* faisalā karūṁ gā**
I'm the one who will make the decision.

میں تو فیصلہ کروں گا (دوسرے کریں نہ کریں) ۔
***maiṁ tō* faisala karūṁ gā (dūsrē karēṁ na karēṁ)**
I'll make a decision (the others may or may not).

bhī also occurs as an emphatic particle following a noun. It emphasizes the comprehensiveness of the idea expressed in the sentence, and is usually translated as 'even'.

بچّہ بھی یہ جانتا ہے ۔
baccā *bhī* ye jāntā hai
Even a child knows this.

ایسی غریبی میں بھی وہ مایوس نہیں ہوا ۔
aisī γarībī mēṁ *bhī* vo māyūs nahīṁ hūā
Even in such poverty, he didn't despair.

Following a verb, it emphasizes it and expresses the speaker's impatience or exasperation.

اب چپ کرو بھی !
ab cup karō *bhī*!
Now *just* keep quiet!

1211 Emphatic and concessive phrases ending in bhī

bhī may follow **phir**, 'then'; **aur**, 'and'; **tō** (§1201) and **par**, 'on'.

phir bhī, 'even so'

غریبی سخت تھی ، پھر بھی وہ مایوس نہیں ہوا -
γarībī saxt thī, *phir bhī* vo māyūs nahīṁ hūā
The poverty was extreme, *even so* he didn't despair.

aur bhī

Qualifying a noun, **aur bhī** means 'even more'.

اور بھی نقصان
***aur bhī* nuqsān**
even more damage

Qualifying an adjective, **aur bhī** means 'even ... -er', 'even more'.

اور بھی سخت نقصان
***aur bhī* saxt nuqsān**
even more severe damage

tō bhī shows contrast and means 'still', 'nevertheless'. It is used like a coordinating conjunction, similar to **phir bhī**.

درد بہت تھا تو بھی وہ نہیں رویا -
dard bahut thā *tō bhī* vo nahīṁ rōyā
The pain was severe, *nevertheless* he didn't cry.

1212 hī nahīṁ ... bhī in parallel clauses

Parallel clauses with **hī nahīṁ** in the first clause and **bhī** in the second clause express an augmentation of the idea in the first clause: 'not only ... but'.

اُس نے خط ہی نہیں بھیجا ، فون بھی کیا -
us nē xat *hī nahīṁ* bhējā, fōn *bhī* kiyā
He *not only* sent a letter, *but* called as well.

1213 Oblique infinitive + par bhī, 'despite'

When **bhī** follows a phrase consisting of OBLIQUE INFINITIVE + **par** it shows strong contrast and means 'even after', 'despite'.

پیسے دینے پر بھی یہاں بجلی نہیں ملتی -
paisē *dēnē par bhī* yahāṁ bijlī nahīṁ miltī
Despite paying money, (we) don't get electricity here.

1214 Indefinite pronouns + bhī, 'at all'

bhī is used as an emphatic particle after the indefinite pronouns **kōī** and **kuch**, most commonly in negative sentences.

kōī bhī, 'anyone at all'

یہاں کوئی بھی نہیں آتا -
yahāṁ *kōī bhī* nahīṁ ātā
No one at all comes here.

kuch bhī, 'anything at all'

کچھ بھی ہو
kuch bhī hō
Come what may.

یہاں کچھ بھی نہیں ملتا -
yahāṁ *kuch bhī* nahīṁ miltā
Nothing at all is available here.

1215 Relative words followed by bhī, '-ever'

The relative words **jō, jahāṁ, jab** and **jaisā**, followed by **bhī**, acquire the meanings 'whoever'; 'wherever', 'no matter where'; 'whenever', 'no matter when'; 'however'. See §1122.

1216 The adjectival particle sā (~ sē ~ sī)

Adjectival phrases are also formed by adding the particle **sā** to adjectives, nouns and pronouns. The particle **sā** is discussed in detail in §310.

INTERJECTIONS

1217 Vocative interjections

Vocative interjections include **ō, ai**, 'o'; and **arē** (f. **arī**), 'oh', 'hey!'.

او رکشے والے !
ō rikśē vālē!
O rickshaw driver!

ارے آپ یہاں ، آپ کب دہلی آئے ؟
arē āp yahāṁ, āp kab dehlī āē?
Oh, you (are) here! When did you come to Delhi?

1218 Free interjections

Free interjections may stand alone as a sentence, or introduce a sentence. A list of the more common includes **vāh** and **śābāś** 'bravo', which express applause; **ō hō** 'oh no!', **ūī** 'heaven forbid (only in women's speech)' and **hāē** 'alas'.

واہ واہ آپ نے تو کمال کر دیا !
***vāh vāh,* āp nē tō kamāl kar diyā!**
Bravo, you have worked a miracle!

او ہو میں بٹوا بھول گیا !
***ō hō,* maiṁ baṭvā bhūl gayā!**
Oh no, (I) forgot (my) wallet!

ہائے ! اب دادی نہیں رہیں !
***hāē*! ab dādī nahīṁ rahīṁ!**
Alas! Grandmother is no more!

Urdu also has many free interjections with religious content, such as **inśāallāh**, 'if God wills' and **bismillāh**, 'in the name of God'. See Chapter 16.

LEADERS AND TAGS

Leaders and tags provide clues about the speaker's mood or intent. Leaders introduce sentences, and are often secondary meanings of common words. They include **kyōṁ** 'well', **kyōṁ na** 'how about...', and **acchā** 'oh', 'well'). Tags conclude a sentence and comment on it. Two common tags are **sahī** and **nā**.

1219 The leaders **kyōṁ and kyōṁ na**

The basic meaning of **kyōṁ** is 'why?'. As a leader, it asks for the other person's reaction to an idea.

کیوں بیٹی ! تو ہمارے ساتھ دعوت میں جانا پسند کرے گی ؟
***kyōṁ* bēṭī! tū hamārē sāth dāvat mēṁ jānā pasand karē gī?**
Well, daughter! Would you like to go to the party with us?

The basic meaning of **kyōṁ na** is 'why not?'. As a leader, it offers a suggestion.

کیوں نہ آج ہم چڑیا گھر جائیں ؟
***kyōṁ na* āj ham ciṛiyā ghar jāēṁ?**
How about going to the zoo today?

1220 **acchā** introducing sentences

The basic meaning of **acchā** is 'good'. As a leader, it expresses surprise and possibly reproof.

اچّھا ! آپ یہاں بیٹھے سو رہے ہیں ! (پڑھنا چاہئے تھا -)
***acchā*! āp yahāṁ baiṭhē sō rahē haiṁ! (paṛhnā cāhiē thā)**
Oh! You're sitting here asleep! ((You) should have studied.)

اچّھا اچّھا ! تو آج آپ کی سالگرہ ہے ! (بتانا چاہئے تھا -)
***acchā acchā*! tō āj āp kī sālgirah hai! (batānā cāhiē thā)**
Well well! Today is your birthday! ((You) should have told (me).)

1221 The concessive tag **sahī**

sahī, 'very well', 'all right'(to be distinguished from **sahīh**, 'right', 'true') is used predicatively and concedes the statement preceding it. In translation the whole sentence must be taken into account.

ایسا ہی سہی -
aisā hī sahī
All right, let it be.

جیسا تم چاہو ویسا سہی -
jaisā tum cāhō vaisā *sahī*
Very well, as you wish.

عشق مجھ کو نہیں وحشت ہی سہی
میری وحشت تیری شہرت ہی سہی
iśq mujh kō nahīṁ vahśat hī sahī
mērī vahśat tērī śohrat hī sahī
All right, I am not merely in love, but in a wild frenzy,
At least concede that you owe your fame to my frenzy (Ghālib)

sahī may be added to **tō**.

وہ آئے گا تو سہی -
vo āē gā tō *sahī*
He's coming *all right* (but I don't know when).

1222 The rhetorical tag nā

The tag **nā** has two functions.
At the end of a statement, it prompts for a reply:

یہ داستان دلچسپ ہے نا !	آپ آ رہے ہیں نا ۔
ye dāstān dilcasp hai *nā*!	**āp ā rahē haiṁ *nā*?**
This tale is interesting, *isn't it!*	You are coming, *aren't you?*

nā makes courteous questions from courteous formal requests ending in **gā**:

چائے پیجئے گا ۔	→	چائے پیجئے گا نا ۔
cāē pījiē gā		**cāē pījiē gā *nā***
Please take tea.		*Would you* please take tea?

Used at the end of a request, it makes it more insistent:

ہمارے گھر تشریف لائیے نا !	بیٹھو نا ! کیوں اِتنی جلدی جا رہے ہو ؟
hamārē ghar taśrīf lāiyē *nā*!	**baiṭhō nā! kyōṁ itnī jaldī jā rahē hō?**
Please *do* come to our house!	Sit down! Why are you leaving so soon?

In requests, **nā** usually corresponds to the **tum**-level of request forms. But see the first sentence in the preceding set, where the formal-polite **taśrīf** makes the request respectful, while retaining some of the informality of **nā**.

CONJUNCTIONS

1223 Coordinating conjunctions

Coordinating conjunctions link two words, two phrases or two clauses of equal weight in the sentence.

aur, 'and'

میں اور آپ	ہم نے چائے پی اور پکوڑے کھائے ۔
maiṁ *aur* āp	**ham nē cāē pī *aur* pakōṛē khāē**
I *and* you	We drank tea *and* ate fritters.

aur may also be used like an adjective to qualify a noun, meaning 'other', 'more'. It often occurs in a phrase with **kuch**, 'some'.

اور چائے ڈالئے ۔	کچھ اور کپڑا دکھائیے ۔
***aur* cāē ḍāliē**	***kuch aur* kapṛā dikhāiyē**
Please pour *more* tea.	Please show me *some more* cloth.

اور کچھ کپڑا دکھائیے ۔
***aur kuch* kapṛā dikhāiyē**
Please show me *some other* cloth.

The noun may be omitted, leaving **aur** to stand as the direct object.

اور لاؤں ، بیگم صاحبہ ؟
***aur* lāūṁ, bēgam sāhiba?**
Shall I bring *more*, ma'am?

aur may be used like an adverb to qualify an adjective.

اور اچّھا کپڑا
***aur* acchā kapṛā**
even better cloth

yā, 'or'

آپ چائے پیئیں گے ، یا کافی ؟
āp cāē pīēṁ gē, *yā* kāfī?
Will you drink tea *or* coffee?

magar, lēkin, 'but'

میں کل آؤں گا مگر (لیکن) جمعے کو نہیں آ سکتا ۔
maiṁ kal āūṁ gā *magar* (*lēkin*) jumē kō nahīṁ ā saktā
I'll come tomorrow, *but* I can't come Friday.

balke, 'rather', 'on the contrary'

balke introduces a clause which contrasts with a preceding negative clause.

وہ سُست نہیں بلکہ بہت محنتی ہے ۔
vo sust nahīṁ *balke* bahut mehnatī hai
He is not lazy, *on the contrary* he is very hard-working.

jab ke, 'while', 'when', 'since'

شادی میں تاجو ڈھولک بجاتی تھی جب کہ عورتیں گاتی تھیں ۔
śādī mēṁ tājō ḍhōlak bajātī thī *jab ke* aurtēṁ gātī thīṁ
In the wedding, Tajo played the drum *while* the women sang.

جب کہ تجھ بن نہیں کوئی موجود
پھر یہ ہنگامہ اے خدا کیا ہے

jab ke tujh bin nahīṁ kōī maujūd
phir ye hangāma ai xudā kyā hai
When nobody is present except You
Then what is this fuss all about, O God (Ghalib)

jaisē hī and jab sē

The relative words **jaisā** and **jab** are used in phrases that are translated by English conjunctions. See §1118 and §1115.

1224 Correlative conjunctions

Correlative conjunctions link two clauses of equal weight. The clauses may be inclusive, asserting two things simultaneously (the 'both ... and' type); or they may be exclusive, presenting two alternatives (the 'either ... or' type).

Inclusive

bhī ... bhī, 'both ... and' links two clauses, usually with omission of the verb in the second clause.

میں بھی جاؤں گا اور آپ بھی (جائیں گے) -
maiṁ _bhī_ jāūṁ gā aur āp _bhī_ (jāēṁ gē)
Both I and you will go.

خاں صاحب سخی بھی ہیں اور مہمان نواز بھی -
xāṁ sāhib saxī _bhī_ haiṁ aur mehmān navāz _bhī_
Mr. Khan is *both* generous and hospitable.

Exclusive

yā ... yā means 'either ... or', 'whether ... or'; **na ... na**, means 'neither ... nor'. They link two clauses, usually with omission of the verb in the second clause.

میں یا دفتر میں ہوں گا یا جلسے میں -
maiṁ _yā_ daftar mēṁ hūṁ gā _yā_ jalsē mēṁ
I will *either* be in the office *or* in the meeting.

یہ کام یا میں کروں یا تم کرو ، کسی کو تو کرنا ہے -
ye kām *yā* maiṁ karūṁ *yā* tum karō, kisī kō tō karnā hai
Whether I do this work *or* you do, someone must do it.

وہ نہ دفتر میں ہے نہ جلسے میں -
vo *na* daftar mēṁ hai, *na* jalsē mēṁ
He is *neither* in the office *nor* in the meeting.

kyā ... kyā links two contrasting adjectives or nouns, which follow a main clause and explicate it.

موت کے سامنے سب برابر ہیں کیا دولتمند کیا غریب -
maut kē sāmnē sab barābar haiṁ, *kyā* daulatmand, *kyā* ɣarīb
In the face of death all are equal, *whether* rich *or* poor.

1225 Causal conjunctions

kyōṁke, 'because'

kyōṁke introduces the answer to a question.

کیوں نہیں آئے ؟—کیونکہ بارش ہو رہی تھی -
kyōṁ nahīṁ āē?—*kyōṁke* bāriś hō rahī thī
Why didn't (you) come?—*Because* it was raining.

cūṁke, 'since', 'because'

When **cūṁke** is used in the causal clause, **is liē** usually introduces the conclusive clause.

چونکہ بارش ہو رہی تھی ، اِس لئے وہ نہیں آئے -
***cūṁke* bāriś hō rahī thī, is liē vo nahīṁ āē**
Since it's raining, they haven't come.

cunāṁce, 'so', 'therefore'

پل ٹوٹ گیا ، چنانچہ بس نہیں آ سکتی -
pul ṭūṭ gayā, *cunāṁce* bas nahīṁ ā saktī
The bridge broke, *so* the bus can't come.

1226 Concessive conjunctions

agarce, 'although', 'even though'

When **agarce** introduces concessive clauses, **phir bhī**, 'nevertheless' usually introduces the conclusion, but is often not translated. The concessive clause stands first in the sentence.

اگرچہ سردی آ گئی ہے پھر بھی پنکھے چل رہے ہیں -
***agarce* sardī ā gaī hai phir bhī pankhē cal rahē haiṁ**
Even though winter has come, the fans are still running.

halāṁke, 'even though'

halāṁke introduces concessive clauses, which may stand first or second in the sentence.

حالانکہ سردی آ گئی ہے پھر بھی پنکھے چل رہے ہیں -
***halāṁke* sardī ā gaī hai phir bhī pankhē cal rahē haiṁ**
Even though winter has come, the fans are still running.

مجھے کوٹ خریدنا پڑا حالانکہ وہ خاصا مہنگا تھا -
mujhē kōṭ xarīdnā paṛā *halāṁke* vo xāsā mahaṁgā thā
I had to buy a coat *even though* it was quite expensive.

1227 Subordinating conjunctions

Subordinating conjunctions introduce a subordinate clause, often with a subjunctive verb (§608), or the simple irrealis (§622).

agar, 'if'

agar introduces the condition clause of conditional sentences (described in detail under §609).

اگر بارش ہوئی تو میں اندر رہوں گی -
***agar* bāriś hūī, tō maiṁ andar rahūṁ gī**
If it rains, I'll stay inside.

tā ke, 'so that' and baśartēke, 'provided that', 'on the condition that'

These subordinating conjunctions take the subjunctive.

تجارت کیجئے تا کہ آمدنی میں اضافہ ہو۔
tijārat kījiē, *tā ke* āmdanī mēṁ izāfa hō
Work in commerce, *so that* (your) income increases.

مریض تندرست ہو جائے گا بشرطیکہ وہ ڈاکٹر کی صلاح پر عمل کرے۔
marīz tandurust hō jāē gā *baśartēke* vo ḍākṭar kī salāh par amal karē
The patient will recover *provided that* he acts on the doctor's advice.

jab tak + negative, 'until'

jab tak + NEGATIVE introduces a relative subordinate clause. See §1114.

ke, 'that'

The conjunction **ke** has a variety of uses, and may introduce both subordinate and coordinate clauses.

1228 ke introducing subordinate clauses

In the following examples, **ke** introduces subordinate clauses which describe the consequence of circumstances set forth in the main clause. It is usually translated as 'that'.

اُس سے میری جان پہچان اِتنی نہیں کہ اُس کا پتہ میرے پاس ہو۔
us sē mērī jān pehcān itnī nahīṁ *ke* us kā patā mērē pās hō
I am not so well acquainted with him *that* I would have his address.

Subordinating expressions + ke

A number of phrases expressing possibility, necessity and wish end in **ke** and introduce clauses with subjunctive verbs. See §608 for additional examples.

ممکن ہے کہ اُسے خبر لگی ہو۔
***mumkin hai ke* usē xabar lagī hō**
It's possible that he has got the news.

چاہئے کہ وہ دوا کھائے۔
***cāhiē ke* vo davā khāē**
He *should* (*needs to*) take medicine.

ضروری ہے کہ وہ دوا کھائے۔
***zarūrī hai ke* vo davā khāē**
It's necessary that he take medicine.

1229 **ke** introducing coordinate clauses

The conjunction **ke** may (a) replace other conjunctions, (b) introduce both coordinate and subordinate clauses.

ke may replace **yā** in questions offering an either ... or choice.

کیا پیئیں گے ، کافی کہ چائے ؟
kyā piēṁ gē, kāfī *ke* cāē?
What will you drink, coffee or tea?

ke may replace **kyōṁke** and **tā ke**, especially in poetry.

بول کہ سچ زندہ ہے اب تک
bōl *ke* sac zinda hai ab tak
Speak, *because* truth still lives (Faiz)

1230 **ke** introducing quotations and reported facts

ke introduces clauses which function as direct objects of verbs like **kahnā**, 'to say', **dēkhnā**, 'to see', **sunnā**, 'to hear', **paṛhnā**, 'to read', **sōcnā**, 'to think', **samajhnā**, 'to understand', etc.

Following **kahnā, ke** introduces a direct or indirect quotation. It is not translated.

Direct quotation

اُس نے کہا کہ میں باغ میں ہوں گا ۔
us nē kahā ke maiṁ bāɣ mēṁ hūṁ gā
He said, 'I will be in the park'.

Indirect quotation

اُس نے کہا کہ وہ باغ میں ہو گا ۔
us nē kahā ke vo bāɣ mēṁ hō gā
He said he would be in the park.

Following **dēkhnā, sunnā, paṛhnā, sōcnā, samajhnā**, etc., **ke** introduces a coordinate clause which reports what is seen, heard, read, etc.

میں نے پڑھا کہ بات چیت ناکام ہو گئی ۔
maiṁ nē paṛhā *ke* bāt cīt nākām hō gaī
I read *that* the talks had failed.

میں نے سوچا کہ آپ اِن دنوں الہ آباد میں ہیں -
maiṁ nē sōcā *ke* āp in dinōṁ ilāhābād mēṁ haiṁ
I thought (*that*) you were in Allahabad these days.

ke introduces a coordinate clause which explicates and shows the direct result of the idea expressed in the main clause.

پتہ نہیں اُس نے کیا کچھ خریدا کہ ایک بھی روپیہ نہ بچا !
pata nahīṁ us nē kyā kuch xarīdā *ke* ēk bhī rūpaya na bacā!
I can't imagine what all she bought, *that* not even a rupee is left!

ke introduces a juxtaposed coordinate clause which stands in strong contrast to the the main clause.

یہ کہاں کی دوستی ہے کہ بنے ہیں دوست ناصح
ye kahāṁ kī dōstī hai *ke* banē haiṁ dōst nāsih
What kind of friendship is this, *that* friends have become moralizers (Ghalib)

The juxtaposition of the two clauses may show identity of time. One may say that here **ke** replaces **jab**, and is preferably translated with some sort of time word.

ایک کام پورا نہیں ہوتا کہ دوسرا آ پڑتا ہے -
ēk kām pūrā nahīṁ hōtā *ke* dūsrā ā paṛtā hai
Before one job gets finished, a second turns up.

گئے دن کہ تنہا تھا میں انجمن میں
gaē din *ke* tanhā thā maiṁ anujman mēṁ
Gone are the days *when* I was alone in the assembly (Iqbal)

ke may replace **jō**, linking juxtaposed contrasting clauses. (See §1106-§1107 for other uses of **jō**.)

میں کہ بیکار ہوں کس طرح شادی کا خرچ اُٹھا سکوں گا !
maiṁ *ke* bēkār hūṁ, kis tarah śādī kā xarc uṭhā sakūṁ gā!
How can I pay the cost of a wedding *when* I'm unemployed!

Compare میں جو بیکار ہوں کس طرح شادی کا خرچ اُٹھا سکوں گا ؟
maiṁ *jō* bēkār hūṁ, kis tarah śādī kā xarc uṭhā sakūṁ gā?
How can I, *who* am unemployed, pay the cost of a wedding?

13 NUMBERS AND TIME

NUMBERS

1301 Cardinal numbers

Table 29 (p. 230-1) shows the spellings of the cardinal numbers from 1 to 100. Table 30 p. 232) shows the numerals in the Urdu orthography. Note that a sequence of *numerals* is written from left to right (just as in European languages), even though Urdu *text* is written from right to left. Urdu numerals are used mainly for pagination and for writing numbers in Urdu texts. They are little used for calculation at present, and children are generally taught to do arithmetic using 'English' numbers (the so-called Arabic numbers) even in Urdu-medium schools.

The first syllables of the numbers in the vertical columns, while not identical, are often similar. Some students find it easier to learn the numbers by memorizing the vertical columns, rather than the horizontal ones.

The numbers **ikāvan** (51), **ikāsī** (81) and **ikānavē** (91) have the variant forms **ikyāvan** اِکیاون, **ikyāsī** اِکیاسی and **ikyānavē** اِکیانوے.

Not shown on the chart are:

ہزار	**hazār**, 1,000	one thousand
لاکھ	**lākh**, 100,000	one hundred thousand
کروڑ	**karōṛ**, 10,000,000	ten million (a hundred **lākh**)
ارب	**arb**, 1,000,000,000	a thousand million (a hundred **karōṛ**)

Numbers are grammatically unmarked adjectives (§302), and precede the noun they qualify. They are treated as masculine, but do not inflect. Cardinal numbers in the 'teens' which end in **-a** (ہ) do not change when qualifying plural or oblique nouns. As is the case with other adjectives ending in **chōṭī hē** (ہ), the **h** is not pronounced.

بارہ قمیص ، چودہ رومال اور پندرہ جوڑے جرّاب
***bāra* qamīs, *cauda* rūmāl, aur *pandra* jōṛē jurrāb**
twelve shirts, *fourteen* handkerchiefs and *fifteen* pairs of socks

مکان نمبر دو سو پچھتّر
makān nambar *dō sau pachattar*
house number *275*

جہاز میں ایک ہزار دو سو پچپن مسافر ہیں -
jahāz mēṁ *ēk hazār dō sau pacpan* musāfir haiṁ
There are *1,255* passengers on the ship.

پانچ لاکھ روپئے کا نقصان
***pāṁc lākh* rupaē kā nuqsān**
a loss of *five hundred thousand* rupees

1302 Ordinal numbers

Ordinals are formed by adding the suffix **-vāṁ** واں to the cardinal number, which makes it a regularly behaving marked adjective (§301). Ordinals agree with the noun they qualify in gender, number and case (see Table 9, §303 and Table 10, §304).

ساتواں باب	**sātvāṁ bāb**, the seventh chapter (m. sg. nom.)
ساتویں باب میں	**sātvēṁ bāb mēṁ**, in the seventh chapter (m. sg. obl.)
ساتویں جلد	**sātvīṁ jild**, the seventh volume (f.)

There are six ordinal numbers which are formed irregularly. These are also marked adjectives.

پہلا – پہلے – پہلی	**pahlā** (~ **pahlē** ~ **pahlī**), first
دوسرا – دوسرے – دوسری	**dūsrā** (~ **dūsrē** ~ **dūsrī**), second
تیسرا – تیسرے – تیسری	**tīsrā** (~ **tīsrē** ~ **tīsrī**), third
چوتھا – چوتھے – چوتھی	**cauthā** (~ **cauthē** ~ **cauthī**), fourth
چھٹا – چھٹے – چھٹی	**chaṭā** (~ **chaṭē** ~ **chaṭī**), sixth
نواں – نویں – نویں	**navāṁ** (~ **navēṁ** ~ **navīṁ**), ninth

The final unpronounced **chōṭī hē** (ہ) in the cardinal numbers 11 through 17 changes to aspiration in the ordinals. The vowel **-a-** remains, but is pronounced very short, and may be elided in fast speech.

گیارھواں	**gyārhavāṁ**, eleventh
بارھواں	**bārhavāṁ**, twelfth
تیرھواں	**tērhavāṁ**, thirteenth
چودھواں	**caudhavāṁ**, fourteenth
پندرھواں	**pandrahvāṁ**, fifteenth
سولھواں	**sōlhavāṁ**, sixteenth
سترھواں	**satrahvāṁ**, seventeenth

Table 29: Cardinal numbers from 1 to 100

1 ایک	2 دو	3 تین	4 چار	5 پانچ
ēk	**dō**	**tīn**	**cār**	**pāṁc**
11 گیارہ	12 بارہ	13 تیرہ	14 چودہ	15 پندرہ
gyāra	**bāra**	**tēra**	**cauda**	**pandra**
21 اِکیس	22 بائیس	23 تیئیس	24 چوبیس	25 پچّیس
ikkīs	**bāīs**	**tēīs**	**caubīs**	**paccīs**
31 اِکتیس	32 بتّیس	33 تینتیس	34 چونتیس	35 پینتیس
iktīs	**battīs**	**taiṁtīs**	**cauṁtīs**	**paiṁtīs**
41 اِکتالیس	42 بیالیس	43 تینتالیس	44 چوالیس	45 پینتالیس
iktālīs	**bayālīs**	**taiṁtālīs**	**cavālīs**	**paiṁtālīs**
51 اِکاون	52 باون	53 تریپن	54 چوّن	55 پچپن
ikāvan	**bāvan**	**tirēpan**	**cavvan**	**pacpan**
61 اِکسٹھ	62 باسٹھ	63 تریسٹھ	64 چونسٹھ	65 پینسٹھ
iksaṭh	**bāsaṭh**	**tirēsaṭh**	**cauṁsaṭh**	**paiṁsaṭh**
71 اِکہتّر	72 بہتّر	73 تہتّر	74 چوہتّر	75 پچھتّر
ikhattar	**bahattar**	**tehattar**	**cauhattar**	**pachattar**
81 اِکاسی	82 بیاسی	83 تراسی	84 چوراسی	85 پچاسی
ikāsī	**bayāsī**	**tirāsī**	**caurāsī**	**pacāsī**
91 اِکانوے	92 بانوے	93 ترانوے	94 چورانوے	95 پچانوے
ikānavē	**bānavē**	**tirānavē**	**caurānavē**	**pacānavē**

6 چھہ	7 سات	8 آٹھ	9 نو	10 دس
chē	**sāt**	**āṭh**	**nau**	**das**
16 سولہ	17 سترہ	18 اٹھارہ	19 اُنّیس	20 بیس
sōla	**satra**	**aṭhāra**	**unnīs**	**bīs**
26 چھبّیس	27 ستّائیس	28 اٹھائیس	29 اُنتیس	30 تیس
chabbīs	**sattāīs**	**aṭhāīs**	**untīs**	**tīs**
36 چھتّیس	37 سینتیس	38 اڑتیس	39 اُنتالیس	40 چالیس
chattīs	**saiṁtīs**	**aṛtīs**	**untālīs**	**cālīs**
46 چھیالیس	47 سینتالیس	48 اڑتالیس	49 اُنچاس	50 پچاس
cheyālīs	**saiṁtālīs**	**aṛtālīs**	**uncās**	**pacās**
56 چھپّن	57 ستّاون	58 اٹھاون	59 اُنسٹھ	60 ساٹھ
chappan	**sattāvan**	**aṭhāvan**	**unsaṭh**	**sāṭh**
66 چھیاسٹھ	67 سرسٹھ	68 اڑسٹھ	69 اُنہتّر	70 ستّر
cheyāsaṭh	**sarsaṭh**	**aṛsaṭh**	**unhattar**	**sattar**
76 چھہتّر	77 ستتّر	78 اٹھتر	79 اُناسی	80 اسّی
chehattar	**satattar**	**aṭhattar**	**unāsī**	**assī**
86 چھیاسی	87 ستاسی	88 اٹھاسی	89 نواسی	90 نوّے
cheyāsī	**satāsī**	**aṭhāsī**	**navāsī**	**navvē**
96 چھیانوے	97 ستانوے	98 اٹھانوے	99 ننانوے	100 سو
cheyānavē	**satānavē**	**aṭhānavē**	**ninānavē**	**sau**

Table 30: Numerals from 1 to 100

NOTE: In Urdu, composite numbers are written from left to right, as they are in English. But a sequence of numerals, as in counting, is written from left to right. Therefore the order of the numerals in this chart is the reverse of the proper order. This reverse order has been used so that the numerals will correspond to the numbers in the chart on the previous page.

۱	۲	۳	۴	۵	۶	۷	۸	۹	۱۰
1	2	3	4	5	6	7	8	9	10
۱۱	۱۲	۱۳	۱۴	۱۵	۱۶	۱۷	۱۸	۱۹	۲۰
11	12	13	14	15	16	17	18	19	20
۲۱	۲۲	۲۳	۲۴	۲۵	۲۶	۲۷	۲۸	۲۹	۳۰
21	22	23	24	25	26	27	28	29	30
۳۱	۳۲	۳۳	۳۴	۳۵	۳۶	۳۷	۳۸	۳۹	۴۰
31	32	33	34	35	36	37	38	39	40
۴۱	۴۲	۴۳	۴۴	۴۵	۴۶	۴۷	۴۸	۴۹	۵۰
41	42	43	44	45	46	47	48	49	50
۵۱	۵۲	۵۳	۵۴	۵۵	۵۶	۵۷	۵۸	۵۹	۶۰
51	52	53	54	55	56	57	58	59	60
۶۱	۶۲	۶۳	۶۴	۶۵	۶۶	۶۷	۶۸	۶۹	۷۰
61	62	63	64	65	66	67	68	69	70
۷۱	۷۲	۷۳	۷۴	۷۵	۷۶	۷۷	۷۸	۷۹	۸۰
71	72	73	74	75	76	77	78	79	80
۸۱	۸۲	۸۳	۸۴	۸۵	۸۶	۸۷	۸۸	۸۹	۹۰
81	82	83	84	85	86	87	88	89	90
۹۱	۹۲	۹۳	۹۴	۹۵	۹۶	۹۷	۹۸	۹۹	۱۰۰
91	92	93	94	95	96	97	98	99	100

گیارھواں مہینہ

gyārhavāṁ mahīna

the *eleventh* month

چودھویں کا چاند
***caudhavīṁ* kā cāṁd**[1]
the moon of the *fourteenth* (i.e., full moon)

اِکیسویں صدی
***ikkīsvīṁ* sadī**
the *twenty-first* century

1303 Fractions

The following fractions are used in referring to quantities, time (§1311) and money. All fractions lesser than **dō**, 'two' are grammatically singular.

Singular fraction words (adjectives)

پون ، پونا	**paun**, **paunā**, less one quarter
سوا	**savā**, plus one quarter
آدھا ، آدھ	**ādhā**, **ādh**, one half
ساڑھے	**sāṛhē**, plus one half
ڈیڑھ	**ḍēṛh**, one and a half

Singular fraction words (nouns)

چوتھائی	**cauthāī**, a quarter
تہائی	**tihāī**, a third

Plural fraction word (adjective)

ڈھائی	**ḍhāī**, two and a half

paun and **ādh** occur before units of measure (including time words), **paunā** and **ādhā** are used with other nouns. **paunā** and **ādhā** are marked adjectives, and agree with the noun they qualify. The remaining fractions are invariable.

آدھ گھنٹہ ، آدھا گھنٹہ
***ādh* ghanṭa, *ādhā* ghanṭa**
half an hour

---

1 **caudhavīṁ** agrees with the deleted word **rāt**, 'night', which is feminine. The reference is to the fourteenth night of the lunar calendar.

صرف پون گز کپڑا چاہئے ۔
sirf *paun* gaz kapṛā cāhiē
Only *three quarters* of a yard of cloth is needed.

پون بجا ہے ۔
***paun* bajā hai**
It's *12:45* (1:00 less one quarter).

پونے دو کیلو چاول
***paunē dō* kīlō cāval**
1.75 kilos of rice.

sāṛhē, 'plus one half'[2] is used only with numbers (including time expressions), whereas **ādhā**, 'half', is used with nouns.

ساڑھے چھہ گز ریشمی کپڑا
***sāṛhē chē* gaz rēśamī kapṛā**
six and a half yards of silk cloth

آدھی پیالی چائے ۔
***ādhī* piyālī cāē**
half a (small) cup of tea

ڈیڑھ بجا ہے ۔
***ḍēṛh* bajā hai**
It's *one-thirty*.

ڈھائی بجے ہیں ۔
***ḍhāī* bajē haiṁ**
It's *two-thirty*.

ڈیڑھ من لکڑی
***ḍēṛh* man lakṛī**
one and a half maunds of wood

The use of fractions with numbers from 20 to 99 is rare, however they *are* used with larger numbers (**sau**, '100', **hazār**, '1,000', etc.), and the combination of fractions and the special words for multiples of thousands account for some typically South Asian expressions for large numbers.

سوا سو	**savā sau**, 125
ڈیڑھ لاکھ	**ḍēṛh lākh**, 150,000
ڈھائی لاکھ	**ḍhāī lākh**, 250,000
سوا دو لاکھ	**savā dō lākh**, 225,000

Note that in the last example, the entire phrase **savā dō** qualifies **lākh** ($2.25 \times 100{,}000 = 225{,}000$).

2 **sāṛhē** never occurs with the singular numeral **ēk** (**ḍēṛh** is used for 'one and a half').

Other expressions for fractions

cauthāī, 'a quarter' and **tihāī**, 'a third' may be used to express fractions. If used alone, they are nouns, but if used before another noun, they function as adjectives.

پانی کا تین چوتھائی حصّہ کھیتوں میں آتا ہے -
pānī kā *tīn cauthāī hissa* khētōṁ mēṁ ātā hai
Three quarters (*a three fourths part*) of the water reaches the fields.

صرف ایک تہائی پیالی دودھ ڈالنا -
sirf *ēk tihāī* piyālī dūdh ḍālnā
Put in only *one third* of a cup of milk.

Cardinal numbers can be used with **hissa**, 'part' to express one part of a whole.

پانی کا چوتھا حصّہ (ایک چوتھائی) بخارات بنتا ہے -
pānī kā *cauthā hissa* (~ *ēk cauthāī*) buxārāt bantā hai
One fourth part (~ a quarter) of the water evaporates (becomes steam).

baṭā (the masculine singular past participle of **baṭnā**, 'to be divided') is used to express remaining fractions.

دو بٹا سات
dō baṭā sāt
two sevenths

baṭā is also used to express the English rendering of the slant ('over') in some street addresses.

اٹھاسی بٹا چار ، شیر شاہ روڈ
aṭhāsī *baṭā* cār, śēr śāh rōḍ
88/4 (eighty-eight *over* four), Sher Shah Road

1304 'Once', 'twice', etc.

'Once', 'twice', etc. is expressed by a phrase consisting of the number plus the nouns **bār** (f.), 'time', 'turn'; **dafa** (f.), 'time' or **martaba** (m.), 'time', 'occasion'. If the number is an ordinal, it agrees with the noun.

میں نے تین بار کوشش کی ، پھر بھی ٹھیک نہ ہوا -
maiṁ nē *tīn bār* kōśiś kī, phir bhī ṭhīk na hūā
I tried *three times* (and) it still isn't okay.

وہ کل صبح دوسری بار آیا ۔
vo kal subah (~ subh) *dūsrī bār* āyā
He came yesterday morning *for the second time.*

اُن سے کئی دفعہ پوچھا ۔
un sē *kaī dafa* pūchā
(I) asked them *several times.*

چوتھی دفعہ پوچھنے پر جواب ملا ۔
***cauthī dafa* pūchnē par javāb mil gayā**
On asking the *fourth time*, (I) got an answer.

The number **dō** coalesces with a following **bār** to form a compound, **dōbāra**, 'again' (a synonym of **phir**).

یہ کام ٹھیک نہیں ہوا ، دوبارہ کیجئے
ye kām ṭhīk nahīṁ hūā, *dōbāra* kījiē
This work hasn't been done right, please do it *again.*

1305 Multiplicatives ('twofold', 'double', etc.)

Multiplicatives are formed by adding the suffix **gunā**, which coalesces with the numbers **dō**, **tīn** and **cār** to make compounds. **gunā** inflects to agree with the noun it qualifies.

دو	**dō**	دُگنا	**dug(u)nā**	double, two times, twofold
تین	**tīn**	تِگنا	**tig(u)nā**	triple, three times, threefold
چار	**cār**	چوگنا	**caugunā**	quadruple, four times, fourfold
پانچ	**pāṁc**	پانچ گنا	**pāṁc gunā**	quintuple, five times, fivefold
چھہ	**chē**	چھہ گنا	**chē gunā**	sextuple, six times, sixfold

آپ کے پیسے دگنے ہو جائیں گے ۔
āp kē paisē *dug(u)nē* hō jāēṁ gē
Your funds will be *doubled.*

آپ کی دولت دگنی ہو جائے گی ۔
āp kī daulat *dug(u)nī* hō jāē gī
Your wealth will be *doubled.*

چار کا دگنا آٹھ ہوتا ہے ۔
cār kā *dug(u)nā* āṭh hōtā hai
Two times four is eight.

چار کا تگنا بارہ ہوتا ہے ۔
cār kā *tig(u)nā* bāra hōtā hai
Three times four is twelve.

1306 Repeated numbers

Repetition of numbers expresses distributiveness.

بسیں دو دو گھنٹے کے بعد جاتی ہیں -
basēm̐ *dō dō ghanṭē kē bād* jātī haim̐
The buses go *every two hours.*

قطار میں کھڑے ہو کر ایک ایک کر کے آئیے -
qatār mēm̐ kharē hō kar *ēk ēk kar kē* āiyē
Please form (stand in) a line and come *one at a time.*

Approximation is expressed with two even numbers in sequence. (There are several exceptions to this rule: the sequence **chē āṭh** does not occur; **dō cār** occurs, but means 'a few'; the odd number sequence **pām̐c sāt** occurs, and is often shortened to **pān sāt**.)

دس بارہ آدمی دکان میں تھے -
***das bāra* ādmī dukān mēm̐ thē**
There were about a dozen (*ten-twelve*) people in the shop.

کتنے لوگ یہاں رہتے ہیں ؟—پتہ نہیں ، پان سات (پانچ سات) ہوں گے -
kitnē lōg yahām̐ rahtē haim̐?—pata nahīm̐, *pān sāt* hōm̐ gē
How many people live here?—I don't know, maybe *half a dozen.*

صرف دو چار آدمی حاضر تھے -
sirf *dō cār* ādmī hāzir thē
Only *a few* people were present.

1307 Numbers with the oblique plural

Numbers may occur in the oblique plural to express totality or an indefinitely large amount (§112).

CALENDAR AND CLOCK TIME

1308 Months

In both India and Pakistan, official business runs on Common Era (C.E.) time, using English months. However the Islamic Hijrī calendar (A.H., 'After Hijra'), which commenced in 622 C.E., is used to determine Muslim religious observances. Because the Hijrī calendar is lunar, the Hijrī year is approximately eleven days shorter than the Common Era Year.

mahīna مہینہ , 'month' may refer to both Common Era and Hijrī months. The names of the days of the Hijrī months (which are all masculine gender) are:

محرّم	**muharram**
صفر	**safar**
ربیع الاوّل	**rabī-ul-avval**
ربیع الثانی	**rabī-us-sānī**
جمادی الاوّل	**jamādī-ul-avval**
جمادی الثانی	**jamādī-us-sānī**
رجب	**rajab**
شعبان	**śābān**
رمضان	**ramzān**
شوّال	**śavvāl**
ذی قعدہ ، ذوالقعدہ	**zīqād**
ذی الحجہ	**zil hij (< zil hijja)**[3]

The names of the Common Era months are:

جنوری	**janvarī** (f.)	January
فروری	**farvarī** (f.)	February
مارچ	**mārc** (m.)	March
اپریل	**aprail** (m.)	April
مئی	**maī** (f.)	May
جون	**jūn** (m.)	June
جولائی	**jūlāī** (f.)	July
اگست	**agast** (m.)	August
ستمبر	**sitambar** (m.)	September
اکتوبر	**aktūbar** (m.)	October
نومبر	**navambar** (m.)	November
دسمبر	**disambar** (m.)	December

3 Sometimes colloquially pronounced **zil haj**.

1309 Days

kal has two meanings: 'tomorrow' with non-perfective tenses, and 'yesterday' with perfective tenses.

> میں کل آیا اور کل پھر جاؤں گا ۔
> **maiṁ *kal* āyā aur *kal* phir jāūṁ gā**
> I came *yesterday* and I will go again *tomorrow*.

parsōṁ means 'the day after tomorrow' with non-perfective tenses, and 'the day before yesterday' with perfective tenses.

> میں پرسوں آیا اور پرسوں پھر جاؤں گا ۔
> **maiṁ *parsōṁ* āyā aur *parsōṁ* phir jāūṁ gā**
> I came *the day before yesterday* and I will go again *the day after tomorrow*.

The names of the days of the week (**hafta** ہفتہ) are:

اِتوار	**itvār** (m.)	Sunday
پیر	**pīr** (m.)	Monday
سوموار	**sōmvār** (m.)	Monday (less common than **pīr**)
منگل	**mangal** (m.)	Tuesday
بدھ	**budh** (m.)	Wednesday
جمعرات	**jumērāt** (f.)	Thursday (lit. Friday-eve)
جمعہ	**juma** (m.)	Friday
ہفتہ ، ہفتے کا دن	**hafta, haftē kā din**	Saturday

jumē kā din is also commonly used for 'Friday'. **juma** originally meant 'congregation (for prayers in the mosque)'.

The primary meaning of **hafta** is 'week', but has also come to be used for 'Saturday' (particularly in Pakistan). It is a shortened form of **haftē kā din**, 'the (last) day of the week'.

When the days of the week are used as adverbs of time in sentences, they appear in the oblique case.

> آج ہفتہ (ہفتے کا دن) ہے ۔
> **āj *hafta* (haftē kā din) hai**
> Today is *Saturday*.

> ہفتے کو (ہفتے کے دن کو) ہم دعوت پر جا رہے ہیں ۔
> ***haftē kō* (haftē kē din kō) ham dāvat par jā rāhē haiṁ**
> *Saturday* we are going to a party.

اگلے پیر عیدالاضحیٰ ہے ۔
aglē *pīr* īd-ul-azhā hai
Next *Monday* is Eid-ul-Azha.

اگلے پیر آپ ہمارے گھر تشریف لائیے ۔
aglē *pīr* āp hamārē ghar taśrīf lāiyē
Next *Monday* please come (honorific) to our house.

1310 Writing the date

Dates are written from right to left in the following order: day, month, year. The numerals for the date are followed by the sign ، , and the year is written over the sign ـــ (**san**), which is followed by a small ء for Common Era dates[4] and a small ھ (**dō caśmī hē**) for Hijrī dates. The ordinal number (**pahlī**, 'first' (agreeing with **tārīx** (f.), 'date')) is used for mentioning the first day of the month. Cardinal numbers are usually used in mentioning the other days, but ordinals may also be used.

۱، جنوری ۱۹۹۵ء
pahlī janvarī unnīs sau pacānavē
1st January 1995 (C.E.)

مئی کی ۳۱ تاریخ
maī kī iktīs tārīx
the 31st of May

۳۱، مئی ۱۹۹۷ء
iktīs maī unnīs sau satānavē
31st May 1997 (C.E.)

محرّم کی ۱۰ / محرّم کی ۱۰ تاریخ
muharram kī dasvīṅ/muharram kī das tārīx
the tenth of Muharram

۸، رجب ۱۴۱۸ھ
āṭh rajab cauda sau aṭhāra
8 Rajab 1418 (A.H.)

4 This sign is derived from the initial stroke of ع (**ain**), for **īsavī** عیسوی (Christian Era).

The first day of a Hijrī month is referred to as چاند کی پہلی **cāṁd kī pahlī**, 'the first of the moon'. The Persian loanword **yakum** (f.) also means 'the first of the month'.

میری تاریخِ پدائش یکم مارچ اُنیس سو ساٹھ ہے ۔
mērī tārīx-e-padāiś *yakum* mārc unnīs sau sāṭh hai
My date of birth is *first* March, 1960.

1311 Telling the time

Divisions of the day

The day (**din** دن) is divided roughly into **subah** (~ **subh**) صبح , 'morning', **dō pahr** دو پہر , 'afternoon' and **śām** شام , 'evening'. Historically, a 24-hour period was divided into three-hour watches, or **pahr** پہر . According to this reckoning, **dō pahr** (watch two) means 'noon', and also the period from noon to 3 p.m. **seh pahr** سہ پہر (watch three) refers to the period from 3 p.m. to 6. **śām** 'evening' begins at about 5 p.m., with fluctuations according to the season. **rāt** رات , 'night' begins at about 9 p.m.

śām and **rāt** are used in adverbial expressions of time with the postposition **kō**. With **subah, kō** is optional, and with **din, mēṁ** is used.

وہ شام کو (رات کو) آئے گا ۔
vo *śām kō* (*rāt kō*) āē gā
He will come *in the evening* (*at night*).

وہ صبح (کو) آئے گا ۔
vo *subah* (~ subh) (kō) āē gā
He will come *in the morning*.

وہ دن میں آئے گا ۔
vo *din mēṁ* āē gā
He will come *during the day*.

Clock time

Clock time is expressed with the perfect participle of **bajnā** بجنا , 'to strike', which agrees in number with the hour. Numbers which express time are treated as masculine nouns.

Stating the time

When clock time is stated, it is expressed in a subject-predicate sentence, with the immediate past tense (§631) of **bajnā**. The perfect participle **bajā** is masculine, and agrees with the subject (the hour) in number and case.

اِس وقت میری گھڑی میں پون بجا ہے -
is vaqt mērī gharī mēṁ *paun bajā* hai
Now it's *a quarter to one* by my watch.

ایک بجا ہے -
***ēk bajā* hai**
It's *one o'clock* (*one has struck*).

سوا ایک بجا ہے -
***savā ēk bajā* hai**
It's a *quarter past one.*

In the first example above, **ēk** is the singular subject of **bajā hai**, which agrees with it. In the second example, **paun** is also singular. **savā**, in the third, does not inflect. (See §1303 for fractions.)

ḍēṛh is singular; plural numbers begin with **dō**, 'two':

اب ڈیڑھ بجا ہے -
ab *ḍēṛh bajā* hai
Now it's *one-thirty.*

دو بجے ہیں -
***dō bajē* haiṁ**
It's *two o'clock* (*two have struck*).

اب ٹھیک ساڑھے چھہ بجے ہیں -
ab ṭhīk *sāṛhē chē bajē* haiṁ
Now it's exactly *six-thirty.*

ہم آدھے گھنٹے میں رات کا کھانا کھائیں گے -
ham *ādhē ghanṭē mēṁ* rāt kā khānā khāēṁ gē
We will eat dinner *in half an hour.*

In the second example above, **dō** is the plural subject of **bajē haiṁ**, which is masculine plural. In the third and fourth examples, **sāṛhē** is used with the number **chē**, 'six', to express 'six and a half'. But **ādhā**, 'half' is used with the noun **ghanṭa**, 'hour', to express 'half an hour'.

Telling time by minutes

To express minutes after or before the hour, the phrases **baj kar**, 'having struck' and **bajnē mēṁ**, 'in striking' are used with the borrowed word **minaṭ**, 'minute(s)'.

پانچ بج کر پندرہ منٹ
pāṁc *baj kar* pandra minaṭ
5:15; fifteen minutes *past* five

پانچ بجنے میں دس منٹ
pāṁc *bajnē mēṁ* das minaṭ
4:50; ten minutes *to* five

Using clock time adverbially

When time expressions are used as adverbs of time (qualifying an action or event), they appear in the oblique case. In the second example, **ēk bajē** is an adverbial phrase; **bajē** is masculine oblique singular.

ہم دس بجے صبح چائے پیتے ہیں -
ham *das bajē subah* (~ subh) cāē pītē haiṁ
We drink tea *at ten o'clock in the morning.*

ڈاکیہ دن کے ایک بجے آتا ہے -
ḍākiya *din kē ēk bajē* ātā hai
The postman comes *at one o'clock in the afternoon.*

میں سات بجے شام گھر پہنچوں گی -
maiṁ *sāt bajē śām* ghar pahuṁcūṁ gī
I will arrive home *at seven o'clock in the evening.*

No postposition is used when **bajē** is used in an adverbial expression of time.

وہ دس بجے آئے گا -
vo *das bajē* āē gā
He will come *at ten o'clock.*

Some idioms referring to divisions of the day

صبح سویرے
subah savērē[5]
early in the morning

بہت صبح
bahut subah
very early in the morning
(much morning)

5 **subah** is an Arabic loanword; **savērā** is an indigenous Urdu word. Both mean 'morning', but together they mean 'early morning'.

پہر دن چڑھے
pahr din caṛhē
about 9 a.m.
(one **pahr** of day having risen)

اِتنا دن چڑھے
itnā din caṛhē
so late
(so much day having risen)

پہر رات گئے
pahr rāt gaē
about 9 p.m.
(one **pahr** of night having passed)

آدھی رات
ādhī rāt
midnight
(half night)

پہر رات رہے
pahr rāt rahē
about 3 a.m.
(one **pahr** of night having remained)

کچھ رات رہے
kuch rāt rahē
very early in the morning
(some night having remained)

MONEY

1312 Contemporary currency

In both India and Pakistan, the rupee (**rupiya** روپیہ) is divided into 100 pice (**paisa** پیسہ). The word **paisā** can mean 'money' or a one-pice coin. Pluralized, it means 'funds', 'money in a physical sense'.

آپ کو کتنا پیسہ چاہئے ؟
āp kō kitnā *paisā* cāhiē?
How much *money* do you need?

اُس نے پیسے گن کر بٹوے میں ڈالے -
us nē *paisē* gin kar baṭvē mēṁ ḍālē
He counted *the money* and put it in the bag.

اُس سے پہلے مجھے پیسے تو بہت ملے تھے ، مگر روپیہ کبھی نہ ملا تھا -
us sē pahlē mujhē *paisē* tō bahut milē thē, magar *rūpaya* kabhī na milā thā
Before that I had got many *pice*, but I had never got *a rupee*. (Rusvā, *Umrāō Jān Adā*)

An English decimal point or a diagonal slant may be used to indicate the decimal point, although fractions of a rupee are usually rounded off.

۵۰.۹۵ ~ ۹۵/۵۰

pacānvē rupaē, pacās paisē
Rs. 95.50

1313 Old currency

In older texts, references to the former system may be found, in which, a rupee consisted of 16 annas (**āna** آنہ ، آنا sg., **ānē** pl.); an anna consisted of 4 pice (**paisē** پیسے), and a pice consisted of 3 pie (**pāī** پائی). The phrase **āṭh ānē** (half a rupee) may occasionally be heard.

14 PERSIAN ELEMENTS IN URDU

Urdu developed in close contact with Persian, which was the language of administration and education during the period of Muslim rule in India. Even after Urdu began to replace Persian as the language of poetry in the eighteenth century, Persian retained its official status for another century, and remained a rich source of literary vocabulary in Urdu. Elements of Persian grammar have been borrowed along with the vocabulary, and a knowledge of them is essential for reading literary Urdu, particularly poetry.

This chapter presents an overview of the more important Persian elements from the perspective of the study of Urdu, but does not, of course, attempt to describe Persian grammar comprehensively.

NOTE: where meanings of the Persian loanwords have changed, the current Urdu meaning, rather than the original Persian one, is given. The Urdu pronunciation, rather than the Persian one, is also shown.

THE ENCLITIC **izāfat** (1401)

izāfat 'increase', 'addition' is an enclitic short vowel, pronounced in Urdu as a short **e** which joins two nouns or a noun and an adjective. It has two grammatical functions.

*Noun-**izāfat**-noun (pronoun)*

In the first function, **izāfat** shows a possessive relationship in which the first noun (or pronoun) belongs to the second.

حکومتِ پاکستان **hukūmat-e-pākistān**, The Government of Pakistan

جانِ من **jān-e-man**, my darling (soul/life of I)

This is the reverse of the possessive word-order in Urdu:

پاکستان کی حکومت **pākistān kī hukūmat**, Pakistan's government

میری جان **mērī jān**, my dear

Often the possessive construction with **izāfat** and the possessive with **kā** have different connotations. For example, **hukūmat-e-pākistān** is a proper noun: the Government of Pakistan in its official capacity; whereas **pākistān kī hukūmat** is a common noun and refers to the sitting government at the time of speaking. Similarly, **jān-e-man** is used to address one's sweetheart, whereas **mērī jān** may be used to address any dear friend.

Noun-izāfat-adjective

In the second function, **izāfat** shows that the noun is modified by the following adjective.

وزیرِ اعظم	**vazīr-e-āzam**, prime minister (lit. great minister)
دیوانِ عام	**dīvān-e-ām**, public hall of audience
دیوانِ خاص	**dīvān-e-xās**, private hall of audience

NOTE: **izāfat** is mostly left unwritten in modern texts, especially since modern computer fonts often do not provide a systematic means of writing it. When written, it is written as follows:

(a) as subscript **zēr** (ِ) when it follows ی (**chōṭī yē**) or any consonant,

(b) as ئے (**hamza** over **baṛī yē**) when it follows a word ending in the long vowels ا (**alif**), or و (**vāō**),

(c) as ۂ (**hamza** over **chōṭī hē**) when it follows a final ہ (**chōṭī hē**),

(d) as zero (it is neither written nor pronounced) when it follows a word ending in ے (**baṛī yē**).

In the spoken language there is an increasing tendency to omit the **izāfat** in pronunciation, especially if a word ends in a single consonant following a short vowel: **tālib ilm**, 'student', for **tālib-e-ilm**; **āxir kār**, 'at last', for **āxir-e-kār**.

(a) وادیِ سندھ
vādī-e-sindh
the Indus valley (lit. valley *of* Sindh)

(b) دریائے سندھ
daryā-e-sindh
the Indus River (lit. river *of* Sindh/Indus)

(c) جذبۂ دل
jazba-e-dil
emotion *of* the heart

(d) رائے عالی
rāē-ālī
a high opinion

WORD-FORMING AFFIXES

Persian has contributed many word-forming suffixes and prefixes to Urdu. The following are some of the most common affixes, including prepositions.
NOTE: Words with Persian suffixes will be found in dictionaries under the same entry as the word to which the suffix is added. Words and phrases beginning with prefixed prepositions must however be looked up under the preposition.

1402 Nominal suffixes

Suffixes forming nouns

The abstract suffix **-ī** (alternating with **-gī** after words ending in **-a** ہ) derives abstract nouns from nouns and adjectives. Compare English '-ness' and '-ship'.

گرم ← گرمی	**garm**, hot (adj.) → **garmī**, heat
دوست ← دوستی	**dōst**, friend (noun) → **dōstī**, friendship
زندہ ← زندگی	**zinda**, alive (adj.) → **zindagī**, life
بندہ ← بندگی	**banda**, slave (noun) → **bandagī**, slavery

The suffixes **-kār**, **-gār**, **-gar** and **-cī**[1] make agent nouns. The new noun shows a person who does, or is involved with, the old noun.

دست ← دستکار	**dast**, hand → **dastkār**, craftsman
گناہ ← گناہگار	**gunāh**, sin → **gunāhgār**, sinner
جادو ← جادوگر	**jādū**, magic → **jādūgar**, magician
افیم ← افیمچی	**afīm**, opium → **afīmcī**, opium addict

New nouns with the suffix **-bān** ~ **-vān** shows the 'keeper' of the old noun.

میز ← میزبان	**mēz**, table → **mēzbān**, host
کوچ ← کوچوان	**kōc**, coach → **kōcvān**, coach-driver

The suffixes **-gāh**, **-ābād** and **-stān** ~ **-istān** form nouns of location.

عید ← عیدگاہ	**īd**, Eid festival → **īdgāh**, place for Eid prayers
آکبر ← آکبرآباد	**akbar**, Akbar → **akbarābād**, city of Akbar[2]
ریگ ← ریگستان	**rēg**, sand → **rēgistān**, sandy desert

1 **-cī** has been borrowed into Persian from Turkish.

2 An old name for Agra.

The suffix **-zār** derives new nouns which show a place characterized by the old noun.

گل ← گلزار	**gul**, rose → **gulzār**, rose garden

The diminutive suffixes **-ca**, **-īca** and **-ak** form diminutives of the old noun.

چمچ ← چمچہ	**cammac**, large spoon → **camca**, teaspoon
دست ← دستک	**dast**, hand → **dastak**, knock on door

The suffix **-dān** ~ **-dānī** shows a container (the suffix should be distinguished from **dān**, present stem of **dānestan**, 'to know', as in **sāinsdān**, 'scientist'). This suffix is added not only to Perso-Arabic words but also to indigenous Urdu words.

چوہا ← چوہے دان	**cūhā**, mouse → **cūhēdān**, mouse trap
چائے ← چائے دانی	**cāē**, tea → **cāēdānī**, teapot

Suffixes forming both nouns and adjectives

Possession is shown by **-dār**, **-āvar** ~ **-var**, **-yār** ~ **-yar** and **-mand**. **dār** is the most productive in forming new derivations, and is suffixed not only to Perso-Arabic words but also to indigenous Urdu words and even English loanwords.

ذمہ ← ذمہ دار	**zimma**, responsibility → **zimmēdār**, responsible
سمجھ ← سمجھدار	**samajh**, understanding → **samajhdār**, sensible
ٹکٹ ← ٹکٹ دار	**ṭikaṭ**, stamp → **ṭikaṭdār**, ready-stamped (envelope)
ہنر ← ہنرور	**hunar**, skill → **hunarvar**, skillful
ہوش ← ہوشیار	**hōś**, senses → **hōśyār**, careful, vigilant
ہوش ← ہوشمند	**hōś**, senses → **hōśmand**, sensible, intelligent
دولت ← دولتمند	**daulat**, wealth → **daulatmand**, wealthy

Suffixes forming adjectives

The adjectival suffix **-ī** makes descriptive adjectives from nouns.

پاکستان ← پاکستانی	**pākistān**, Pakistan → **pākistānī**, Pakistani
محنت ← محنتی	**mehnat**, effort → **mehnatī**, hard-working

The suffix **-a** derives attributive adjectives from predicate adjectives (§306).

موجود ← موجودہ	**maujūd**, present → **maujūda**, present

Predicative adjective

جج صاحب عدالت میں موجود تھے
jaj sāhib adālat mēṁ *maujūd* thē
The judge was *present* in the court.

Attributive adjective

موجودہ حکومت
***maujūda* hukūmat**
the *current* (sitting) government

The suffix **-āna** derives adverbs and adjectives of quality from nouns and adjectives. Compare English '-ly'.

دوست ← دوستانہ	**dōst**, friend → **dōstāna**, friendly
ظالم ← ظالمانہ	**zālim**, unjust → **zālimāna**, unjust, unjustly

The suffixes **-nāk** and **-gīn**, 'full of' make new adjectives of quality from nouns. Compare English '-ous', '-ful'.

خطر ← خطرناک	**xatar**, danger → **xatarnāk**, dangerous
شرم ← شرمناک	**śarm**, shame → **śarmnāk**, shameful
شرم ← شرمگین	**śarm**, shame → **śarmgīn**, bashful

1403 Prefixes

The negative particle **nā-** occurs as a prefix to nouns and Persian verb stems.

ناکام	**nākām**, unsuccessful (< **kām**, desire)
نادان	**nādān**, ignorant, foolish (< **dān** < **dānestan**, to know)

ham- 'same' is productive as a prefix in Urdu.

ہم ذات	**hamzāt**, of the same caste (< **zāt**, caste)
ہم مذہب	**ham mazhab**, co-religionists (< **mazhab**, religion)

1404 Prepositions

Persian prepositions are usually used as prefixes in Urdu (the exceptions are **az**, **bar** and **tā**, which are less productive than the others). Most have their own entries in Urdu dictionaries.

***az*, 'from', 'of'; 'by (authorship)'**

کم از کم	**kam az kam**, at least (< **kam**, less, few)
از خود	**az xud**, voluntarily (< **xud**, self)
از علامہ اقبال	**az allāma iqbāl**, by Allama Iqbal

***ba*, 'with', 'by'**

بخیر	**baxair**, in safety (< **xair**, good, goodness)
بزور	**bazōr**, by force (< **zōr**, power, force)

***bā*, 'with', 'along with'**

بااصول	**bāusūl**, principled (< **usūl**, principle)
باادب	**bāadab**, courteous (< **adab**, courtesy)

***bar*, 'on', 'over'**

بر طرف کرنا	to dismiss (< **bar taraf**, aside < **taraf**, side, direction)

***bē*, 'without'**

bē is usually written as a separate word.

بے شک	**bēśak**, doubtless (< **śak**, doubt)
بے حد	**bē had**, extremely (< **had**, limit)
بے بس	**bē bas**, helpless (< **bas**, control, power)

***dar*, 'in'**

در حقیقت	**dar haqīqat**, in fact (< **haqīqat**, fact, reality)
درخواست	**darxāst**, application (**dar** + **xāst** < **xāstan**, to wish)

***tā*, 'up to'**

تا حال	**tā hāl**, hitherto (< **hāl**, state, present state)

ba, bā, bar and **dar** derive compound postpositions (§531).

بطور **bataur**, as, in the capacity (of)
بغیر **baɣair**, without
بہ نسبت **banisbat**, in comparison (with)
باوجود **bāvujūd**, in spite (of)
درمیان **darmiyān**, between

1405 Plural suffixes

Persian distinguishes two numbers, singular and plural.

Nouns representing animate beings take the plural suffix **-ān** (often pronounced **-āṁ** in Urdu). In Persian, inanimate nouns take the plural suffix **-hā**, but in Urdu this suffix occurs only in a few set expressions.

بزرگان **buzargān**, elders (< **buzarg**, elder)
طالبان **tālibān**, students (< **tālib**, seeker, student)
سالہا سال **sālhā sāl**, for years on end (< **sāl**, year)

Animate nouns ending in **-a** ہ change **-ān** to **-gān**.

نمائندگان **numāindagān**, representatives (< **numāinda**, representative)

Animate nouns ending in **-ā** ا change **-ān** to **-yān**.

گدایان **gadāyān**, beggars (< **gadā**, beggar)

Only words of Persian origin (or Arabic loanwords which have been assimilated into Persian) may take Persian plural suffixes. Some Persian loanwords in common use have both Persian and indigenous Urdu plural forms: **numāindē** نمائندے ~ **numāindagān** نمائندگان, 'representatives'; **sāhib** صاحب ~ **sāhibān** صاحبان, 'gentlemen'. In such cases, use of the Persian plural is usually typical of a formal or literary style.

Words ending in Persian plural suffixes do not take the Urdu oblique plural suffix in **-ōṁ**. (**sāhibōṁ nē**, but **sāhibān nē**, 'gentlemen' (subject of a perfective transitive verb)). However Persian plurals occur mostly in the nominative case.

VERB FORMS

1406 Present and past verb stems

The Persian verb forms which occur most commonly in Urdu are the present and past stems. Both are formed from the infinitive, which ends in **-tan**, **-dan** and **-īdan**. The past stem is formed by dropping **-an**. The present stem of regular verbs is formed by dropping the full infinitive suffix.

INFINITIVE	MEANING	PAST STEM	PRESENT STEM
kuśtan	to kill	**xuśt**	**xuś**
xōrdan	to eat	**xōrd**	**xōr**
fahmīdan	to understand	**fahmīd**	**fahm**

Irregularities in the formation of the present stem are common.

dādan	to give	**dād**	**dah**
xāstan	to wish, want	**xāst**	**xāh**
dāśtan	to know	**dāśt**	**dār**
guzāśtan	to pass (trans.)	**guzāśt**	**guzār**
śudan	to be, become	**śud**	**śav, śau**
būdan	to be	**būd**	**bāś**
raftan	to go	**raft**	**rav, rau**
āmadan	to come	**āmad**	**ā**
yāftan	to obtain	**yāft**	**yāb**

Past participles are formed by suffixing **-a** to past stems, and present participles by suffixing **-inda**, **-āṅ** or **-ā** to present stems.

Occasionally a past stem occurs as an Urdu noun:

نشست **niśast**, seat (past stem of **niśastan**, to sit)

آمد **āmad**, arrival (past stem of **āmadan**, to come)

Both past and present stems occur in Urdu in borrowed compounds. Compounds with past participles are also frequent. In dictionaries, compounds are listed under the first element in the compound.

COMPOUNDS (1407)

Compounding is a very productive process in Persian. Compounds can be made with two independent words (such as nouns and adjectives), and also with independent words and verb stems, and with verb stems themselves. The compound constitutes a single word in Urdu, although the elements are sometimes written with intervening spaces.

Adjective + noun

The elements are simply juxtaposed. When an adjective is compounded with a following noun, the result is an adjective meaning 'possessing the thing or idea expressed by the two words'.

کمبخت	**kambaxt**, unfortunate (**kam**, less + **baxt**, fortune)
خوبصورت	**xūbsūrat**, beautiful (**xūb**, good + **sūrat**, appearance)
خوشحال	**xuśhāl**, prosperous (**xuś**, happy + **hāl**, state)
بدصورت	**badsūrat**, ugly (**bad**, bad + **sūrat**, appearance)
تنگ دل	**tang dil**, mean, miserly (**tang**, narrow + **dil**, heart)

Noun + adjective

حقیقت پسند	**haqīqat pasand**, realist (**haqīqat**, truth + **pasand**, liked)

Noun + noun

The elements may joined with **o**, 'and', or simply juxtaposed.

روز و شب	**rōz o śab**, around the clock (**rōz**, day + **śab**, night)
روز نامہ	**rōznāma**, daily newspaper (**rōz**, day + **nāma**, letter)
کارخانہ	**kārxāna**, workshop, factory (**kār**, work + **xāna**, house)

Compounds with present stems as the second element

Here the present stem acquires the sense of a present participle.

کامیاب	**kāmyāb**, successful (**kām**, desire + **yāb** < **yāftan**, to obtain)
مفت خور	**muft xōr**, freeloader (**muft**, free + **xōr** < **xōrdan**, to eat)
شکر گزار	**śukr guzār**, grateful (**śukr**, thanks + **guzār** < **guzāśtan**, to pass)
گھڑی ساز	**gharī sāz**, watchmaker (**gharī**, watch + **sāz** < **sāxtan**, to make)
پابند	**pāband**, restrained, bound (**pā**, foot + **band** < **bastan**, to bind)

Reduplicative compounds of present stems

خواہ مخواہ **xāh maxāh**, unnecessarily (**xāh**, present stem of **xāstan**, to want)
کش مکش **kaś makaś**, struggle (**kaś**, present stem of **kaśīdan**, to pull)

Compounds with past stems as the second element

درخواست **darxāst**, application (**dar**, in + **xāst** < **xāstan**, to wish)

Compounds with past participles as the second element

شادی شدہ **śādī śuda**, married (**śādī**, marriage + **śuda**, become < **śud** < **śudan**, to be, become)
تعلیم یافتہ **tālīm yāfta**, educated (**tālīm**, education + **yāfta**, obtained <**yāft** < **yāftan**, to obtain)
پیش کردہ **pēś karda**, presented (**pēś**, before + **karda**, did < **kard** < **kardan**, to do)

*Compounds of verb stems joined by **o**, 'and'*

بندوبست **bandobast**, arrangement (**band**, present stem + **bast**, past stem < **bastan**, to bind)
آمدورفت **āmad-o-raft**, traffic (**āmad**, past stem < **āmadan**, come + **raft**, past stem < **raftan**, to go)

NOTE: Nominal suffixes may be used to form new words from compounds, and compounds may be further compounded:

کامیابی **kāmyābī**, success (**ī** + **kām**, desire + **yāb** < **yāftan**, to obtain)
تنگ دلی **tang dilī**, meanness (**ī** + **tang**, narrow + **dil**, heart)
کارخانہ دار **kārxānadār**, mill owner (**dār** + **kār**, work + **xāna**, house)
درخواست دہندہ **darxāst dehinda**, applicant (**dar**, in + **xāst** < **xāstan**, to wish + **deh** < **dādan**, to give + **-inda**, noun of agent suffix)

MISCELLANEOUS

1408 Comparison of adjectives with **tar**, **tarīn**

The comparative and superlative of Perso-Arabic adjectives can be formed in Urdu with the Persian suffixes **tar** تر (comparative) and **tarīn** ترین (superlative). Some of these Perso-Arabic comparatives are used in colloquial spoken Urdu, whereas others are used in literary Urdu. In Urdu, Persian comparatives and superlatives often lose their comparative or superlative force and merely intensify the adjective.

Examples of the use of Persian comparatives and superlatives in sentences may be found in §315.

*Comparative: adjective + **tar***

بد ← بدتر	**bad**, bad → **badtar**, very bad
خوب ← خوب تر	**xūb**, well → **xūb tar**, better
کم ← کمتر	**kam**, less, few → **kamtar**, even less, fewer
بہ ← بہتر	**beh**, good → **behtar**, better, very good
خراب ← خراب تر	**xarāb**, bad → **xarāb tar**, worse
دلچسپ ← دلچسپ تر	**dilcasp**, interesting → **dilcasp tar**, more interesting
تیز ← تیز تر	**tēz**, sharp, fast → **tēz tar**, faster
خاص ← خاص تر	**xās**, special → **xās tar**, more special

*Superlative: adjective + **tarīn***

بد ← بدترین	**bad**, bad → **badtarīn**, worst
خوب ← خوب ترین	**xūb**, well → **xūb tarīn**, best
کم ← کمترین	**kam**, less, few → **kamtarīn**, fewest, least
بہ ← بہترین	**beh**, good → **behtarīn**, best, very very good
خراب ← خراب ترین	**xarāb**, bad → **xarāb tarīn**, worst
تیز ← تیز ترین	**tēz**, sharp, fast → **tēz tarīn**, fastest
خاص ← خاص ترین	**xās**, special → **xās tarīn**, most special, intimate

1409 Persian numbers

Persian cardinal and ordinal numbers occur in Urdu compounds and idioms.

یک	**yak**, one
دو	**du**, two
سہ	**se**, three
چہار	**cahār**, four
پنج	**panj**, five
شش	**śaś**, six
ہفت	**haft**, seven
ہشت	**haśt**, eight
نہ	**nuh**, nine
دہ	**dah**, ten

Ordinals: **yakum**, **duvum**, **sivum**, **cahārum**, etc.

یکم جون
***yakum* jūn**
the *first* of June

سہ پہر
se paher
the *third* watch (approximately 3 p.m. to 6 p.m.)

یکدلی
yakdilī
unanimity

15 ARABIC ELEMENTS IN URDU

As Urdu borrows much vocabulary from Arabic, elements of Arabic word formation are present in Urdu. This chapter presents an overview of some of the more important Arabic elements in modern Urdu.

Although many Arabic words occur in everyday Urdu, heavily Arabicized Urdu is found mostly in literary language, and is particularly typical of administrative language or newspaper texts.

The phonemic transcription used in other parts of this grammar is necessarily replaced in this chapter by a transliteration representing the Arabic characters.

NOTE: where meanings of the Arabic loanwords have changed, the current Urdu meaning, rather than the original Arabic one, is given. The Urdu pronunciation, rather than the Arabic one, is also shown.

TRILITERAL ROOT STRUCTURE OF ARABIC WORDS

The TRILITERAL ROOT is the basic structure of the Arabic word. Most Arabic words consist of three root consonants, or radicals (a few consist of four). The vowels do not belong to the root, but to the grammatical structure of the language. Various derived verbs, with their associated participles and verbal nouns, are formed by adding affixes and vowel patterns to the root (§1501). The derived participles and verbal nouns (rarely the finite verbs) have been borrowed into Urdu, and the Arabic grammatical patterns are evident mainly in semantic relationships between words with the same root:

محنت	امتحان	محن
meḥnat	**imtiḥān**	**meḥan**
effort	examination	sufferings

قبول	قابل	مقبول	اقبال	استقبال
qabūl	**qābil**	**maqbūl**	**iqbāl**	**istiqbāl**
acceptance	capable	popular	prosperity	reception
علم	عالم	معلوم	تعلیم	معلّم
ʿilm	**ʿālim**	**maʿlūm**	**taʿlīm**	**muʿallim**
knowledge	scholar	known	education	teacher

نظم	منظوم	تنظیم	منظّم	انتظام	نظام
naz̤m	**manz̤ūm**	**tanz̤īm**	**munaz̤z̤am**	**intiz̤ām**	**niz̤ām**
poetry	metric	organization	organized	arrangement	system

1501 Arabic derived verb forms

Arabic derives nine verb forms from simple verbs.[1] The simple verb is designated as 'Form I', and the remaining forms are numbered from Form II to Form X. Form IX does not occur in Urdu. Each verb form has its own verbal noun[2] (VN), active participle (AP) and passive participle (PP). Arabic verbal nouns and participles are common in Urdu, and the student will find it rewarding to learn the formation of verbal nouns and participles.

The Arabic root فَعَلَ (**faᶜala**), which means 'do', is traditionally used as a key to demonstrate the affix and vowel patterns in the derived forms. The function, derivation and formation of Forms I-VII and X of فَعَلَ are shown in Table 31 on p. 260. The verbal nouns and participles belonging to these forms are shown in Table 32 on p. 261. Strong verbs (verbs which do not have the letters ء و ی (**'vy**) as one of their radicals) conform to the pattern of فَعَلَ. Platts, *Dictionary of Urdu, Classical Hindi and English* may be consulted for information about the derivations of Arabic vocabulary.

The aspects distinguished in the derived verbs (intensive, causative, reflexive, passive, etc.) are the traditional ones in Arabic, not in Urdu, which has its own means of forming causatives or passives. The Arabic aspects help to shed light on the semantic links between related words, but do not substitute for a dictionary in finding the meaning of a borrowed Arabic word.

---

1 There are in fact 14 derived forms, but Forms 11 to 15 are too rare to be important for Urdu.

2 Called the 'infinitive noun' in Platts, *Dictionary of Urdu, Classical Hindi and English*.

Table 31: Forms I-VII and X of فَعَلَ **faᶜala**

Form	Function in Arabic	Derived from	Formation	Form	
I	Primary meaning	Root		فَعَلَ	**faᶜala**
II	Intensive of I	Form I	Doubling the second radical	فَعَّلَ	**faᶜᶜala**
III	Reciprocal of I, showing the attempt to perform I	Form I	Lengthening the vowel after the first radical	فاعَلَ	**fāᶜala**
IV	Causative of I	Form I	Prefixing أ (**-a**)[1] and dropping the vowel between the first and second radicals:	أفعَلَ	**'afᶜala**
V	Reflexive of II	Form II	Prefixing تَـ (**ta-**)	تَفَعَّلَ	**tafaᶜᶜala**
VI	Reflexive of III	Form III	Prefixing تَـ (**ta-**)	تَفاعَلَ	**tafāᶜala**
VII	Passive of I	Form I	Prefixing إنـ (**in-**)	إنفَعَلَ	**infaᶜala**
VIII	Reflexive of I, reciprocal	Form I	Prefixing إ (**i-**), and infixing ـتـ (**-t-**) after the first radical	إفتَعَلَ	**iftaᶜala**
IX	(Does not occur in Urdu)				
X	Desiderative of IV	Form IV	Prefixing إستَـ (**ista-**)	إستَفعَلَ	**istafᶜala**

1 The initial أ (**-a**) in Form IV is actually a consonantal ء **hamza** in Arabic: ہمزة القطع (**hamzat al-qaṭᶜ**). The alif is the seat of the **hamza**.

1502 Arabic verbal nouns and participles

Strong verbs

Form I verbal nouns do not have a predictable pattern. The active and passive participles of Form I have the patterns **fāʿil** and **mafʿūl** respectively. The participles of the derived Forms II-X all prefix **mu-**. Active participles contain a short **-i-** in the final syllable, while passive participles contain a short **-a-**.

Table 32: Verbal nouns and participles of فَعَلَ and its derived forms

Form	Verb	Verbal Noun	Active Part.	Passive Part.
I	فَعَلَ	فِعل etc.	فاعِل	مَفعُول
II	فَعَّلَ	تَفعِيل	مُفَعِّل	مُفَعَّل
III	فاعَلَ	مُفاعَلَت فِعَال	مُفاعِل	مُفَاعَل
IV	أَفعَلَ	اِفعَال	مُفعِل	مُفعَل
V	تَفَعَّلَ	تَفَعُّل	مُتَفَعِّل	مُتَفَعَّل
VI	تَفَاعَلَ	تَفَاعُل	مُتَفَاعِل	مُتَفَاعَل
VII	اِنفَعَلَ	اِنفِعَال	مُنفَعِل	مُنفَعَل
VIII	اِفتَعَلَ	اِفتِعَال	مُفتَعِل	مُفتَعَل
X	اِستَفعَلَ	اِستِفعَال	مُستَفعِل	مُستَفعَل

Examples

Form I (simple verb)

نَظم **naẓm**, order, poetry, is VN I of نظم , arrange, join.
ناظِم **nāẓim**, administrator, manager, is AP I of نظم .
مَنظوم **manẓūm**, metric, in verse, is PP I of نظم .
عِلم **ʿilm**, knowledge, science, is VN I of علم , know.
عالِم **ʿālim**, scholar, Muslim theologian, is AP I of علم .
مَعلوم **maʿlūm**, known, is PP I of علم .

Form II (intensive)

Form II verbal nouns are always feminine in Urdu.

تَعلیم **ta'līm**, education, is VN II of علم , know.
تَنظیم **tanẓīm**, organization, party, is VN II of نظم , arrange, join.
مُعَلِّم **mu'allim**, teacher, instructor, is AP II of علم .
مُنَظَّم **munaẓẓam**, organized, is PP II of نظم .
تَصویر **taṣvīr**, picture, is VN II of صور , form.

Compare the active and passive participles of صَوَّر Form II of صور:
مُصَوِّر **muṣavvir**, painter, مُصَوَّر **muṣavvar**, illustrated.

Form III (conative, reciprocal)

Form III is not so common as the previous two.

جِہاد **jihād**, holy war, is VN III of جہد , strive.
مُجاہَدہ **mujāhada**, endeavour, strife,[3] is VN III of جہد .
مُجاہِد **mujāhid**, fighter in holy war, is AP III of جہد .

Form IV (causative)

Form IV has many examples in Urdu. The verbal noun and active participle are the parts of speech usually found.

اِسلام **islām**, Islam, is VN IV of سلم , be safe.
مُسلِم **muslim**, Muslim, is AP IV of سلم .
اِقبال **iqbāl**, prosperity; confession, is VN IV of قبل , receive, accept.

Forms V to VII

These are less frequently found.

تَعَلُّق **ta'alluq**, connection, relation, is VN V of علق , hang or cling to.
تَصَوُّف **taṣavvuf**, mysticism, is VN V of صوف .

---

3 The two verbal nouns of Form III will have different but related meanings. In the case of the root جہد, the verbal noun on the pattern of **fi'āl**, **jihād**, has a religious sense, whereas the verbal noun on the pattern **mufā'alat**, **mujāhada**, has a secular meaning. Arabic ـت has been changed to Urdu ہ (**-a**).

مُتَعَلِّق **muta'alliq**, concerning, is AP V of علق.
تَعاوُن **ta'āvun**, cooperation, is VN VI of عون, help.
اِنقِلاب **inqilāb**, revolution, is VN VII of قلب, turn, change.

Form VIII

This form occurs frequently.

اِنتِظام **intizām**, arrangement, is VN VIII of نظم, connect.
مُنتَظِم **muntazim**, manager, master of ceremonies is AP VIII of نظم.
اِنتِخاب **intixāb**, selection, choice, is VN VIII of نخب, extract.
مُنتَخَب **muntaxab**, chosen, elected, is PP VIII of نخب.
اِختِلاف **ixtilāf**, disagreement, is VN VIII of خلف, be left behind.
مُختَلِف **muxtalif**, various, is AP VIII of خلف.

Assimilation of ت t to dental consonants and و ء (' v) takes place in verbal nouns of Form VIII. (See also 'Weak verbs', on p. 264.)

اِطّلاع **ittilā'**, announcement, is VN VIII of طلع, ascend, appear.
اِتّحاد **ittihād**, union, is VN VIII of وحد, to be one.
مُدّعا **mudda'ā**, wish, claim, is PP VIII of دعو, ask, desire.[4]

Form X

اِستِعمال **iste'māl**, use, is VN X of عمل, do, act.
مُستَعمَل **musta'mal**, current, in use, used, is PP X of عمل.
اِستِقبال **istiqbāl**, reception, welcome, is VN X of قبل, receive, accept.
مُستَقبِل **mustaqbil**, future, is AP X of قبل.

Doubled radicals

Roots which have the same consonant in the second and third place may lose short vowels, unless one of the radicals is further doubled in the pattern.

Some very common Urdu words contain doubled radicals, but this is not apparent until the roots are inflected, because in Urdu a final doubled consonant is not pronounced, and **tašdīd** is usually not written.

4 The spelling has been assimilated to Urdu. The Arabic spelling is مُدّعى with the pronunciation **mudda'ā**.

خاص **xāṣ**, special, ← خاصّ **xāṣṣ**
خط **xaṭ**, letter, ← خطّ **xaṭṭ**
حق **ḥaq**, right, ← حقّ **ḥaqq**

Example

مُحِقّ **muhiqq**, speaking the truth, is AP IV(**mufᶜil**) of حقّ , be just.

Compare: مُحَقِّق **muhaqqiq**, research scholar (AP II of حقّ)
تَحقِيق **taḥqīq**, research, inquiry (VN II of حقّ)

Weak verbs

Roots which contain ء و ی (' v y) have irregular inflectional patterns:
(a) initial و **v** may be assimilated to a following **i**, **u** or **t**; initial ء **hamza** (represented in Urdu by ا **alif**) is usually retained, but may be assimilated to the vowel **-a** in the prefix ت **ta-** ;
(b) medial و ی (**v y**) are assimilated to a following vowel;
(c) final و ی (**v y**) is written as ی in derived participles; in active participles ی is pronounced **-ī**, and in passive participles it is pronounced **ā** and may be written یٰ. The passive participles are sometimes spelled with ا **alif** in Urdu.

Examples

مُؤَثِّر **mu'aṣṣir**, effective, is AP II (**mufaᶜᶜil**) of اثر , make an impression.
تاثُّر **ta'aṣsur**, impression, is VN V (**tafaᶜᶜul**) of اثر .
تاثِیر **tāṣīr**, effect, efficacy, is VN II (**tafᶜīl**) of اثر .

قائِم **qā'im**, fixed, established, is AP I (**fāᶜil**) of قوم , stand.
مَقام **maqām**, place, site, is VN I of قوم .
مُقیم **muqīm**, residing, is AP IV (**mufᶜil**) of قوم .

راضی **rāẓī**, pleased, consenting, is AP I (**fāᶜil**) of رضی , approve.
مُرتضیٰ **murtazā**, chosen, is PP VIII (**muftaᶜal**) of رضی .
مُدّعا **muddaᶜā**, wish, claim, is PP VIII of دوی , ask, desire[5]

5 The original Arabic spelling is مُدّعیٰ with the pronunciation **muddaᶜā**.

NOUN DUALS AND PLURALS

Arabic distinguishes three numbers: the singular, dual and plural.

1503 Dual form of Arabic nouns

The Arabic dual suffix occurring in Urdu is **-ain**.

> والدین
> **vālidain** (< **vālid**, father)
> parents

1504 Plural forms of Arabic nouns

Strictly speaking, only Arabic loanwords may take Arabic plural suffixes. Many Arabic loanwords have both Arabic and Urdu plural forms. In such cases, use of Arabic plural forms is usually typical of a formal or literary style.

Sound (regular) plurals

The plural suffix **-īn** is used mainly with participles.

> منتظمین **muntaẓimīn**, administrators
> بند کے متاثرین **band kē muta'as̤s̤irīn**, those affected by the dam

The plural suffix **-āt** is used with nouns, including verbal nouns. Plurals in **-āt** are normally the same gender as their singulars. The plural in **-āt** is sometimes used with words of Persian or Indic origin.

> حالات ← حال **hāl** → **hālāt**, circumstances
> کاغذات ← کاغذ **kāgaẕ** → **kāgẕāt**, papers, documents
> جنگلات ← جنگل **jangal** ← **janglāt**, forests

The Urdu names of branches of learning are formed with the suffix **-iyāt** (**-ī** and the plural in **-āt**).

> لسانیات **lisāniyāt** (f.), linguistics < لسان , tongue
> معاشیات **maᶜāśiyāt** (f.), economics < معاش , means of livelihood

Broken (irregular) plurals

Broken plurals are formed by changing the vowel patterns of the singular noun. There are numerous broken plural patterns, of which the more common are listed below. Broken plurals in Urdu are normally the same gender as their singulars.

The real structure of words with doubled radicals becomes apparent from their broken plurals.

(a) ا (**a**-) is prefixed, and the vowels are changed, to the pattern **afᶜāl**:[6]

حُکم ← اَحکام **ḥukm** → **aḥkām**, orders

خَبَر ← اَخبار **xabar**, news → **axbār**, newspaper

(b) The vowels are changed, to the pattern **fuᶜūl**:

عِلم ← عُلوم **ᶜilm** → **ᶜulūm**, sciences

حَق ← حُقوق **ḥaqq** → **ḥuqūq**, rights

(c) The vowels are changed, to the pattern **fuᶜul**:

کِتاب ← کُتُب **kitāb** → **kutub**, books

(d) The vowels are changed to the pattern **fuᶜalā** (**fuᶜalā'** in Arabic, but the final ء is generally not written in Urdu). This pattern is typical of participles of the pattern **faᶜīl** and also in some cases of **fāᶜil**.

عالِم ← عُلَما **ᶜālim** → **ᶜulamā**, religious scholars

طالِب ← طُلَبا ، طُلَباء **ṭālib** → **ṭulabā, ṭulabā'**, seeker

(e) The vowels are changed to the pattern **faᶜāil** (originally **faᶜā'il** in Arabic). This pattern may occur with AP I **fāᶜil**, but typically handles derived four-consonant patterns which do not contain long vowels.

فائِدہ ← فَوائِد **fā'ida** → **favā'id**, benefits (< VN I of فید, accrue)

مَسجِد ← مَساجِد **masjid** → **masājid**, mosques (noun of place of سجد)

(f) The second radical is doubled, and the vowels changed, to the pattern **fuᶜᶜāl**. This is typical of AP I **fāᶜil**.

حاکِم ← حُکّام **ḥākim** → **ḥukkām**, rulers, officials, commanders

6 The initial اَ (-**a**) of this plural pattern is actually the consonantal ء **hamza** in Arabic: ہمزۃ القطع (**hamzat al-qaṭᶜ**). The alif is the seat of the **hamza**.

(g) ا (-ā-) is infixed, and the vowel pattern will be **a-ā-ī**. This pattern typically handles derived four-consonant patterns which contain a long second vowel. Verbal nouns of Form II (**tafʿīl**) always contain a long **ī** as the second vowel.

تَصویر ← تَصاویر **taṣvīr → taṣāvīr**, pictures
تَفصیل ← تَفاصیل **tafṣīl → tafāṣīl**, details

(h) ا (**a**-) is prefixed, and the vowels changed, to the pattern **afiʿlāʾ**. This is common when the root is weak, the second radical is doubled and the noun refers to a rational being.

وَلی ← اَولیاء **valī → auliyāʾ**, saints
طَبیب ← اَطِبّاء **ṭabīb → aṭibbāʾ**, physicians (with assimilation of the doubled radical ب)

Urdu nouns with Arabic dual or plural forms do not take the Urdu oblique plural suffix in **-ōṁ**.

والدین کی اجازت
vālidain kī ijāzat
the permission of one's parents

طلبا نے عرضی پیش کی
tulabā nē ʿarzī pēś kī
The students presented a petition.

Compare: طالب علموں نے عرضی پیش کی
tālib ilmōṁ nē ʿarzī pēś kī
The students presented a petition.

ARABIC PREPOSITIONS AND PARTICLES

1505 Prepositions

NOTE: The following are only a few Arabic prepositions. Phrases beginning with Arabic prepositions must be looked up under the preposition in dictionaries.

فی *fī, 'per'*

فی صدی **fī ṣadī** per cent
فی سال **fī sāl** per year

ب ***bi***, *'with', 'in'*

بالکل **bilkul**, completely (**bi** + **al-kull**, see §1507)

بالتفصیل **bittafṣīl** detailed (**bi** + **at-tafṣīl**, see §1507)

In the above example, the definite article **al** is assimilated to the ت **t** in **tafṣīl**, because **t** is a **śamsī** (sun) letter. See §1507.

ل ***li***, *'for', 'to'*

الحمد الله **al ḥamdu li'llāh**, Praise be to God!

1506 Negative particles

لا *lā, 'no', 'not', 'without' (absolute negation)*

لا علاج **lā ʿilāj**, incurable (**lā** + **ʿilāj**, treatment)

لا جواب **lā javāb**, answerless, matchless (**lā** + **javāb**, answer)

غیر ***γair***, 'im-', 'un-', 'non-'

γair is a noun in Arabic ('stranger'), and the words below would be analysed as NOUN + NOUN compounds in that language. In Urdu, it occurs as a noun only in the compound postposition **baγair** (§531).

غیرحاضر **γairḥāẓir**, absent (**γair** + **ḥāẓir**, present)

غیرملکی **γairmulkī**, foreign(er) (**γair** + **mulk**, land + **ī**, adjectival suffix)

MISCELLANEOUS

1507 The definite article

The Arabic definite article, **al-**, occurs in some borrowed phrases and proper names. The vowel **a-** in the article is assimilated to the final vowel of the preceding noun (**-u**, **-i** or **-a**[7]).

یوم الحساب (< ***yaumu al-ḥisāb**)
yaum ul-ḥisāb
the Day of Reckoning

---

7 The nominative, genitive and accusative suffixes of nouns.

عبد الحق
ᶜabd-ul-haqq (< ***ᶜabdu al-haqq**)
Servant of the Truth (God)

بالکل
bilkul (< * **bi al-kull**, in the whole; **bi** is a preposition (§1505))
completely

If the definite article occurs before a word beginning with any of the following (dental or alveolar) consonants: ت ث د ذ ر ز س ش ص ض ط ظ ل ن (called **śamsī** or 'sun' letters[8] in Arabic), the -**l**- is assimilated to the following letter in pronunciation. It is written as though it were pronounced **l**.

عبد الرحمٰن
ᶜabd-ur-raḥmān (< ***ᶜabdu al-raḥmān**)
Servant of the Compassionate (God)

السلام علیکم
as-salāmu ᶜalaikum (< * **al-salāmu ᶜalaikum**)
Peace be on you.

1508 Nouns of place

Nouns of place have the patterns **mafᶜal** and **mafᶜil**:

مکتب **maktab**, school (< کتب, write)
مسجد **masjid**, mosque (< سجد , prostrate oneself in prayer)

1509 Nouns of instrument

Nouns of instrument have the patterns **mifᶜāl** and **mifᶜala** (the second is rare in Urdu):

مفتاح **miftāḥ**, key (< فتح , open)
میزان **mīzān**, scales (< وزن , weigh)

8 The remaining letters are called **qamrī**, or 'moon' letters.

1510 Elative

The elative (comparative and superlative of adjectives) has the pattern **'af‘al**:[9]

> اکبر **akbar**, bigger, biggest ← کبیر **kabīr**, big
> اکثر **akṣar**, usually, often ← کثیر **kaṣīr**, abundant

1511 Suffixes

tanvīn

Arabic adverbs ending in **-an** have been borrowed into Urdu. These are written with ً (**tanvīn**), which is usually written over ا , but may be written over ہ . The Arabic noun from which the adverb is derived may also found in Urdu, although the semantic connection between the two is not always obvious.

> فور > فوراً
> **fauran < faur**
> immediately < hurry, haste

> تقریب > تقریباً
> **taqrīban < taqrīb** (VN II of قرب)
> approximately < bringing near; ceremony

The noun may have lost its original Arabic pronunciation and spelling:

> (دفعۃ <) دفعہ > دفعتہً ، دفعتاً
> **daf‘atan < daf‘a**
> suddenly < time, moment

Abstract suffix -iyat

Many abstract nouns in Arabic have the pattern **fa‘lat**, e.g. کثرت **kaṣrat**, 'abundance'. Abstract nouns of quality can also be formed by adding **-iyat** (**-iyyat** in Arabic). They are all feminine in Urdu.

> شخص ← شخصیت
> **šaxṣiyat**, personality ← **šaxṣ**, person

---

9 The initial ا (**-a**) of the elative is actually the consonantal ء **hamza** in Arabic: ہمزۃ القطع (**hamzat al-qaṭ‘**). The alif is the seat of the **hamza**.

انسانیت ← اِنسان
insāniyat, humanity ← **insān**, human being

Adjectival suffix -ānī

The adjectival suffix forms adjectives from nouns.

جسمانی ← جسم
jismānī, physical ← **jism**, body

روحانی ← روح
rūḥānī, spiritual ← **rūḥ**, spirit

16 CEREMONIOUS AND PIOUS SPEECH

GREETINGS AND INTRODUCTIONS

1601 Greetings

ādāb arz is a greeting which may be exchanged by Muslims and non-Muslims. The reply is also **ādāb arz**.

آداب عرض
ādāb arz
hello (may I present my respects)

as-salāmu alaikum is a greeting given by Muslims, generally to other Muslims. The reply is **va alaikum as-salām**.

السلامُ علیکم — و علیکم السلام ۔
as-salāmu alaikum—va alaikum as-salām
Peace be on you.—And on you, peace.

xudā hāfiz, 'goodbye (God keep you)' is said to members of any religion. **allāh hāfiz** is a neologism and means the same. The same phrase is repeated in reply.

خدا حافظ	اللہ حافظ
xudā hāfiz	**allāh hāfiz**
God keep you.	God keep you.

When someone is travelling away from home, the following phrases may be added to **xudā hāfiz** or **allāh hāfiz**:

فی امان اللہ	اللہ کے حوالے
fī amān illāh	**allāh kē havālē**
in the protection of God	(in) God's care

When a child greets an elder, the elder responds with short phrases that are in effect short prayers (**duā**) for the child's welfare, and usually places his hand on the child's head in blessing:

جیتے رہو
jītē rahō
May you remain alive! (to a boy)

جیتی رہو
jītī rahō
May you remain alive! (to a girl)

سلامت رہو
salāmat rahō
May you remain safe!

خوش رہو
xuś rahō
May you remain happy!

السلام علیکم دادی جان ! کیسی ہیں آپ ؟
— وعلیکم السلام بیٹا ! جیتے رہو ! خوش رہو !
as-salāmu alaikum, dādī jān! kaisī haiṁ āp?
—va alaikum as-salām bēṭā! ***jītē rahō! xuś rahō!***
Hello, grandmother! How are you?
Hello, son! *May you remain alive! May you be happy!*

1602 Introductions and polite exchanges

Traditional polite phrases of introduction are socially asymmetrical. Courtesy demands that the person who asks about someone's name, health, etc. use respectful, even ceremonial language, while the other person should respond with modest simplicity, or even ceremonious self-deprecation. This formal etiquette is called **takalluf** تکلّف in Urdu.

اِسم شریف ؟
ism-e-śarīf?
What is your name (lit. noble name)?

آپ کی تعریف ؟ \ جناب کی تعریف ؟
āp kī ***tārīf?*** **/janāb kī** ***tārīf?***
What is your name/your honour's name (lit. *praise*)?

Examples

اسم شریف ؟ — مجھے نسیم کہتے ہیں -
ism-e-śarīf? **— mujhē nasīm kahtē haiṁ**
(Your) *noble name*?—They call me Nasim.

جناب کی تعریف ؟ — ناچیز (بندے) کو عابد کہتے ہیں -
janāb kī ***tārīf?*** **—** ***nāciz*** **(*bandē*) kō ābid kahtē haiṁ**
Your honour's *praise*?—They call the *worthless thing/slave* Abid.

One may reply respectfully to inquiries about one's health by alluding to the efficacy of the other person's prayers, or by thanking God (§1604).

مزاج شریف ؟
mizāj śarīf?
How are you?[1]

مزاج کیسا ہے ؟
mizāj **kaisā hai?**
How is (your) *disposition*?

مزاج بخیر ؟
mizāj baxair?
How are you?[2]

آپ کی دعا ہے — آپ کی دعا چاہئے
āp kī *duā* hai — āp kī *duā* cāhiē
It is your *prayer* — your *prayer* is needed.

Examples

مزاج شریف ؟ — آپ کی دعا ہے -
mizāj śarīf?—āp kī duā hai
How are you?—I am fine (due to your prayer).

اور سناؤ نسیم بیٹا ، کار و بار کیسا ہے ؟
— بس چچا جان آپ کی دعا چاہئے ، بالکل ٹھیک چل رہا ہے -
aur sunāō nasīm bēṭā, kār-o-bār kaisā hai?
—bas cacā jān, *āp kī duā cāhiē*, bilkul ṭhīk cal rahā hai
What else (tell more), Nasim son, how is business?
—It's going just fine, uncle dear, *with your prayer.*

With similar asymmetry, one refers to another's house as a mansion (**daulat xāna** دولت خانہ) or at least a 'residence' (**rihāiś** رہائش), and to one's own in modest terms or even self-deprecating terms.

آپ کی رہائش کہاں ہے ؟ — میں وارث روڈ پر رہتا ہوں -
āp kī *rihāiś* kahāṁ hai?—maiṁ vāris rōḍ par rahtā hūṁ
Where do you live (lit. Where is your *residence*?)?—I live on Waris Road.

آپ کا دولت خانہ کہاں ہے ؟ — میرا غریب خانہ گلبرگ میں ہے -
āp kā *daulat xāna* kahāṁ hai?—mērā *γarīb xāna* gulbarg mēṁ hai
Where is your *mansion*?—My *humble dwelling* is in Gulberg.

---

1 Originally **mizāj-e-śarīf**, with **izāfat**. It means 'your noble disposition'.

2 An abbreviation of **kyā āp kā mizāj baxair hai**, 'Is your disposition well?'

One may ask about a person's nationality with the term 'connection' (**taalluq** تعلق). In asking about the duration of a person's stay, the term 'stay', 'establishment' (**qeyām** قیام) is appropriate in the question, whereas the response should be plain and straightforward.

آپ کا تعلق کہاں سے ہے ؟ — جناب ، میں اِنگلینڈ کا ہوں ۔
āp kā *taalluq* kahāṁ sē hai?—janāb, maiṁ inglaiṁḍ kā hūṁ
Where are you from (your *connection*)?—Sir, I'm from (lit. of) England.[3]

لاہور میں آپ کا قیام کب سے ہے ؟ — میں یہاں دو مہینے سے ہوں ۔
lāhaur mēṁ āp kā *qeyām* kab sē hai?—maiṁ yahāṁ dō mahīnē sē hūṁ
How long have you been in Lahore?—I have been here for two months.

When asking someone how his family is, one should rather ask about his home, particularly when a man asks another man if his family is well. This is because women may observe **parda** پردہ or seclusion, and it is inappropriate for a man to inquire about the welfare of the women in another man's household.

اہل خانہ تو خیریت سے ہیں ؟
***ahl-e-xāna* tō xairiyat sē haiṁ?**
Is your family well (lit. Are *the people of the house* well?)?

گھر میں سب خیریت ہے ؟
***ghar mēṁ* sab xairiat hai?**
Is everything okay *in* (your) *house*?

When leaving a social gathering, it is polite to ask permission (**ijāzat** اجازت) to leave, or ask for leave (**ruxsat** رخصت).

اب مجھے اجازت دیجئے ۔
ab mujhē *ijāzat* dījiē
May I leave now (lit. Please give *permission* now.)?

اب میں جناب سے رخصت چاہوں گا ۔
ab maiṁ janāb sē *ruxsat* cāhūṁ gā
I have to leave now (lit. Now I will wish *leave* from your honour.).

3 An alternative reply, if one lives in England but is travelling abroad, is **maiṁ inglaiṁḍ sē āyā hūṁ**, 'I have come from England.' If one is living in England, one can say **maiṁ inglaiṁḍ mēṁ rahtā hūṁ**, 'I live in England.'

FORMAL AND CEREMONIOUS SPEECH

1603 Formal polite requests

Formal polite requests or inquiries to strangers of equal or superior status use verb phrases with **taśrīf** تشریف , 'one's honourable self'. (See 'Other request forms', §610.) **taśrīf** is never used in the response.

کیا آپ کل کی دعوت میں تشریف لا سکتے ہیں ؟
— جی ہاں انشاء اللہ میں ضرور آؤں گا ۔
kyā āp kal kī dāvat mēṁ *taśrīf lā saktē haiṁ*?
—jī hāṁ inśā allāh maiṁ zarūr āūṁ gā
Can you come to tomorrow's party?
—Yes, I'll definitely come, God willing.

السلام علیکم ، کیا ڈاکٹر صاحب تشریف رکھتے ہیں ؟
— و علیکم السلام میں ڈاکٹر وحید بول رہا ہوں ۔
as-salām alaikum, kyā ḍākṭar sāhib *taśrīf rakhtē haiṁ*?
—va alaikum as-salām, maiṁ ḍākṭar vahīd bōl rahā hūṁ
Hello, *is* the doctor *available*?
—Hello, this is Doctor Vahid speaking

Two respectful ways of asking for a favour are:

کیا آپ میرے لئے ایک تکلیف کریں گے ؟
kyā āp mērē liē ēk taklīf karēṁ gē?
May I bother you with a favour (lit. Would you take a trouble for me)?

میری ایک گزارش ہے کہ ...
mērī ēk guzāriś hai ke ...
I have a request, that ...

1604 Thanking someone

Expressions of thanks (**śukriya** شکریہ , 'thank you', and **meharbānī** مہربانی , **navāziś** نوازش , and **karam** کرم , all meaning 'kindness') are often countered with a modest disclaimer: **mērā farz thā**, 'It was my duty.'

آپ نے میرے لئے وقت نکالا ۔ بہت شکریہ ۔
āp nē mērē liē vaqt nikālā. bahut *śukriya*
You found time for me. *Thank you* very much.

— اِس میں شکریہ کی کیا بات ہے ۔ یہ تو میرا فرض تھا ۔
is mēṁ śukriya kī kyā bāt hai. ***ye tō mērā farz thā***
There is no need of thanks. *It was my duty.*

1605 Congratulations

Congratulations are expressed with **mubārak** مبارک, 'blessed', 'fortunate' or **mubārakbād** مبارکباد, 'blessing(s)', 'congratulation(s)'. The response is **āp kō bhī mubārak (hō)**, 'May you also be blessed.'

بھئی نئے گھر کی بہت مبارک — شکریہ ، آپ کو بھی مبارک ۔
bhai, naē ghar kī bahut ***mubārak (mubārakbād)*****—śukriya, āp kō bhī** ***mubārak***
Friend, hearty *congratulations* on the new house.—*Congratulations* to you, too.[4]

عید مبارک ! — آپ کو بھی عید مبارک
īd ***mubārak*****!—āp kō bhī īd** ***mubārak***
Happy Eid!—*Happy* Eid to you too.

A person may be congratulated on a job well done with **śābāś**, 'bravo':[5]

شاباش حامد تم نے آج بہت اچھا کام کیا ۔ تمھیں انعام ملنا چاہئے ۔
śābāś **hāmid, tum nē āj bahut acchā kām kiyā. tumhēṁ inām milnā cāhiē**
Bravo Hamid, you did a fine job today. You deserve a prize.

PIOUS PHRASES AND EXCLAMATIONS

A **muslim**, a believer in Islam, means one who has submitted his will to God. The more common term in spoken Urdu is **musalmān** مسلمان . Thus in a range of everyday actions, the Muslim alludes to the sovereignty of God in human life, through a variety of pious expressions, many borrowed from Arabic.

---

4 **mubārakbād** is the Persian equivalent of Urdu **mubārak hō**, 'May blessings be.' **bād** is the optative of **būdan**, 'to be'.

5 Originally Persian **śād bāś**, 'remain happy'.

1606 Mentioning holy prophets

Whenever the name of the Prophet Mohammad (PBUH) is uttered or written, the following phrase is added:

> صلّی اللہ علیہ و سلّم
> **sallallāhu alaihi va sallam**
> May God's peace and blessings be upon him!

In writing, this is usually abbreviated to the sign ؐ (and in English, 'PBUH' an abbreviation for 'Peace be upon him.'). The third person pronoun used to refer to the Prophet is **āp** (§203). The title **hazrat** حضرت, 'lord', 'sir', 'master' is prefaced to the name of the Prophet as well as to the names of others considered prophets in Islam, as well as saints and highly respected persons.[6]

> حضرت محمد صلّی اللہُ علیہ و سلّم...
> **hazrat muhammad *sallallāhu alaihi va sallam* ...**
> Muhammad, *may God's peace and blessings be upon him* ...

Another phrase is added to the names of prophets other than Muhammad (PBUH):

> علیہ السلام
> **alaihissalām**
> on whom be peace

> حضرت عیسیٰ علیہ السلام...
> **hazrat īsā *alaihissalām* ...**
> Christ, *on whom be peace* ...

1607 Phrases for planning or beginning something

inśā allāh is prefaced to expressions of future plans, since according to Islamic belief it is presumptuous of human beings to think that the future can be ordered otherwise than God wills.

> انشاء اللہ
> **inśā allāh**
> if God wills

6 The plural, **hazrāt**, means 'gentlemen': **xavātīn o hazrāt**! 'Ladies and gentlemen!'

کل ہمارے ہاں دعوت ہے ۔ کیا آپ تشریف لا سکیں گے ؟
— جی ہاں انشاء اللہ میں ضرور آؤں گا ۔
kal hamārē hāṁ dāvat hai. kyā āp taśrīf lā sakēṁ gē?
—jī hāṁ *inśā allāh* maiṁ zarūr āūṁ gā
Tomorrow there's a party at our place. Can you come?
Yes, I'll definitely come, *God willing*.

One mentions God when starting something new, or beginning a new day.

بسم اللہ الرحمٰن الرحیم
bismillāhir-rahmānir-rahīm
in the name of God, the merciful and the compassionate

اچّھا تو آئیے ہم آج کا کام شروع کرتے ہیں ۔
— بسم اللہ الرحمٰن الرحیم ۔
acchā tō āiyē ham āj kā kām śurū kartē haiṁ
—bismillāhir-rahmānir-rahīm
Come on, we'll begin today's work.
—in the name of God, the merciful and the compassionate

1608 Phrases invoking protection and short prayers

One of the following two phrases is prefaced to any expression of praise. The first, **māśā allāh**, is addressed to those younger in age when giving blessings or compliments. The second, **subhān allāh**, is not age-restricted.

ماشاء اللہ	سبحان اللہ
māśā allāh	**subhān allāh**
what God wills	God be praised; with the grace of God

There is a belief that praise can attract evil to the person or thing praised, the above phrases, which give the real credit to God, are a way of invoking protection for the person or thing praised.

ماشاء اللہ جناب ۔ آپ کا بیٹا تو اب خاصا بڑا ہو گیا ہے ۔
***māśā allāh* janāb, āp kā bēṭā tō ab xāsā baṛā hō gayā hai**
My goodness sir, your son has grown quite big (*as God wills*).

The following phrases may be prefaced to a compliment to invoke protection from the evil eye (**caśm-e-bad** چشم بد , **burī nazar** بُری نظر).[7]

چشم بد دور
caśm-e-bad dūr
(May) the evil eye (remain) far.

نظر نہ لگے
nazar na lagē
May the evil eye not affect.

خدا بری نظر سے بچائے
xudā burī nazar sē bacāē
May God save from the evil eye.

چشم بد دور۔ بہت ہی خوبصورت بچہ ہے ۔
***caśm-e-bad dūr.* bahut hī xūbsūrat bacca hai**
The evil eye (be) far. What a beautiful child.

allāh karē and **xudā karē** are used in wishing for something (a form of prayer).

اللہ کرے
allāh karē
May God grant ...

خدا کرے
xudā karē
May God grant ...

اللہ نہ کرے
allāh na karē
May God forbid ...

خدا نہ کرے
xudā na karē
May God forbid ...

خدا نخواستہ
xudā naxāsta
May God forbid ...

allāh is the name of God used by Muslims, while **xudā** may be used by both Muslims and non-Muslims. In the negative, these prayers invoke protection from misfortune. **xudā naxāsta** is the Persian form of **allāh na karē**. All these phrases take the subjunctive form of the verb. With **allāh na karē** and **xudā naxāsta**, the *negative* of the subjunctive may be used to express the possibility of an undesirable event (§608).

اللہ نہ کرے وہ بیمار ہو ۔
***allāh na karē* vo bīmār hō**
God forbid (that) he should be sick.

اِس وقت باہر مت جاؤ خدا نہ کرے کچھ ہو نہ جائے ۔
is vaqt bāhar mat jāō, *xudā na karē* kuch hō na jāē
Don't go out now, *God forbid* (that) something might happen (to you).

---

7 **burī nazar** is usually shortened to **nazar**, and the meaning understood from the context. The primary meaning of **nazar** is 'sight', 'vision'.

If someone wishes for another person's benefit in a prayer, the second person responds with **āmīn** آمین, 'amen'.

اللہ کرے آپ کے کھوئے ہوئے پیسے مل جائیں — آمین ۔
allāh karē āp kē khōē hūē paisē mil jāēṁ—*āmīn*
God grant that you get your lost money back.—*Amen*.

If a situation is truly hazardous, the phrase **xudā burī ghaṛī sē bacāē**, 'God save from the evil moment' may be said.

بھئی زمانہ بہت خراب ہے ۔ خدا بری گھڑی سے بچائے ۔ آپ خیال رکھیں ۔
bhaī zamāna bahut xarāb hai. *xudā burī ghaṛī sē bacāē.* āp xyāl rakhēṁ
Brother, the times are very bad. God save you in the evil moment, you take care.

1609 Phrases of repentance and requests for forgiveness

The following expressions are used when one hears of something reprehensible. **tauba tauba** توبہ توبہ is a mild expression of repentance, said while touching one's earlobes, and is variously translated 'God forbid!' 'Never again!' **astaγfirullāh** استغفر اللہ means 'God forgive me' and is said when a serious mistake has been committed, to ask God and the person offended for forgiveness. **lā haula va lā quvvat** (a shortened form of لا حول و لا قوۃ الا باللہ **lā haula va lā quvvata illā billāh**) means 'There is no force or strength (other than of God)' and is said to banish Satan or curse something evil.

توبہ توبہ کیا آپ نے سنا کہ راشد رشوت لیتا ہے ۔
— استغفر اللہ ۔ بہت ہی بری بات ہے ۔ اللہ معاف کرے ۔
***tauba tauba,* kyā āp nē sunā ke rāśid riśvat lētā hai**
—*astaγfirullāh.* bahut hī burī bāt hai. allāh muāf karē
Heaven forfend; did you hear that Rashid takes bribes?
—*God have mercy*; that's terrible. May God forgive (him).

کیا آپ نے یہ کتاب پڑھی ہے ؟ کیسی ہے ؟
— لا حول و لا قوت نہایت فضول کتاب ہے ۔
kyā āp nē ye kitāb paṛhī hai? kaisī hai?
***lā haula va lā quvvat* nehāyat fuzūl kitāb hai**
Have you read this book? How is it?
To hell with it, it's an utterly worthless book.

If someone says something offensive to or about an elder or respected person, or offensive to God, one must promptly say **maāz allāh**, 'May God defend me!' It is also a rejection of blasphemy. **maāz allāh** معاذ اللہ may be said with **lā haula va lā quvvat**

بھئی میں اُن بزرگ کی بات نہیں مانتا ۔
— توبہ توبہ ۔ استغفر اللہ ۔ ایسی بات نہیں کہتے ۔ معاذ اللہ گناہ ہو گا ۔
bhaī maiṁ un buzurg kī bāt nahīṁ māntā
—*tauba tauba, astaγfirullāh.* aisī bāt nahīṁ kahtē. *maāz allāh,* gunāh hō gā
Pal, I won't obey that elder.
—*God forbid, God have mercy*, you're not saying such a thing. *God protect you,* it would be a sin.

1610 Phrases for sad occasions

The following phrases are used when the speaker finds himself helpless in an unfortunate situation, for example, in responding to condolences upon a death.

جیسے مولا کی مرضی
jaisē maulā kī marzī
As God wills ...

جیسے اللہ کی رضا
jaisē allāh kī rizā
As God wills ...

بہت افسوس ہوا — جیسے اللہ کی مرضی ۔
bahut afsōs hūā—*jaisē allāh kī marzī*
(I was) very sorry (to hear about it).—*It was as God willed.*

1611 Phrases for happy occasions

God is praised or thanked when the speaker reports on a favourable situation.

الحمد للّٰہ
alhamdu lillāh
Praise be to God!

اور سنائیے ، کیا ہو رہا ہے ؟ سب ٹھیک ہے ؟
— الحمد للّٰہ سب ٹھیک ہے ۔
aur sunāiyē, kyā hō rahā hai? sab ṭhīk hai?
—*alhamdu lillāh* sab ṭhīk hai
Tell (me) more, what's happening? Is everything okay?
—*God be praised*; everything is okay.

اللہ کا شکر ہے

allāh kā śukr hai

Thanks (is) to God.

چچا جان ! آپ کی طبیعت اب کیسی ہے ؟

— اللہ کا شکر ہے بیٹی ! بہت بہتر ہوں ۔

cacā jān! āp kī tabiat ab kaisī hai?

—*allāh kā śukr hai* bēṭī, bahut behtar hūṁ

Uncle dear! How is your health now?

—*Thank God*, daughter! I am much better now.

Note that **śukr** can only be used with reference to God; if a person is to be thanked, **śukriya** must be used instead. See §1605.

BIBLIOGRAPHY

The bibliography is adapted and expanded from Frances Pritchett, *Inventory of Language Materials*, at the web site:
gopher://gopher.cc.columbia.edu:71/11/clioplus/scholarly/SouthAsia/Teaching/ILM.

Textbooks

Barker, M.A.R., *et al.* (1993) *Spoken Urdu*, 3 vols (with cassettes), Ithaca, NY: Spoken Language Services.

Bhatia, Tej K. and Koul, Ashok (1999) *Colloquial Urdu: A Complete Language Course*, London: Routledge.

Glassman, Eugene H. (1995) *Spoken Urdu: A Beginning Course* (with cassettes), Lahore: Nirali Kitaben Publishing House.

Grainger, Peter L. (1986) *Making a Sound Start in Urdu* (with cassettes), Lahore: Nirali Kitaben Publishing House. (Pronunciation drills, explanations, dialogues; correlates with Barker, *Spoken Urdu*.)

Matthews, D.J. and Shackle, C. (1982) *Introduction to Urdu*, London: School of Oriental and African Studies.

Naim, C.M. (1999) *Introductory Urdu*, 2 vols, Chicago: Center for South Asian Studies, University of Chicago.

Platts, John T. *A Grammar of the Hindustani or Urdu Language*. 1967 reprint of London 1904, Delhi: Munshiram Manoharlal.

Russell, Ralph (1981-86) *A New Course in Urdu and Spoken Hindi*, vol. 1, vol. 2, *An Outline of Grammar and Common Usage*, vol. 3, *Rapid Readings*, vol. 4, *The Urdu Script*, London: School of Oriental and African Studies.

Urdu Writing System

Hanaway, William L. and Spooner, Brian (1995) *Reading Nastaᶜliq, Persian and Urdu Hands from 1500 to the Present*, Costa Mesa, CA: Mazda Publishers.

Koul, Omkar N. (1991) *Urdu Script: Reading and Writing*, New Delhi: Creative Publishers.

McGregor, R.S. (1991) *Urdu Study Materials* for use with *Outline of Hindi Grammar*, New Delhi: Oxford University Press.

(See also sections of textbooks by Barker 1993, Naim 1999 and Russell 1986 which are devoted to the writing system.)

Glossed readers and glossaries for published short stories

Ahmad, Mumtaz (1985) *Urdu Newspaper Reader* (with cassettes), Wheaton, MD: Dunwoody Press.

Barker, M.A.R. et al. (1968) *An Urdu Newspaper Reader*, Ithaca, NY: Spoken Language Services.

Kalsi, A.S. *et al.* (1991) *Modern Urdu Texts. Urdu Short Stories*, London: School of Oriental and African Studies. (A glossary to accompany selected short stories by Prem Chand, Manto, Krishan Chandar, Bedi, Intizar Husain, and Mazhar ul Islam.)

Matthews, D.J. and Shackle, C. (1991) *A Selection of Twentieth Century Urdu Verse*, London: School of Oriental and African Studies.

Matthews, D.J. (1994) *Ghalib: Eight Letters and Fifteen Ghazals*, London: School of Oriental and African Studies.

Taj, Afroz (1996) *Tanhaiyan, Ankahi and Ahsas* (Companion), Raleigh, NC: Hillsborough Street Textbooks. (Summaries of Pakistani television series, episode by episode, with brief vocabularies, followed by discussion questions, in both Urdu calligraphy and typeset Devanagari script.)

Shackle, C. and Snell, R. (1990) *Hindi and Urdu since 1800: A Common Reader*, London: School of Oriental and African Studies.

Dictionaries and glossaries

Ferozsons Urdu-English Dictionary: A Comprehensive Dictionary of Current Vocabulary (1983), Lahore: Ferozsons.

Kitabistan's Twentieth Century Standard Dictionary. Lahore: Kitabistan Publishing Company (Urdu-English and English-Urdu).

Platts, John T. *A Dictionary of Urdu, Classical Hindi, and English*, reprint (1977) of 1930, New Delhi: Oriental Books Reprint Corp. (Also: reprint (1994) of 1911, Lahore: Sang-e-Meel. Original edition 1884.)

الحاج مولوی فیروز الدین (۱۹۸۷) جامع فیروزاللغات - دہلی : انجم بک ڈپو

(Alhaj Maulvi Firozuddin (1987) *Jame Firoz-ul-Lughat*, Delhi: Anjum Book Depot.)

Schomer, K. *et al.* (1983) *Basic Vocabulary for Hindi and Urdu*, Berkeley, CA: Center for South Asia Studies, University of California.

INDEX

D

E

F

G

H

O

U

V